ORDINARY
HEROES

BOOKS BY PETER HAY

Ordinary Heroes
Theatrical Anecdotes
A Book of Business Anecdotes
All the Presidents' Ladies
A Book of Legal Anecdotes
Broadway Anecdotes

ORDINARY HEROES

HEROES

*The Life and Death
of Chana Szenes,
Israel's National Heroine*

PETER HAY

PARAGON HOUSE
NEW YORK

First paperback edition, 1989

Published in the United States by

Paragon House Publishers
90 Fifth Avenue
New York, NY 10011

Grateful acknowledgments are made to the Jewish Publication Society for kind permission to quote the poem "Blessed is the Match" in Marie Syrkin's translation, from her book of the same title; and to Vallentine, Mitchell & Co. Ltd. for kind permission to quote all other poems in English translation from *Hannah Senesh: Her Life and Diary*.
    All translations of letters, diaries and poems are by the author unless otherwise stated; permission to quote these and to reproduce photographs was most generously granted by Katherine and Giora Szenes.

Library of Congress Cataloging-in-Publication Data

Hay, Peter, 1944–
    Ordinary heroes : the life and death of Chana Szenes, Israel's
national heroine / by Peter Hay. — 1st pbk. ed.
        p.   cm.
    Reprint, with new introd. Originally published: New York : Putnam,
c 1986.
    Bibliography: p.
    Includes index.
    ISBN 1-55778-276-8 : $10.95
    1. Senesh, Hannah, 1921–1944.   2. Jews—Palestine—Biography.
3. Holocaust, Jewish (1939–1945)—Hungary. 4. World War, 1939–1945—
—Underground movements, Jewish—Hungary. 5. Hungary—Ethnic
relations. I. Title.
[CT1919.P38S365   1989]
940.53'18'09439092—dc290
    [B]   89-32873
                                                                   CIP

*To the memory of
my Grandmother
Edith Singer
and
to my Mother
Éva Háy
who lived through it*

ACKNOWLEDGMENTS

I owe many debts to many people without whom this book would not have been possible. I want to thank especially Katherine and Giora Szenes for their untiring cooperation during hours of interviews about painful details of their lives, for giving me generous access to their private papers, diaries, and photographs, for their constant encouragement.

The following also provided firsthand accounts of their part in this story: Reuven Dafni, Éva Háy, Elisabeth Marton, Miriam Neeman, Miriam Pergament, Yonah Rosen, Lydia and Pál Sas, Judith Schanda, Magda Zimmering, members of Kibbutz Sedot Yam and the Nahalal Agricultural School.

I am grateful for advice and support from Professor János Bak, Charles Bloch, Herb Brin, Dr. Ebelin Bucerius, Dr. Gerd Bucerius, Dr. Miriam Buk, Rabbi Abraham Cooper, Rabbi William Cutter and Georgianne Cutter, Marilyn Gross, Licci Habe, Rabbi Marvin Hier and Malka Hier, Paul Jarrico, Yvette Jarrico, Eva and Paul Kolozsváry, Dan Leon, Jay Levine, Niv Neeman, Nessa Rapoport, Eve Tettemer Siegel, Ginnosra Szenes, Ilana and David Szenes, Lydia Triantopoulos, and Simon Wiesenthal.

I am indebted to Livia Rothkirchen at the archives of Yad Vashem, and to Yaffa Weisman at the library of Hebrew Union College in Los Angeles. In the same city, I have also made use of the libraries of the University of Judaism, and of the Simon Wiesenthal Center.

I have been fortunate in my talented editor, Nancy Perlman, who has labored long and hard in shaping a vast amount of heterogeneous material. I am also grateful for the many useful suggestions from my copy-editor, Sean Devlin.

Richard Kahlenberg was instrumental in encouraging and persuading me to undertake this book; his advice and friendship have been essential.

I wish to thank, in particular, my friend Didi Conn, an outstanding actor, whose enthusiasm about Chana Szenes brought us to collaborate on a play about her, to make our first trip to Israel, which in turn led to this book.

My mother, herself a figure in this story, read the manuscript twice and made many invaluable suggestions. Her response to the book has meant a great deal to me.

Finally and mostly, I am much indebted to my dear wife, Dorthea Atwater, both for her patient support and for her unfailing expertise as a professional editor and author of three books.

CONTENTS

NOTE ON NAMES

There have been several different spellings of names that occur in the book. For example, Chana Szenes has appeared in English-language editions mainly as Hannah Senesh (sometimes the Germanic Senesch). While this might make pronunciation easier, it is difficult to argue that one pays tribute to historical figures by arbitrarily altering the spelling of their names. I happen to believe in the magic of names and, in trying to restore them to the original, I used the name that belonged not only to the person but to a period in his or her life. That is why Anikó becomes Chana when she moves from Budapest to Palestine.

In Hungarian the family and first names are inverted: Chana Szenes was Szenes Anna; Anikó is what everybody called her. It is pronounced Un-eko, with the stress on the first syllable. Chana in Hebrew is pronounced Hannah with an aspirant (a slight hint of a k in front of the word).

Katherine Szenes's original name in Hungary was Katalin, but everybody used the more familiar form of Kató, (which in Hungarian is pronounced Cut-oh). In Israel she is known as Ima (Mother) Szenes.

Gyuri is the familiar form of György; in Israel he is called Giora. Gyuri is pronounced as Yuri with D in front of it (stress on first syllable); Giora is phonetic, with the stress on the second syllable.

In all Hungarian words and names the stress always falls on the first syllable. Strokes on a vowel means a long or rounded sound: a is pronounced as the u in cut, but with an accent it is á as in are. A short e as in melt becomes, with an accent, long é as in "make": Éva is pronounced Ava. A stroke on í, ó, or ú simply makes those vowels long. Umlauts on o and u can be short (dots: ö) or long (strokes: ő); ö is pronounced as e in her, ü is like trying to say ee with the lips rounded.

The consonant combination cs is ch in English; sz is s (hence Szenes is pronounced Senesh); zs is zh; ny is the soft n as in Russian nyet, gy is the soft g (the closest pronunciation is dy); j is always pronounced y.

Hebrew names, because they are transcribed from a different alphabet, are more or less phonetic.

I have kept most of the street names in Hungarian: utca = street; út = road or boulevard; körút = ring-road (literally); tér = square.

PREFACE
TO THE PAPERBACK EDITION

The name and story of Chana Szenes have become better known in America since I began working on her biography some six years ago, and especially in the three years since this book was published. There have been a couple of other books inspired by her diaries and poetry, a one-woman show which has toured widely, and recently a film. Yet I still meet many, in and out of the Jewish community, who have not heard about her, or have only the vaguest notions about what she did and stood for. This is true even in Israel, where everybody knows the name of Chana Szenes and the fact that she had been a parachutist who jumped out of a plane somewhere, in some war. Many, who were born after the foundation of Israel, know little else about one of their national heroes. Her diaries and poems have been in print for more than forty years, but no full-scale biography written for an adult readership has ever appeared in Hebrew.

Name recognition by itself does not mean that Chana's actions are now better understood or even universally admired. Although much has been written to mitigate the image of European Jewry all passively surrendering to the Nazi Holocaust, that frightened figure of a little girl in hiding who is finally taken away and murdered has endured, at least outside Israel, as the human embodiment of what happened to a whole people. Anne Frank is obviously not responsible for that: we are. *Ghetto*, Joshua Sobol's apologist play which glorifies the morally ambivalent actions of the doomed inhabitants of the Vilna ghetto at the expense of the Jewish partisans outside, has been the only Israeli drama in recent memory to be exported on a global scale, just as American television epics which have shown Jews, blacks, or women being victimized, humiliated, and sometimes annihilated, have proven to be among the most popular.

I had already finished *Ordinary Heroes* when a friend gave me a 1960 article written by Bruno Bettelheim in Harper's, *The Ignored Lesson of Anne Frank* (reprinted in his book *The Informed Heart*). In it, the distinguished psychoanalyst argued that the Frank family was culpable, within the context of the times, for what happened to Anne, by not fleeing Holland when there was still time, by not building even an escape route from their hideout, and by clinging to material goods that represented the illusion of normalcy. A part of Anne Frank's universal appeal is her unshakable belief in basic human goodness. Yet, as Dr. Bettelheim, himself a survivor of concentration camps, wrote with clinical logic:

> If all men are basically good—if going on with intimate family living, no matter what else, is what is to be most admired—then indeed we can all go on with life as usual and forget about Auschwitz. Except that Anne Frank died because her parents could not get themselves to believe in Auschwitz. And her story found wide acclaim because for us too, it denies implicitly that Auschwitz ever existed. If all men are good, there was never an Auschwitz.

This warning, made almost thirty years ago, has been ignored in much the same way as was the real lesson of Anne Frank. There are those around us who deny that Auschwitz ever happened, and some of us who fear that its recurrence cannot be prevented. There are people, from so-called respectable, intellectual circles and not on the lunatic fringes, who have persuaded themselves that Zionism is an ideological phenomenon similar to fascism. Somehow, Jews are supposed to have both escaped and perpetrated the horrors of Nazism; Israel, which was created anew to provide a haven for persecuted Jews, is being turned into a nation of persecutors. Such tortured thinking is not new or that unusual, and it has brought us plenty of trouble already during the course of this terrible century. And yet the ultimate horror is the thought that Auschwitz may have been extreme but not exceptional: that it is the fundamental paradigm of the human condition.

Is there a middle ground between self-blinding optimism and an equally paralyzing despair? The world was dark already before Auschwitz, when Chana Szenes, pacifist and poet, put down the pen and picked up the plough, and then exchanged both for a parachute and a gun. But what did she actually accomplish, I am sometimes brought to task, whom did she save, how many Nazis did she kill? Was not her mission a complete failure? Did she not die?

It is easy to miss and ignore the lesson of Chana Szenes, too. Though not much older than Anne Frank, Chana recognized that evil exists in the world, and that good people must face up to it or the evil will destroy them. She joined a tiny group among Jews when she became a Zionist and went to Palestine. She was among fewer than three dozen Jewish commandos who were parachuted into occupied Europe. And she was practically alone when she insisted on crossing back into Hungary to face the evil there. Each step was opposed by people who loved her and whom she admired. Many were older or male authority figures, and she won for herself the right to take each step at the partial cost of their approval. In preparing for their mission, Chana told her fellow parachutist Yoel Palgi that the chances of military success seemed miniscule. But she also intuited correctly that the greatest weapon the Nazis used in weakening resisters was to increase their sense of isolation and complete abandonment. Chana felt that if just one Jew in hiding, in prison or in a concentration camp was given new courage by the fact that Jewish commandos dropped from the sky to bring aid, the mission would be worthwhile. That, and much more was accomplished. The example of the parachutists, the seven who died and the many more who survived, inspired generations of Israelis to take action into their own hands and to fight for what they love.

The struggles of the Szenes family and of many other ordinary heroes encountered in this story, embody different and more hopeful symbols of the Holocaust and of the Zion that they have built. Chana may have been unusually clairvoyant in the darkness of those days, but there is nothing unusual about the darkness itself. And it was not enough to see clearly what needed to be done. Chana acted because *she* needed to do something; in the fact and the way of her doing lie both her success and her lesson.

For an author among the lasting benefits of publishing a book are friendships and professional associations formed with readers. In this context, I mention with pleasure the names of Kit Anderson, Marilyn and Michael De Guzman, Michael Donaldson, Rebekah Finer, Mania Goren, Dennis Klein, Ruth Liepman, Jenny Magid, Laurence Salzmann, Alan Shayne, Loren Stephens, Norman Stephens, Ivan Szenes and his family, Lori Wilner, and the many people whom I met in synagogues and churches, senior citizen homes and community centers, where I was invited to talk about *Ordinary Heroes*. I also want to thank editors Don Fehr and Juanita Lieberman, and the whole staff of Paragon House for making this paperback edition possible.

PETER HAY
Los Angeles, March 1, 1989

FOREWORD

In our times young people often find it hard to choose an example to follow. They feel that there is little opportunity nowadays to show personal courage. Amid all the evil in the world, what difference can one person make? The bravery and self-sacrifice of Chana Szenes, the sufferings of her family and other ordinary people who become heroes under extraordinary circumstances, provide inspiration that even the greatest evil can be defeated.

Chana's aspirations for a normal life as a teacher and poet were interrupted in Budapest by homegrown anti-Semitism and the Nazi menace from outside. At seventeen she took her first independent step by becoming a Zionist: "This word conveys so much," she wrote in her diary in October 1938, "but to me it means this: I have developed a stronger consciousness and pride in being Jewish. My aim is to go to Palestine and help build the country . . . I have become a new person and it feels right. One must have a strong idea to feel enthusiastic about, one must feel that one's life is not superfluous or spent in vain, that one is needed—and Zionism gives me this purpose."

Chana Szenes was working in her kibbutz in Eretz Israel at a safe distance from the Holocaust in Europe, but her conscience and her courage would not let her rest. She volunteered on a seemingly hopeless mission to organize Jewish resistance against the Nazi machinery of death. Again, nobody urged her to go; quite the contrary, all her friends and comrades tried to dissuade her. Chana went because she believed that one woman could make a difference.

It has been a matter of special pride to me that the Institute that bears my name, the Simon Wiesenthal Center in Los Angeles, has recently honored two individuals, both of whom volunteered to go to Nazi-occupied Hungary and there fulfill their destinies. One was Raoul Wallenberg, the young Swedish diplomat who saved thousands of lives as a "righteous Gentile." The other was Chana Szenes, who brought hope to her deserted people and later became a national symbol for the reborn Zion in Israel. There have been many books about Raoul Wallenberg, but this is the first one that presents the story of Chana Szenes as a heroine for today's world, while remembering why she needed to act as she did in the context of the Holocaust. It is wholly appropriate that this heroic story should be told now by a Hungarian born in the year of Chana's death, one whose family were neighbors and close friends of the Szenes family, and whose father was saved by Raoul Wallenberg.

Just a few months before she made the decision that would lead to her martyrdom, Chana quoted in her diary this sentence from a Jewish writer: "All the darkness cannot extinguish the light of a single candle, yet one candle can illuminate all the darkness." The life of Chana Szenes was one such candle.

—Simon Wiesenthal
Dokumentationszentrum,
Vienna, Austria
March 1986

private code of last resource. To be captured as British airmen who turned out to be Jews would place them in double jeopardy.

Chana had always, at every training session, volunteered to jump first. It helped to enhance her growing reputation for courage, but she knew better. She needed to prove herself, not so much to the thirty other commandos, all of whom were men, as to the *chaverim*, her friends and fellow workers left behind. Many had opposed her going. There were those who loved her and wanted to save her from danger. Others thought she was being impulsively romantic. They said she should fight the war by building peace. There was plenty of work to be done at the kibbutz, clearing centuries of dunes.

The arguments within the secretive Haganah, the Jewish self-defense organization, were more detached. Nobody doubted her talents, they said, but the chief consideration must be whether these would serve or endanger the mission. Did she fully realize what was involved? Would a twenty-two-year-old middle-class girl from Hungary withstand the Gestapo's tortures? Her stubbornness was legendary, but would she obey orders if they were contrary to what she thought best? Did she believe in the conditions of the mission, as the Haganah had thrashed them out with the British, or would her actions be guided by a more personal agenda? In the end, it was her stubbornness that had won both camps over. Month after month, without letup, she pestered them. With relentless logic she argued every objection, removing every trace of specific emotion that might be held against her candidacy. She wore them down and they yielded to her will. They were loath to let her go into certain danger; at the same time they were proud of her.

The training proved both them and her right. But Chana had hoped, desperately, that after her first few jumps the fear that dried out the throat and turned cartilage into jelly would surrender to her will. It didn't. She hated to see her comrades trying to shake their uncontrollable trembling by tensing and relaxing muscles, clamping jaws tight to prevent any tell-tale chattering of their teeth. She could not stand the idea of drawing out her agony by watching them jump. It was easier to be a hero by going first. After a dozen jumps, after two dozen, the fear never stopped, despite the exhilaration that followed the letting go. Each time beforehand she had to bite her tongue to prevent herself blurting out some excuse, saying that she would jump in the morning instead.

Now there was no next day. The mission, which she had joined by employing every ounce of her will and ingenuity, had begun. As the bomber droned its way from Italy toward their destination in the mountains of Yugoslavia, Chana felt the surfeit of excitement turning into weariness, draining all the thrill out of her. She caught sight of Reuven's ghostly face. The unofficial commander of the mission, he had doubts about having this

DESCENDING

Chana had volunteered to jump first.

She groped toward the green light in the forward section of the four-engine Halifax bomber. Her movements were awkward and unsure; she felt like an adolescent again, made self-conscious by the excessive bulk of her flyer's equipment. Her suit had several zipped pockets on the hips and the legs, and each pocket was crammed with tools and essential items for survival: revolver, flashlight, compass and maps, a tiny first-aid kit. She was also carrying forged documents, money, and mail for the partisans. The parachute itself was stowed in a bulky capsule on her back.

She had sat for hours in a cramped corner of the aircraft. Moving at last toward the long-awaited goal, she could feel her tense muscles responding, each limb scrambling to catch up with her eager mind. The round flight helmet swallowed her soft, wavy hair and cast the high forehead into shadow, making her indistinguishable from the men on board. Each man was coping silently with his private demon; some with their eyes wide open, others still trying to ward off sleep. Conversation was futile against the roar of the engines. And everything had been said many times during the enforced togetherness of training. Graffiti scratched in English on the leather brims of their helmets summed up their situation: "Don't follow me," or "I must be mad." The desperate military humor seemed flat now.

There had been laughter during the practice jumps. From both nerves and high spirits they cracked Hebrew jokes that annoyed their British officers, who kept reminding them in accents of enervated superiority that they were now representing His Britannic Majesty and should behave accordingly. No yellow streak, no unbecoming jollity; above all, try not to sound like bloody foreigners. Some of the Palestinian volunteers hardly knew English, despite their RAF uniforms. They were selected because they had come originally from Central Europe. Yet they now had to be ready to disguise knowledge of the local language. Hebrew was to be a intense young woman on his team. She forced a smile and gave him the thumbs-up. There was nothing left to say. One of the flight crew had already removed the circular lid over the hatch. He reached out for Chana's hand to make sure she would not accidentally step into the gaping hole. As she carefully lowered both legs into the void, a rush of cold night air brutally revived her. The moon had just risen, throwing a sharp silhouette over the wing of the aircraft. Below, there was only darkness, with white patches of snow amidst the black forests. It was all utterly unlike the maps she had been studying for weeks. She hovered, hanging on to the hatch, knowing from training that the hardest thing now was to wait for the green light to turn red. Even a few seconds too soon in the air could make a difference of several miles on the ground. Given the sketchy intelligence provided, and the fortunes of war that kept the partisans constantly on the move with the shifting boundaries, those few miles could mean landing in German-held territory. But like a racehorse in the starting gate, she could hardly hold herself back.

"Go!" The command exploded as the light changed to red (or did she imagine that?), the roar of the engine suddenly fell away, and she crashed down into the black void so rapidly that her mind could concentrate only on one thought—the parachute that wasn't opening and probably wouldn't open and that this was her fear every time she had jumped—and she felt the strange freedom that comes from not being able to do anything about it because things were for once beyond her control. Now a sharp jerk checked the free fall, and even before she looked up, the reassuring rocking of her body told her that she was not going to die—at least not yet. The white giant billowed above her like a genie from the bottle, taking her where she wanted to go.

Chana had covered two thirds or more of the mile-long drop when she began to make out some black valleys below the peaks where the snow and the moon met. The March wind was cold against her face. It was much stronger than she had expected, and she wondered whether it would take her too far off course. At the same time her mind was liberated from the terrible fear of the jump and she felt too peaceful to be practical for the moment. She was content to be just floating.

Her thoughts began to wander. A ruddy-cheeked face came to her, with a wisp of blondish mustache; it belonged to the young English sergeant in charge of the supply depot at the air base in Bari, where she had gone to pick up equipment for the mission.

"Looking forward to your brolly-hop?" She smiled at the RAF slang for the jump. He advised her to choose carefully the color and number of her parachute, knowing that many paratroopers were superstitious about them. The chutes lay on open shelves, each clearly labeled with a number and the name of the persons who folded and inspected it. The young man readily explained the reason: "S'ppose somebody was goofing off, thinking about her evening date, for instance, and the thing failed to open. You'd have somebody to curse during those last seconds."

"What good would that do?" Chana wondered aloud. The young man, hungry for conversation, had no answer. It was obvious that he rarely met women in that warehouse, or anywhere else. They talked for a few minutes. Soon he wanted her to promise to visit England and meet his mother once the war was over.

"Don't laugh, but she would want me to marry some girl just like you." Chana did laugh.

"What about you?" she teased, but she relented when she saw his confusion. He was handsome enough, in an English sort of way. She knew the type from the British forces that tried to keep order in Palestine.

"The poor lad is head over heels in love with you," Yoel, a fellow commando, told her afterward. "He found out that I knew you and he kept saying that he could only marry someone like you. What on earth did you do to that chap?"

Remembering, Chana felt her cheeks blush against the cold air. This man had met her for just a quarter of an hour and imagined spending the rest of his life with her. Maybe there *was* such a thing as love at first sight. Would she ever feel that sure about any man? Was it even important, compared to the great events convulsing the world? She indulged in a moment of self-pity. If the mission turned out badly, she could never become a woman, never have the chance to love that way.

She tried to conjure up more pleasant thoughts, and immediately her mind was crowded with the faces of her family, now scattered far apart. She saw the intent, questioning face of her brother, Gyuri, during their brief goodbye in Tel Aviv, only six weeks ago. It was their first and last meeting after a separation of five years. By coincidence she had learned of his arrival in Palestine on the same day that she was to leave for her training in Egypt. She managed to win a twenty-four-hour postponement, but she was not permitted to breathe a word about the mission to him.

She blamed herself now for not finding better words to reassure him about his new life in Eretz Israel. Chana had arranged for Gyuri to join a group of young Zionists from Transylvania who were starting a kibbutz by the Sea of Galilee. Chana already felt close to these young pioneers, because Yoel and two other friends of the mission, Yonah and Peretz, all came from that kibbutz.

The thought of her recent reunion with Gyuri immediately drove Chana's thoughts to their mother, Kató, who was so much the quintessential mother that Chana could barely imagine her in any other role. Widowed very young, it never occurred to Kató to remarry. Her whole life was consecrated to her children and keeping her husband's memory and literary works alive.

Chana's early love of literature and writing made that bond with her parents particularly strong; mother and daughter had enjoyed an unusually close relationship, unaffected by adolescence. Thus, when she became a Zionist at the age of seventeen, Chana knew that she faced a terrible choice—to stay near her mother, who was also her best friend, or to build, as she felt obliged to, a new life in Palestine. The guilt she felt for abandoning her mother in Budapest grew more fierce with each year of separation; often it throbbed through her body like physical pain.

As Chana descended from the sky into the mountains of Yugoslavia, she tried to peer beyond the northern horizon. She wanted to glimpse the bright lights of Budapest and the little house where she had lived happily with her family for eighteen years. But there was nothing in the distance except profound darkness. She was falling fast, watching the horizon recede until it was no more. She hit the snowy ground hard, and then came the cold reality that she was utterly alone and far from any place that could be called home.

ONE

ASCENDING

.

Until the day she left her home in Budapest everybody knew Chana as Anikó. Early that day, in September 1939, she and her mother were finishing a night of frantic packing. The train was leaving at noon; they had learned only the day before that Anikó would get her long-awaited passage to Palestine with a group of young Zionists fleeing from Czechoslovakia. The affectionate bickering that punctuated their activity helped to ease their sadness at the imminent and sudden separation. Kató Szenes tried to stuff everything possible into the huge trunk; her daughter was eager to leave as much as possible behind. Finally there was nothing more to be negotiated, except for the raincoat.

"Will you carry it, darling, or shall I squeeze it into this second suitcase?" But Anikó did not want a raincoat.

"Mother, the biggest problem in Palestine is drought. The annual rainfall . . ." But she saw from her mother's energetic folding of the coat that it was useless to argue.

"All right, I'll carry it on my arm, but only because you were gracious enough not to insist on my debutante ball dress for the desert."

"Only because it won't fit you, darling, you've filled out so much in the past year. But I'm sure you can find a dressmaker somewhere. Did I give you Mrs. Kraus's address in Haifa?"

"Yes, Mother."

Anikó had earlier lost the struggle to leave behind half her mother's trousseau of expensive linen, satin bedclothes, brocade table covers, napkins, and dishcloths. What if she were to get married one day in that godforsaken place and Kató couldn't send all this to her because of the war? Anikó countered that even if she could use such finery in Palestine, who would have time to wash and iron everything? She watched in frustration as her mother filled the trunk with accessories for her hypothetical marriage. At the same time she was willing to defer to Kató's wishes in such matters, having exacted her prized permission to leave. In the months ahead Anikó would miss this unconditional dedication to her welfare. Excited as she was by the future, what she felt most acutely right now was the reality of separation from the person who had been not only her mother, but also her best friend and ally.

Brute force was required to close the trunk and old leather suitcases. Anikó bounded with zest onto her bed while Kató, with the strong, straight back of a piano teacher, tried valiantly to pummel the recalcitrant luggage into submission. All at once, Anikó lost her balance and rolled off the bed. Now both of them sat on the floor, helplessly hooting with laughter, with the carefully layered contents spilling over them.

"May I be of help, Madame Kató?" Rózsi, the fresh-cheeked maid, paused a moment in the doorway to take in the scene. She was used to high spirits from Anikó; it was much more unusual to see her widowed employer laugh so heartily, especially with Anikó's departure so near at hand. At last, the three women fastened the suitcases and Rózsi carried them into the hallway, withdrawing into the kitchen to pack lunch for her favorite. With the tactfulness of long-term domestics, she tried to leave mother and daughter alone as much as possible during these last few hours.

It was time now for Anikó to clear her desk. Here were the relics that fused childhood with the most grown-up part of her, the photographs and precious objects that inspired her. These she would carry in her overnight bag, never letting it out of sight. There was the sepia picture of a balding man who looked older than his years, his expression confident and yet melancholy. Anikó kissed the framed photograph before packing it. She talked to this picture every night before going to sleep, telling him about her problems that day and seeking his approval for the way she had coped with them.

The Daddy of her memories was much warmer and less formal than the photograph, but she always remembered those sad eyes. Béla Szenes learned at eighteen about his defective heart. From then on, he was a man in a hurry, marrying younger than was customary and before he could really afford it. He wanted to prove to all the Schlesingers—his own family of honest merchants, with a rabbi in his mother's family—that being a professional writer did not necessarily make him a *Luftmensch*—a dreamer. Then he had to prove himself all over again to the Salzbergers, when he wooed the third of the family's four daughters. Kató's grandfather owned a haberdashery business at Jánosháza, but by the First World War the family had become middle class, and the other daughters married professionals. Béla in fact worked much harder than most lawyers or doctors: he wanted to accomplish as much as possible in the short life predicted for him and to provide for his young family's future. By the time his heart gave out at the age of thirty-three, he had written comedies, novels, poems, and count-

less articles. Eight of his plays were hits in the Budapest theaters, and
some were also produced abroad in German, French, and Czech. He was
the toast of the town and king of the coffee houses, where everybody
enjoyed the whimsical columns by "The Coalman." This was a pun on his
adopted name of Szenes, assimilated from "Schlesinger" at a time when
Jews wanted to blend into Hungarian society. The outwardly sunny, hu-
morous, gentle man was under the constant pressure of newspaper and
theater deadlines, which probably hastened the course of his ailment. Despite the demands of his work, Béla lavished attention on his two small
children, hoping that they would store up enough memories of him to last
a lifetime. When he suddenly collapsed in the race to finish his latest
comedy, literary Budapest mourned a major loss. Gyuri was six, Anikó
five years old.

Rummaging in a desk drawer, Anikó now found an old magazine clipping
featuring a photograph of herself sitting on a bench with a man, and Gyuri
standing behind them. Little Anikó was about eight, looking extremely
demure, with an expression of anxious concentration on her face. It had
been Anikó's first interview with a real journalist, and she clearly wanted
to make sure that he got things right. The man from *Theater Life* magazine
wanted to know what the Szenes children felt about the musical version
of their father's hit comedy opening that week. Reading the fading news-
print of ten years before, Anikó smiled as much at the patronizing tone as
from the remembered pleasure of seeing herself in print for the first time:

> This premiere is a very personal affair for the little Szenes children!
> One can tell from all the excited pushing and shoving around me:
> Anikó is wearing a fluffy white dress making her look like a little
> angel. On Gyuri's sturdy torso his vest is fairly bursting with pride.
> "Is Labass playing the lead?" he asks.
>
> They know the play like the back of their hands! They have only
> seen two other plays by their papa: *I'll Never Marry* and *House Guest*.
> But *Rich Girl* remains their favorite.
>
> "That's the one we understood most," Gyuri explains. Anikó has
> a sentimental attachment to this comedy. She was born during its first
> run.
>
> What else can I tell you about the little Szenes children? Both of
> them are intelligent and well-mannered. And they're already possessed
> of the real artistic spirit. Gyuri paints and plays the piano superbly. I
> asked him what he wants to be. Most of all he would like to be famous.
> But he will also express his doubts quite truthfully. In his view Anikó
> is more likely to achieve greatness. As a poet. She writes beautiful
> poems. Here is one of the most moving ones, which has been published
> already in their own *Little Szenes Gazette:*

Oh you happy children
You who have parents
You can be together
And live happily forever

Oh you happy children
How I'd like to join you
Laughing and playing
Just happily living . . .

Anikó blushed now at the naive sentimentality of her early effort. Being eight seemed no excuse to the eighteen-year-old. She had come to despise self-pity and worked hard to purge her writing of it. She had begun to admire toughness of style and mind.

She now picked up another picture, this time of her mother sitting in the garden with Gyuri, a gangling teenager, next to her. Anikó teasingly called him her "old man," because Gyuri was a year older. Actually, she had always felt like the older sibling. She was fiercely protective of her brother in this household of adoring females, which had included until recently Fini-mama, their grandmother, who had died the year before. Anikó had defended Gyuri's right to be withdrawn and moody. She understood why he had seized the first opportunity to go abroad to study. He was now in France, learning about textiles; it was sensible to have a trade, all of Kató's friends agreed, in case things got worse, which they did every day. Anikó and Kató had visited him in Lyons the previous spring, and the "old man" seemed to be thriving on his own. What made Anikó even happier was that Gyuri had also become a Zionist in France and hoped to join her in Eretz Israel after he finished his studies. The two of them spent those few days in Lyons feverishly planning their lives, while their mother listened quietly, desolate at the prospect of losing both of her children but knowing that there was no future for them at home.

Gazing at the picture of the two people who were closest to her, Anikó felt her heart tighten as she thought of this miniature Diaspora, a family of three scattered into three different countries.

She had fought hard for permission to pursue the dream of Zion that had captured her heart and imagination almost a year before. Every step had been blocked by officialdom, by uncomprehending friends and the silent martyrdom of her mother's love. Still, Anikó had persevered, plotting her course with steady determination. After deciding to make her *aliyah*—"the ascent," as the return to Palestine was called—she realized that she would probably not get the certificate that was needed for immigration. There were simply too many other candidates with much stronger Zionist credentials. She worked to improve her slender chances, planning each move carefully. She chose to study agriculture, because that would be of immediate value to the struggling pioneers on the land. When she had to write her application letter to the Agricultural School in Nahalal, Anikó struggled to explain her purpose in Hebrew, which she had been studying for less than a year. Those few imperfect sentences cost her days of labor, but she wanted to impress the school authorities with the sincerity of her goals. She had succeeded, and admission to the school had made it much easier to obtain the coveted certificate.

This was by far the hardest thing Anikó had ever done. In this summer of graduation from high school it was also her first act of independence as an adult. Despite her success so far, the journey ahead was full of unpredictable difficulties. As she dreamed of building a new land, the war that she had spent the past few years dreading, the war that would soon engulf the world for the second time in one generation, had already begun ten days before. Borders were closing all over Europe except to invading armies. Anikó was in a hurry to leave home before she was trapped. Still, as thrilled as she was at the new future opening before her, she yearned for the moment when her mother, brother, and closest friends might join her in the land that Zionists called Eretz Israel—the land of Israel.

The anxious sadness in her heart reminded her of a recent scare, which had followed the arrival of the longed-for certificate. Anikó had felt so much joy and anticipation, and so much sorrow about parting from her mother, that her heart would not stop aching, a small persistent pain that tormented her day after day. She was filled with dread: what if she had inherited her father's sickness? Perhaps they would not admit her to Palestine if she couldn't do the heavy physical labor. Anikó lived in the anguish of uncertainty for days. Finally, not wanting to worry her mother, she phoned the family doctor in secret. After a careful examination, the doctor reassured her that he found no heart defect. It was all nervous tension, he told her. From that moment on, her diary reflected only a growing impatience to move on.

Rereading her diary reminded Anikó that she needed to find a thicker folder in which to carry her writings. She had neatly transcribed most of her poetry into a notebook, but there were some loose pages, including those unfinished verses she was planning to polish during the trip. Two other notebooks, with blue covers and lines to guide her oversized, childish handwriting, contained the diaries that she had kept more or less regularly for the past five years. She kept the diaries for her eyes only, and many people who thought they knew her would have been astonished by their contents. Gregarious as she was, Anikó very rarely talked about herself, allowing her outgoing public personality to act as a mask to deflect questions back to the questioners. She was genuinely interested in other people and external events, but she also used this interest to protect her deeply introspective self. More serious than her schoolmates, she had no close friends in whom to confide.

There were two exceptions: One was her cousin Évi Sas, who was exactly Anikó's age and lived in the country at Dombovár, where Anikó usually spent a part of the summer. Occasionally Évi came up to Budapest, and within hours the two would be caught up with intimate confidences and lively gossip. Mrs. Szenes was always happy to see Évi, whose striking beauty and sweetness also appealed greatly to Gyuri; had he not left for France, their flirtations might have developed into something serious.

Another occasional confidante was Éva Singer,* six years older than Anikó. She was the only child of Leó and Edith Singer, who lived on the same street as the Szenes family. When Anikó was about fifteen, Éva taught her and Gyuri the rudiments of ballroom dancing, an essential accomplishment for middle-class life in Budapest. Éva, who was bright and glamorous, got married when Anikó was only twelve and their relationship for a number of years thereafter was based on a much closer friendship between their mothers. It was Edith, for example, who found for Gyuri the textile school in Lyons, after a plan to attend a similar school in Milan fell through.

Éva remembers, during her frequent visits back home, an adolescent Anikó who was always serious, quiet, and mature beyond her years. About six years later, Éva separated from her husband and moved back into her parents' home. She visited the Szenes's home daily during the difficult last weeks before Anikó's departure. The two young women, now grown closer, had many serious conversations about why one was leaving and the other staying; Anikó came as close as with anyone in confiding her deeper hopes and fears to Éva, who recalls the almost fanatical earnestness with which Anikó talked about her need to go where she could feel useful: "She saw her goals so clearly, and yet—having won over her mother and successfully battled skeptical friends and relatives—she still had this great need to justify her decision."

In the absence of regular outlets for her confidences, Anikó held imaginary conversations with Béla before going to sleep and shaped her thoughts into poems, which she showed to her mother and teachers. But her deepest feelings she poured into her diaries, which contain a full record of a young girl's intellectual and emotional development from the age of thirteen in a world bent on self-destruction. Night after night Anikó set down her views about the deteriorating political situation at home and abroad and worried about the difficult decisions she had to make. But just as often, and sometimes even in the same entry, she would write about the casual concerns of a gregarious schoolgirl, talking of classes and school dances,

*Now Éva Háy, the author's mother.

and sometimes wondering why boys were beginning to behave toward her in such exquisitely silly ways.

At last, with the diaries and photographs safely stowed in her folder, Anikó packed the final odds and ends into her overnight bag. She draped the raincoat over one arm, and picked up her final piece of baggage, a light portable typewriter on which she had splurged uncharacteristically the day before. She intended to start using it on the train, to record for her anxious mother all the minutiae of the trip and to dispose of any last-minute correspondence for which she knew there would be no time in her new life.

The leave-taking from Rózsi was brief but warm. They embraced; Anikó begged Rózsi to look after Mama and Rózsi entreated Anikó to remember her crash course in domestic skills like making her own bed, washing dishes, and ironing her clothes. Like most of the girls she knew, she had never done housework before, and was a bit worried about how she would manage on her own at the boarding school in Palestine. But Rózsi had been a willing teacher.

"Next time you see me, you'll be proud of me," Anikó promised. Rózsi cried but Anikó forced herself to remain dry-eyed as she took a last mental snapshot of the house and its lovely garden.

The taxi had been loaded already and now Kató and Anikó climbed into the comfortable back seat for the ten-minute drive to the train station. The September air was warm; the city glowed in the gold of late summer. The taxi left 28 Bimbó-út and descended from the Rózsadomb, or Rose Hill, the residential quarter where many artists and writers lived. Anikó peered eagerly out the taxi window, wanting to capture forever in her memory the sights and vistas of her home. Along one of the downhill curves she caught a glimpse of one of those exhilarating views that gives Budapest the epithet "Queen of the Danube."

The city consists of two halves—Buda and Pest—with the great river dividing her in the middle. Buda, on the western bank, is mountainous and easily defensible, a center of civilization since Roman times. The Danube, in places half a mile wide, had provided a formidable natural frontier against waves of barbarians who stampeded from Asia across the vast steppes into the Carpathian basin. Among them, Attila the Hun occupied the Great Plain on the eastern bank of the river, followed half a millennium later by the savage and nomadic Magyars, who decided to remain. These Hungarians, as their western neighbors called them, entered Europe as a scourge of Christendom; around the year 1000 they converted from their pagan ways under their king, Saint Stephen, and became the reluctant guardians of Christendom against other invaders, notably the Mongols and the Turks. The latter came, conquered Buda, and stayed for a century and a half. The scent of their rose gardens still lingers around the tomb of the dervish Gül Baba, a Moslem shrine close to Anikó's home.

The name of Rose Hill also endures, along with a few Turkish baths and minarets and the passion for strong coffee, as continuing reminders of the Oriental connection.

The taxi was crossing Margit Bridge over to Pest, and now Anikó glanced back at the classic view of Castle Hill, dominating the skyline of medieval Buda. Much of the history at which she had excelled in school was crammed into that one inspiring tableau: the nubby Gothic spires of the Coronation Church rising above the white stones of Fisherman's Bastion; all of this overwhelmed by the vast length of the Royal Palace, which had been vacant of resident royalty for centuries. The Hapsburg emperors, who claimed the crown of Saint Stephen from the Turks, had preferred the safety of Vienna, except for the ceremonial visits they occasionally paid to their hotheaded subjects. Since 1920, the year of Gyuri's birth, the castle had been occupied by the regent, Miklós Horthy. In a typically Hungarian contradiction, Horthy claimed to govern in the name of a monarch who was deposed, and he sported the title of admiral in a navy that did not exist.

Between the two world wars, when Gyuri and Anikó were growing up there, Budapest was an exotic and romantic mecca for rich foreigners who flocked to the magnificent hotels along the river embankment for the un-inhibited enjoyment of good wine, bad women, and intoxicating music. Visitors like the Prince of Wales were guaranteed a certain anonymity by the distance of the city from Western capitals and the impenetrability of the language, which made it harder for foreign journalists to collect gossip. People also came for the thermal spas and medicinal waters. Budapest offered a rich variety of swimming pools and mud baths, of foul-smelling and fouler-tasting waters for a variety of ailments that only the very healthy cultivate. The hedonistic, hypochondriacal, aquatic culture provided a sort of national therapy to heal the wounds of history.

Having been for centuries part of a multinational empire, Hungarians preserved a distinctive and exotic culture through their language and lit-erature. Life, with its political uncertainties, was made bearable with good music and theater, rich food and plenty of whipped cream on everything. After 1867, a series of relatively enlightened policies were introduced throughout the Austro-Hungarian monarchy, removing restrictions on higher education and opening most professions to Jews, who had lived in Hungary since the early Middle Ages. Within the patchwork of nationalities that made up the sprawling Hapsburg empire, Jews could now move with rel-ative ease from the crowded *shtetls* of Silesia and Galicia to the cosmo-politan centers of commerce, learning, and the arts in Vienna and Budapest. By the turn of the twentieth century many prominent Jewish industrialists, bankers, and landowners had been raised to the peerage for services ren-dered to the emperor. These Jewish barons lived like other barons, just as the new Jewish middle classes had adopted standard bourgeois values. But their very success in assimilation, which included conversion to Christianity on a massive scale and the adopting of ultra-nationalist attitudes along with Hungarian-sounding names, made the Gentile majority uneasy, if not outright hostile, about what they perceived as Jewish ambition at the expense of declining influence by the landed gentry and the Church.

Although the Szenes family had become assimilated into the mainstream of cultural life in Budapest, they did not convert to Christianity. High holidays and rites of passage were observed. The children learned about Judaism from Aunt Györgyi, a kindly old teacher for whom Anikó composed a valedictory speech. Gyuri quickly lost interest in religion, but Anikó took seriously the vows she had made at her Bat Mitzvah, which she recited so memorably that Dr. Arnold Kiss, the chief rabbi, commended her: "I have not heard such a fine speech so well delivered since Franciska Gál," referring to a famous actress who had subsequently left the Jewish faith. Which well-known fact prompted the thirteen-year-old Gyuri to forget that he was in temple and call out, "Franciska may have made fine promises, but Anikó will also keep them!"

Anikó recalled this family anecdote as she tried to catch a last glimpse of the great synagogue that occupied a whole city block on busy Dohány-utca and now incorporated the house where Theodor Herzl, the founder of Zionism, had been born. This seemed to Anikó an ironic commentary on the way her own religious feelings during the past year had been gradually supplanted by the practical agenda of Zionism. Instead of uniting her with other Jews, as the synagogue had absorbed Herzl's birthplace, her Zionism had further isolated her.

In 1939 almost one quarter of Budapest's population was Jewish, but even with Hitler ensconced in neighboring Austria, only a few thousand would have considered leaving comfortable Budapest and going to Palestine. There were 570 coffee houses in Budapest by the turn of the century, and many intellectuals and artists worked, wrote, dreamed, and practically lived there. Café life provided a natural breeding ground for a secular Jewish culture, and it created a new kind of urban literature—light poems, feuilletons, boulevard comedies, and political cabaret—imbued with Jewish sensibility and humor, which was then exported in great quantities to Vienna, Berlin, Paris, and then Broadway and Hollywood.

Anikó felt a twinge of regret, passing the busy sidewalk cafés on the wide boulevards. On the threshold of adulthood, she was just beginning to taste this intense cultural world of her father and now she was already leaving it. Nobody could tell how long it would all last. Only wiser ears might have detected an uneasy undercurrent as the regulars made fewer jokes while scrutinizing the news pages. From inside the taxi, it would have been hard to realize that Hitler had moved into Poland only ten days before and that a state of war existed between the principal powers of Western Europe.

Even as Poland was being swallowed by Nazi Germany and its unlikely ally, Soviet Russia, Hungarians were divided about their own alliances with Fascist Italy and Nazi Germany. The majority felt triumph and vindication when Hitler dismembered neighboring Czechoslovakia and returned parts of southern Slovakia to Hungary. There was more rejoicing in March 1939 when Hitler helped Hungary repossess the province of Carpatho-Ruthenia. Like most Hungarian patriots, the Jews felt keenly the humiliations of the Treaty of Trianon, signed at Versailles in June 1920, which deprived Hungary of two thirds of her prewar land area and population. The promise of recovering at least the Hungarian-speaking portions of these provinces drove even liberal governments closer to Fascist Italy and Hitler's resurgent Germany. But the Hungarians were also afraid of German expansion into Austria and Czechoslovakia and tried in vain to reach out to their hostile Balkan neighbors. In a precarious tightrope act, the cabinet of Count Pál Teleki, with its strong sympathies with Great Britain and France, had refused the German armies passage through Hungary to invade Poland. On the other hand, successive Hungarian governments were forced, because of a growing Fascist movement at home, to listen to Berlin. And Berlin was increasingly telling Budapest to act on the so-called Jewish problem or the Germans would step in and help them solve it.

Most Hungarians believed that after Hitler got redress for Germany's wrongs, he would stop his war against the Jews. Yet Hungary had also been the first modern European state to reintroduce anti-Semitic legislation, during the right-wing backlash against the abortive Communist regime that was in power for three months during 1919. Béla Kún, the leader of that Soviet government, happened to be Jewish, and the new regent, Admiral Horthy, cannily posed as Hungary's savior against both Communists and Jews, whom he blamed for losing the war and for the dismemberment of Greater Hungary. In 1920 a new law limited the number of Jews admitted to universities and hence to most professions of public influence to 6 percent. In 1932, as the Depression wreaked havoc with Hungary's postwar recovery, Gyula Gömbös, a well-known anti-Semite of the radical right, came to power. He died four years later, but the right did not: the fascist Arrow Cross party was founded in 1935 and immediately captured one sixth of the seats in the Lower House of Parliament. From May 1938 the government of Béla Imrédy kept passing anti-Jewish bills, which caused increasing anxiety among the Jewish community but were too mild to appease either the Germans or their vocal supporters in Hungary. Anti-Semitism, while not yet triumphant, was out in the open. The Arrow Cross still lacked the muscle to stage a Kristallnacht riot, and they did not have the parliamentary votes to confiscate Jewish property, businesses, and jobs. So many thousands of refugees from neighboring countries flocked to what seemed a relative haven. With the recovery of adjacent territories, and as the war spread in Central Europe, the Jewish population of Hungary gradually swelled from under half a million to about double that number—a statistic not lost on Germany.

Anikó followed political events keenly and discussed them at length in her diary. She deplored Mussolini's invasion of Ethiopia and recoiled at the thought of Hitler being welcome in Vienna. And in May 1937, she described an incident that presaged her future. Anikó was so active in her school's Literary Society that she was nominated by all the senior classes to be its secretary. It was a high honor for a girl who was only fifteen. Bármadas was a private Protestant school for girls, which charged Catholics double and Jews triple the regular tuition fees. An exception was made in Anikó's case, because of her outstanding grades and her famous father. For accounting purposes, they agreed that she would be treated as a Catholic. Even so, Mrs. Szenes could barely afford the tuition. Now, with Anikó's impending election, another rule came to light. Officers of school societies had to be Protestant, and in the uneasy political climate no exception could be made. Aunt Boriska, Anikó's favorite teacher, tried to comfort her, saying that this decision was not meant to reject her personally. But the situation posed a dilemma to the sensitive adolescent girl. She had been the undisputed star of the Literary Society: how could she remain a member after what had happened? Her mother was sympathetic but helpless. So Anikó began the long journey that led to Palestine. She confided to her diary:

> It is so hard to find a way out of this without humiliation or false pride, that won't be seen as a retreat, or be considered too pushy. One has to be so careful with every move, because each fault becomes stereotyped. The way I see it, fighting anti-Semitism requires individual qualities—I mean moral ones. It is the most difficult kind of fight. Only now I am beginning to see what it means to be Jewish in a Christian society. But I don't mind it, because it is that struggle to reach our goals that helps us develop exceptional qualities. If I had been born Christian, I could enter any profession, be a teacher perhaps. . . . I would not convert to Christianity under any circumstances, not just because of me but for the sake of my children. I would never force them into the dishonorable position of having to deny or to be ashamed of their origin. And I would not want to deprive them of their religion, as converted parents must. I think religion is very important and I find the modern belief that God is only a crutch

for the weak laughable. It is precisely that faith which gives one strength
and makes other means of support unnecessary.

For a while Anikó sought refuge in a stronger religious faith. She also
began to see the Literary Society as a microcosm: her country did not want
her. She might not even be admitted into the university, despite her brilliant
grades. And if she changed her religion, as many did, she would be doubly
despised: still considered a Jew by those she had joined, and outcast by
those she had abandoned. Worst of all, she would despise herself. Despite
her mental precocity, Anikó possessed the simple, straightforward logic of
a child: if Hungary was not home, she must find her home elsewhere. In
the year following her withdrawal from the Literary Society, she became
a Zionist. This meant finding new friends, because most of her closest
relatives, teachers, and classmates could not comprehend her decision.
Some even considered her a deserter, but Anikó knew in her heart that it
was Hungary that had deserted her. She was not leaving home but going
home—to Eretz Israel.

As the taxi finally arrived at the massive glass-and-iron construction of
the Oriental Station, Anikó was moved to see a small group of friends
waiting on the platform. They were mostly fellow Zionists from the Maccabean Society, whose meetings she had attended regularly during the past
year. They were still waiting for their certificates that would permit them
to join her in Palestine. There were also a few boyfriends with whom she
had gone to the movies and danced at parties. They stood on the platform,
looking awkward and solemn and seeking encouragement from Mrs. Szenes,
who unobtrusively took charge of the generous but impractical bon-voyage
bouquets. What would Anikó do with roses on a five-day journey? The
farewells were brief. Everyone promised to write, though there was no
certainty about how the mail would function in wartime.
As she finally embraced her mother, the forced gaiety, the excitement
about the future, and all her cherished self-control left Anikó. Tears choked
all words inside. All she could think of was that her mother would be
lighting the candles and greeting the Jewish New Year alone. Kató thought
with horror of letting this precious child go all alone into an unknown land
and future. They held each other for a long moment, knowing there was
nothing left to say. The next time they embraced it would be under very
different circumstances.
At the last possible moment, Anikó tore herself from her mother and
climbed onto the train, as it pulled out of the station. With gathering speed
the images of her homeland flew by the train windows. She sat alone in
the crowded compartment, tracing the Hebrew letters of her new name
on the front of her diary: CHANA. . . .

TWO

LOVER OF ZION

Chana left Hungary of her own will, not as a result of direct persecution. She could easily have found better educational opportunities in France, with Gyuri, or in England, where she might have stayed with Éva Singer's parents, who had emigrated just when Anikó was leaving home. Her family and friends would have readily supported such an idea. But she chose instead a poor, backward, and remote place where she must learn to work the arid soil with her hands. She was completely unsuited for such work and knew nothing about it; it is not surprising that almost everyone she knew was baffled by her decision. The fact is that Chana would never have dreamed of going to Palestine, let alone achieved her goal, without the inspiration of a powerful ideal.

Zionism, as a word, was invented less than a century ago. But when Chana fell in love with Zion at the age of seventeen, the idea was already three thousand years old. Like most "isms," the concept of Zionism has become obscured by both the great spiritual battles and the petty regional squabbles that have always characterized human history, and perhaps nowhere more bloodily than on a tiny piece of waterfront on the Mediterranean.

Throughout its recorded history the land of Israel has been composed of two separate realities, both of which interested Chana. It is first a physical entity, at one time flowing with milk and honey, but more recently strewn with sand and rocks, or malignant with disease-bearing swamps. Yet the landscape is full of surprises, packing into a few thousand square miles an immensely diverse geography and varied climate, from snowy mountains to burning deserts, subtropical gardens and pine forests, grotesque salt rocks and silky beaches.

For three thousand years another reality has coexisted in this physical landscape, the intangible idea of the One God. The earth has several spots that are sacred to a particular people or deity. Jerusalem, once considered the center of the earth, is still holy to one out of every three human beings walking on the planet. They belong to many different faiths and sects that have been waging war on each other for centuries; here they coexist, however uneasily. Right above the heads of the Jews bending to the remaining Wall of the Second Temple, Arabs are filing into the Dome of the Rock. The Church of the Holy Sepulchre is divided among four different Christian sects. This is the only land on earth that is called holy by hundreds of millions of people who have never even set eyes on it.

The land changed names—Canaan, Judah, and Israel, Judaea and Palestine, the Patriarchate under Byzantium, the Latin States of the Crusaders, the Sanjaks of the Ottoman Empire, then Palestine under the British Mandate and finally Israel once more. And it changed its rulers—the Hyksos and the Hittites, the Philistines and the Canaanites, the Egyptians and the Jews, the Greeks and the Romans, the Arabs, the Mamluks, the Turks, and the British; Jews and Arabs again and still. Throughout three thousand years of coming and going, that other reality, the grand concept, remained unchanged and had only one name—Zion. The Bible is the spiritual history of a people who believed in Zion. For the children of Israel this was the land where their invisble, omnipotent, and One God lived. And from the time of David there has been no doubt in their minds that His dwelling place was on Mount Zion. That is why the Jews have never been able to abandon Zion altogether. The Jews who were forced to leave carried one promise on their lips—that soon, as soon as next year, they would be in Jerusalem.

For a thousand years, except for the servitude in Babylon, the proud city of David stood, a formidable fortress and a spiritual stronghold. And then, in A.D. 70 a Roman general took this most holy of cities and systematically destroyed it. The general later became Roman emperor and was remembered in history as Titus the Good. For eighteen long and dark centuries, the Land was physically neglected, fought over by lion-hearted saints and greedy pirates. But its holiness grew until it became no less sacred to the Christians, and then to the Moslems, than it was already to Jews. Jerusalem blossomed in the iconography and poetry of the nations. Saint Bernard's words, written in the twelfth century, are still sung today:

> *Jerusalem the golden,*
>   *With milk and honey blest,*
> *Beneath thy contemplation*
>   *Sink heart and voice opprest.*
> *I know not, O I know not*
>   *What joys await us there,*
> *What radiancy of glory,*

What bliss beyond compare.
They stand those halls of Zion,
All jubilant with song . . .

The whole of Western civilization had been Zionist in essence for centuries when Nathan Birnbaum coined the word in the 1890s. Zion had inspired the Crusades, the Puritans who founded New England, and the Mormons who built their Zion in Utah. Long before it became a political or a nationalist Jewish movement, Zionism represented the human quest for the city of God, for the vision of how life ought to be lived beyond mere brutishness. The idea had been more Christian than Jewish, more spiritual than geographical, until the early days of June 1895, when journalist and playwright Theodor Herzl began feverishly to write his manifesto about the Jewish state—the seminal document for modern Zionism.

Like Chana Szenes, Herzl was born in Budapest and spent his first eighteen years there. And like Béla Szenes, Herzl was a writer who died young of exhaustion. Had he lived out his days, he would have been sixty-one when Chana was born, and eighty-four when she died.

In the finest Messianic tradition, Herzl came circuitously and reluctantly to his mission of leading the persecuted Jews of the Diaspora back to the original Promised Land. While writing about the sensational trial of Alfred Dreyfus in Paris, the secularized and assimilated Theodor Herzl began to think about the Jewish question. Witnessing firsthand in both Paris and Vienna the unleashing of anti-Semitism in the wake of the trial, he became convinced that the only solution to the Jewish question (it was mainly anti-Semites who called it a problem) was the re-establishment of a Jewish nation in its old homeland, which was now an all-but-forgotten province of the Ottoman Empire. The idea was not in itself new. In 1862 a Polish rabbi, Zvi Hirsch Kalischer, published a book called *Seeking Zion,* which propounded the idea of Jewish redemption through physical labor in the land of Israel. In the same year a German intellectual and early socialist, Moses Hess, published his *Rome and Jerusalem,* which first formulated the modern idea of a Zionist state. By the end of the century about 4,500 Jews actually farmed land in Palestine as part of agricultural experiments funded by wealthy Jewish philanthropists, such as Sir Moses Montefiore and Baron Edmond de Rothschild. But it was Herzl who formulated a plan for the founding of a modern Jewish nation-state, and who had the charismatic personality to persuade others that the plan could work.

When Herzl finally got to the Promised Land—ironically, in order to meet Kaiser Wilhelm during his pilgrimage to Jerusalem in October 1898—he found the reality of Palestine in shocking contrast with the psalmist's resplendent halls of Zion, which led him to write in his diary: "When I remember thee in days to come, O Jerusalem, it will not be with delight.

The musty deposits of two thousand years of inhumanity, intolerance, and foulness lie in your reeking alleys. The one man who has been present here all this while, the lovable dreamer of Nazareth, has done nothing but help increase the hate."

And he adds with that characteristic sigh of ironic world-weariness which he shared with the greatest prophets of Israel: "If Jerusalem is ever ours, and if I were still able to do anything about it, I would begin by cleaning it up."

Herzl founded a worldwide movement with the first Zionist Congress held in Basel in 1897. It was a secular movement, but the dream of Zion that gave it fire was the same that had burned for three thousand years in the human imagination.

Such were the forces that helped to bring Chana to Zionism, and in the year before she left Budapest she studied its tenets intensely. Despite the fact that Herzl and his earliest supporter, the writer Max Nordau, were both from Hungary, the Zionist movement there remained fairly small. Still, as a member of the Maccabean Society, Chana saw the Zionist cause gaining some ground as the government and the press became increasingly anti-Semitic. In a talk she gave to her Bible group in 1939, she remarked that

> five or even two years ago if anybody talked about Zionism in Hungary, Jewish opinion would attack him as an unpatriotic traitor, or laugh at him as a dreamer, but certainly nobody would have wanted to listen. Today, because of increasing misfortunes, Hungarian Jews are beginning to deal with Zionism, or at least that is what they think they are doing when they start asking: how large is Palestine? How many people can be accommodated there, and would there be any room for [us] in that developing country?

As she became interested in Zionism, Chana tried to learn all she could about Palestine. She read everything she could find and talked to anybody who had visited or lived there. In less than a year she was committed to the movement and could marshal eloquent arguments to propound its tenets. Describing in a speech the achievements of the Palestinian Jews—whose numbers had grown from fifty thousand at the time of Herzl's visit to half a million—she said:

> Diaspora cannot be a goal . . . We don't want handouts, but our lawful rights and our freedom, whatever we have achieved with our own hands. We must demand this as our human right, to have our own homeland for the Jewish people. The solution is so clear: we need a Jewish state . . . If we renounce Zionism, we give up our

traditions, our dignity, truth, our right to live. This small piece of land on the shores of the Mediterranean, that Jews after two thousand years once more feel is their own, has been large enough for the flowering of new Jewish life and culture, grown organically from its ancient roots. Even in its incomplete shape today, it is large enough to be an island in the sea of hopeless Jewish destinies, where we can build a lighthouse of the Jewish spirit to shine a beacon of eternal values into the darkness, the light of faith in the One God.

Less than six months later Chana stood on that island, learning to build that lighthouse with her bare hands. Despite her intellectual and spiritual commitment to the ideal, nothing in her preparations could have anticipated the shock of actually confronting her dreams. When she landed in Haifa some forty years after Herzl, many of the latter's utopian musings had been fully realized. Some of the ancient filth had been cleaned up and new towns had been built. There were tree-shaded boulevards with busy shops and European-style cafés. The foundations for a life dominated by Jewish values had been laid. But this Zion was real and in many respects it jarred with what Chana had imagined. She came to recognize that this was inevitable; yet part of her still clung to the dream.

THREE

THE LAND

"I have been in Eretz four days now. A little sabra, a child, is climbing the olive tree behind me; in front there are cypresses, a cactus, the Emek Valley. I am in Nahalal; I am in the Land; I am home."

Around the time of her eighteenth birthday Chana had adopted a new policy of trying to write her diary in Hebrew. The overwhelming impressions of her arrival, and the fact that this was her first Yom Kippur—the solemn Jewish Day of Atonement—in Palestine, left her at a loss for words even in Hungarian. But the photograph taken on September 19, 1939, the day of her disembarking in Haifa, is more eloquent than words. She is wearing a simple black dress and black patent-leather shoes, looking serene and self-possessed against an overexposed desert landscape. She appears older than eighteen, more woman than girl, radiant with the fulfillment of a dream. No amount of self-consciousness could disguise her smile of triumph and contentment at the sheer achievement of simply having arrived.

She had spent an arduous week of traveling—two days on the train and five on a Romanian liner called the *Bessarabia*. It was an enormous journey for a young girl from Central Europe, even in peacetime. But for Chana it seemed like a pleasure cruise, even though she had to be satisfied with viewing the exotic ports only from afar. The ship stopped three hours in Istanbul, but she was not permitted to disembark. She had to be content with a dockside view of the minarets, bazaars, and cafés, the street vendors hawking watermelons.

Her fellow passengers were mainly Polish and Slovak refugees, but there were also several Jewish citizens of Palestine who were thankfully returning home after visiting relatives. Once having made their acquaintance, Chana questioned them endlessly about life in her chosen land; they generally seemed happy with their lot and anxious to get back to their daily routine, whether home was a kibbutz or town. Chana was particularly enchanted with the sabra children on board, who gave her an opportunity to practice her Hebrew. She marveled how easy it was for them to speak a tongue that she found so difficult, and one that had been dead for two thousand years. Having grown up hearing it only in religious services, she was amazed to hear vernacular Hebrew.

In the course of the journey, she wrote several letters and postcards home, not neglecting to answer mischievously the questions she knew her mother would most want to ask: "I'm wonderfully equipped in terms of clothes, sitting here on deck in my gray pants and checked blouse. I try not to look too unkempt, purely out of regard for your feelings." Her spirits were irrepressible; she had been up on deck since six, thrilling her landlocked senses with the vastness of sunrise at sea. Five weeks after her arrival in Eretz Israel, she was still under the spell of her first impressions, as she wrote enthusiastically to the Zionist friends left behind in Budapest: "If only you could have been with me sailing into the beautiful port of Haifa, if you could have marveled at her natural geography, seen the old city and the new parts, how happy you would have been to see all the Hebrew signs on the stores and buses." And, as always, she is most struck by the people:

> I must be exceptionally lucky, because I've only met wonderful and helpful people everywhere. It's no coincidence, because one keeps hearing how hospitable everybody is toward total strangers. Older people here are still defined by the culture from which they came, and there are greater cultural differences among them. But even such differences don't create any conflicts, and they disappear altogether with the second generation. I'm glad to be able to confirm all that you have heard about the new, free Jewish generation—they were not empty phrases. Not just the sabras, but anyone who has spent some time here and has had a chance to absorb the feel of this country, seems to exude a spirit of freedom. Most immigrants work in much harder circumstances than they left behind, but I doubt if you'd find many who want to go home again.

After two days in Haifa, Chana boarded a bus for the short trip to Nahalal, which lies less than half an hour southeast on the main road to the ancient town of Nazareth. It was the first, and a still relatively young, settlement founded by Zionist pioneers on the northern edge of the fertile Jezreel Valley, also called simply the Emek, or "the Valley" in Hebrew. The bus left the highway, passing a group of primitive shacks where Arab nomads tended their flocks. Chana marveled at the greenness of the countryside, despite the scorching heat. She had never seen cactus growing several feet high. Eagerly, she watched as the bus bounced past modern settlements, whitewashed buildings hidden among lush orchards. And then came Nahalal.

The Agricultural School for Girls at Nahalal was like a small village inside a larger one. Three main buildings contained dormitories, dining halls, classrooms, the library, the reading room, and "countless other rooms." Chana mentions the "gorgeous kitchen" with a note of pride. There were also several outbuildings for the laundry, the dairy, the stables, the poultry, and the apiary, and at the bottom of the garden a nursery, where precious saplings were kept until ready for replanting in a permanent location. There were several gardens, one for flowers and another for vegetables, and orchards spread over several acres of attached land. A long path flanked with olive trees led through these orchards; and beyond the thick stands of grapefruit, lemon, and other exotic fruits, Chana found more familiar trees: apple, pear, walnut, and quince. Further still, extensive vineyards basked in the sun. Looking at this living cornucopia, she could hardly believe that less than twenty years before her arrival the valley's chief product had been malaria, which had killed hundreds of settlers.

Nahalal was the first *moshav,* or cooperative settlement, built in Palestine. In a moshav each family owns its own land, house, animals, and goods (in contrast to the kibbutz, where all property is communal, its use assigned to individual members according to need). Moshe Dayan grew up in Nahalal; his father, Shmuel Dayan, was one of the original thirty founders and wrote a book about the early years of the settlement. Chana, who quickly made friends in the village, must have heard the stories of the founding of Nahalal, which happened to take place the same summer that she had been born in Budapest.

In the summer of 1921, the group that formed the cooperative sent out Shmuel Dayan and two others to scout for land that they could purchase for farming. One piece was too close to the temptations of Haifa to form a cohesive, pioneering community, so they ventured farther into the Emek, which was then settled mostly by Arab shepherds. The would-be settlers saw the occasional fig tree and citrus grove grown wild. There was even a small spring that could be used for irrigation and for domestic animals. Encouraged, they went into the nearby village where they met an old man whom they questioned about some ruined dwellings they had seen. Yes, there used to be a settlement there, he could remember seeing it as a child. Built by Germans, he thought. What happened to them? They all died. Later an Arab village was built on the site. What happened to them? They, too, had all died. Dayan and his companions asked the old man, "Why is it impossible to live here?"

"Foul wind and foul water," replied the Arab. "The bowels of any man who drinks the water shrivel up, and within three days he is dead."

The three scouts returned to Haifa and described their find to the whole

group. Every disadvantage they raised was debated. Yes, there were poisonous swamps and springs; but the land had to be reclaimed somehow
and pioneers do not shirk that responsibility. Yes, the land they would
purchase had poor soil; still, the valley seemed fertile and it would be their
task to improve their land with fertilizers and careful management. Finally,
the moshav would be two hours' walking distance from the nearest Jewish
settlement, surrounded by Arab villages. Nearby Nazareth, associated by
Christians with the Prince of Peace, was known as a hotbed of hatred
against the Jewish immigrants. But the settlers felt that this too was actually
an advantage. They wanted to be far enough from the city so that their
sons and daughters would form an attachment to the soil. The presence
of enemies would help to make them brave and appear strong among the
Arabs, which was essential if there was to be a future for Jews in Palestine.
The cooperative agreed to proceed with the purchase.

The pioneers remembered that first winter as one of back-breaking preparation—clearing the land, removing the stones, and readying it for the
plow. The men, who formed the vanguard until spring, lived in tents. The
unusually wet winter turned everything into mud. The road from Haifa
passed nearly two thousand yards from the site so that all building materials
and provisions had to be dragged through the dirt by hand or mule. Arab
nationalists posed a constant and grave threat that required unremitting
vigilance. Among the residential tents a large pit was dug and secured with
a wall of sandbags. In case of attack, this fortress was large enough for
the isolated pioneers to dig in and find protection against small arms fire.

A greater enemy was malaria, as the old man had warned. Despite a
growing membership, 10 percent of the young moshav died each month
during that first year. With financial help from the Jewish National Fund
four hundred extra workers were hired to drain the swamps. The results
of this heavy and dangerous labor were spectacular. By the second summer,
the mortality rate due to malaria was cut to 1 percent a month and soon
malaria was entirely eliminated.

The settlers did not forget their philosophy, which called for private
ownership of the land. The time had come to divide it into equal portions.
Shmuel Dayan describes the Shabbat morning when all the members gathered to draw lots:

> Hearts pounded with excitement as each member read the number
> of his plot. Immediately the lower fields around the hill were filled
> with men, women, and children bending over to examine the numbers
> on the stakes. For a long time there was a shuffle, each one searching
> for, and finding, his own land. By evening every member had brought
> his belongings to his plot, spread sacks and canvas on the ground, set
> up a crude table on a cement barrel, and had a fire burning in the

stove. A lantern lighted the scene as our people returned into full possession of the land of their forefathers.

The pioneers turned to the book of their forefathers to find a suitable name. Nahalal appears in the Book of Joshua (22:34), a city belonging to one of the twelve tribes of Israel. The word means "a richly watered pasture" and reflected eloquently the hope these children of Israel had for their new home.

Nahalal was a planned settlement from the start, designed by a German architect, Richard Kaufmann. The houses are arranged around a large oval, like the camp made by the pioneers' wagon trains in the American West. In the inner ring of the oval are the public buildings, including the kindergarten and the school. The private plots fan out from a narrow frontage on the inner oval, for the private use of each member. The inner circle, therefore, goes past each house, while another road that connects to the highway to Nazareth and Haifa dissects the circle and runs right into the middle of the settlement.

Chana and Nahalal were officially of the same age, but the school was not established until 1926. It was supported by the Women's International Zionist Organization (WIZO) and the Canadian Hadassah. The principal was the well-known Chana Meisel, a pioneer of agricultural training for women. By the time Chana arrived, Nahalal boasted electric lighting, piped water, a general store, and three buses a day to Haifa along a paved road. It was the focal point for a number of less developed settlements nearby. Still, it had fewer than a thousand people.

Despite their proximity, Nahalal and the Agricultural School were wholly separate entities. One was a practical world of collective experience; the other was preparing for that world through education and practical training. Still, they shared the same land and followed equally exhausting schedules that left little room for social life.

The school's population included the teaching staff and about one hundred and fifty girls who stayed there for two years. Chana's high school in Budapest had had a much higher enrollment, over a thousand students, but all of them had lived at home. Chana had never lived in a boarding school and she was unprepared for the close and sometimes abrasive intimacy produced by people living, working, and studying together twenty-four hours every day. While at home she had always enjoyed ample solitude to balance her active social life, she was now forced to break her habits of aloofness. She could no longer shut the door of her own bedroom, withdrawing into poetry or her diaries.

Fortunately, her two roommates at Nahalal became close friends as well. Miriam, like Chana, had just arrived in Eretz and had had the same kind of upbringing, in Sofia, the capital of Bulgaria. The two were the same age, and absorbed the new experiences through the same fresh eyes. They became inseparable during their two years at Nahalal; and Chana often spoke of Miriam as her only confidante. Pnina was originally from Poland. Having already spent some time in Eretz Israel, she was a source of information and assistance to the two newcomers.

The three girls mirrored the Jewish Diaspora, speaking Hungarian, Bulgarian, and Polish. They had also a rough working knowledge of Western European languages—such as English, German, and French—which had been part of their upbringing as accomplished young ladies. But Chana knew that the key, both symbolic and practical, to their new life here lay in a single shared language. From the first day, she insisted they speak only Hebrew among themselves, both for practice and as a sign of commitment to their new home, which was still struggling to become a country with its own national language.

There was much more to learning Hebrew than the words and the grammar. Pnina introduced Chana to the rich literature and lore of the shtetl, a joyous revelation to her. Although Chana's background could not have been more literary, it was almost entirely focused on Hungarian and Western literature. She was astonished to find how little she knew of Jewish poets, novelists, and playwrights, like Mendele Mocher Sefarim and Sholom Aleichem. Pnina was struck by Chana's hunger to make the entire Jewish heritage her own.

The rigorous daily schedule did not leave much time for extra reading and recreation. Each weekday morning, the wake-up bell rang at 5:30. In the beginning, Chana studied two subjects that were familiar to her from Budapest—chemistry and botany—as well as two that were new to her: an introduction to agriculture and a more specialized course in fruit-growing. Each class was divided according to language skills, with one section for beginners and one for advanced. It says much about Chana's diligence that she was immediately placed in an advanced class.

Chana was impressed at once by the relaxed style of Nahalal, compared to the more rigid academic system to which she had been accustomed. Teachers, most of whom were in their twenties, did not mind being called by their first name. If called upon to answer a question, the student could remain in her seat; in Budapest, classroom response was a much more formal proposition, requiring the student to deliver in front of the class what amounted to a short lecture in imitation of the teacher. Chana had been an outstanding student in Hungary, and this was reflected not only in her report cards but also in the genuine affection she inspired in her teachers. They recognized in her an unusual combination for a student of her age: a dedication not just to the mastery of individual subjects but to the importance of education as a whole. She had trained her mind to question and evaluate everything it encountered.

In Nahalal, too, Chana made an early impression on her teachers and the principal of the school, who was also called Chana. In one of her first letters home the new student reported hearing about a meeting between the principal and the Hebrew teacher, in which the two women discussed the slow progress some of the girls were making in Hebrew. Chana's name apparently came up as a positive example of somebody who insisted on speaking nothing but Hebrew, and whose progress in that language was already significant. Chana was pleased that she had been noticed, especially since almost everything in Nahalal, both in and out of school, was new and hard for her.

In the beginning, the challenge of Hebrew, the new environment, and Chana's Zionist zeal hid the fact that her rigorous education had prepared her mind for something more intellectually demanding than agriculture. After months of working in the orchards, the dairy or the chicken coop (which became her specialty), Chana became increasingly aware that her mind was still not sufficiently engaged. She needed constant mental stimulation and challenge, and it was painful to admit to herself that her mother might have been right in advising her to enroll at Hebrew University instead of an agricultural school. She soon found an outlet for her energy in tutoring other students.

Chana had always shown a talent for teaching and took it seriously. Since her early teens she had tutored pupils, enjoying both the help she was giving someone and the extra pocket money that allowed her to supplement her mother's slender resources. One of her former Budapest pupils, Magda Radó (now Zimmering), recalls Anikó's quiet professionalism: "I looked up to Anikó. She was very businesslike during these tutoring sessions, kept exact time and never said anything outside the topics she came to discuss. She seemed at times preoccupied—almost too mature, I thought then—for the little age difference there was between us [2 years]. There was never any word of personal discussion; an air of distance prevailed."

Within two months of arriving at Nahalal, Chana was tutoring two sabras in chemistry, one of the subjects she knew thoroughly from her former schooling. She exchanged her knowledge of chemistry for Hebrew practice.

Breakfast followed the early morning class, a simple and hearty affair consisting of bread and butter, cheese, and tomatoes. The only rationed luxury was the lump of sugar for tea. After breakfast came chores: general cleaning and tidying of the bedrooms, tasks that the girls shared or took in turn. Pnina was astonished at first by Chana's ineptitude. Despite Rózsi's crash course in domesticity, Chana did not know what to do with a broom and simply had no idea how dishes were washed. Pnina recalled: "One could see immediately that this kind of work was unfamiliar to her. But she mastered everything very quickly, step by step. Her common sense helped her and so did her initiative, which was very much a part of her personality."

At 8:00 the students were sent out to the orchard to spend the morning in nature's laboratory. In one of her many self-deprecating letters Chana described to her mother a zestful morning spent harvesting olives and sorting them by size. After a row and a half, however, her muscles ached from the unaccustomed labor. But at least it was preferable to hauling manure to fertilize the vines, which she had done the week before. She was also glad to be working in the shade of the olives, finding the traditional wide-brimmed hat, sun-screen, and dark glasses insufficient protection against the merciless sun.

By noon, the girls were hungry for lunch. Ten to a table they sat down to a healthy meal of fruit, eggs, and vegetables—all home-grown. In her letters home Chana praised the food, knowing that her mother would be concerned: food is important in both Jewish and Hungarian cultures, much more so than in Israel. Chana was enchanted with the variety of exotic fruits. Like most Northerners, at first she was moved by the mere sight of oranges growing on a tree. Citrus had always been a rare delicacy at home and Chana particularly took to *eskoliot,* which she translated into the English "grapefruit" for her mother, since she wasn't sure if a name even existed for it in Hungarian.

After lunch the students were given an hour's break, which Chana often used to read and answer her mail, wash her hair, or take a much-needed nap. Then it was back to work in the orchard, the dairy, or wherever they were assigned until 3:00, when the students trooped back into the dining hall for midafternoon refreshments of bread and tea; only the quickest got jam. The girls then showered and changed for their 3:30 class, followed at 4:30 by a two-hour break. This luxurious free time was quickly consumed by mending clothes, washing the delicate items that one did not want to entrust to the communal laundry, and ironing—not to mention homework and letter-writing, for which Chana never felt she had sufficient time. The two-hour break was also the best time for outsiders to visit, especially those from neighboring settlements. Relatives and friends usually came on the Shabbat. A third class began at 6:30 followed by supper. In the evenings, some students listened to the radio—the local and international news or classical music. At about 9:30, after more homework and perhaps some quiet conversation, it was time for bed. Chana usually dropped instantly into a deep sleep, helped by physical exhaustion, the fresh air, and her strictly enforced rule that she would read only in Hebrew.

But life at Nahalal was not only studying. Every Friday work stopped at noon in anticipation of the Shabbat. The afternoon was free, and the girls usually seized the time for catching up on personal chores. At half past six everyone gathered to welcome the Shabbat, singing and reading the Torah. As time went on these festivities became more elaborate. Less than a month after her arrival Chana wrote to her mother that she was on the Cultural Committee, which had been entrusted with the task of making these *oneg shabbat* events longer and more colorful. The Shabbat meal, joyful and solemn at once, appealed to both religious and nationalist sentiments, and Chana responded on both levels. After the Shabbat dinner, which always featured special food, the girls would walk in the village, mixing with members of the moshav, singing and dancing with them. In a community where Jews had come from many different countries, there was a lively cultural exchange. Chana loved singing and she taught the sabras wild Hungarian dances, such as the *Csárdás*.

The festive spirit carried over into the Shabbat activities. On a typical Saturday morning Chana played Ping-Pong with some of the good players in the school. She was a fair player herself, having had years of practice with Gyuri, who had been champion at school and played at a professional level. After lunch Miriam and Chana, sometimes accompanied by other girls, would visit one of the neighboring kibbutzim. In the evening special events were held at the *bet ha-am*, or assembly hall. Chana mentions a series of lectures on Freud, which almost put her to sleep; the subject proved too complicated for her knowledge of Hebrew. Another night she watched *The Good Earth*, a movie she had seen in Budapest, but from her new and closer experience of the soil she understood and appreciated it more.

What Chana missed most were live performances. She had acquired her interest in theater from her father, a love of music from her mother. Throughout childhood and adolescence she was always involved in school productions, and she had authored a number of amusing skits for parties and private performances. The cultural richness of Budapest and her family background formed a large appetite that Palestine could not possibly satisfy. However, the village doctor organized weekly chamber concerts at his house, which Chana attended as often as she could. And within weeks of her arrival, she even saw a touring production of the Habimah, the world-famous Hebrew theater company that had emigrated from Moscow to Tel Aviv in 1931. The ticket cost her a hefty five piasters, but she did not hesitate.

Given her single-minded intensity, her love of privacy, and her desire to excel, one might have expected Chana to be unpopular among her classmates in Nahalal. This does not seem to have been the case. For one thing, she was genuinely modest. But more important, she worked very hard to be liked. She was thoughtful of others; her roommate Pnina remembers "how much attention she paid to small things to make our lives more beautiful. She was concerned with expression and form—how a picture was hung—and cared for the needs of others. She never forgot a birthday; she would always surprise friends with a bunch of flowers or some simple gift."

Those who knew Chana at Nahalal speak about her great charm. She was not conventionally pretty, but this does not seem to have bothered her or made her self-conscious. People remember her radiant personality, striking blue eyes, and distinctive features, which were always animated with mischief or heated with passionate argument. Communal life and shared Zionist ideals brought out a more gregarious, activist aspect of Chana's character, but it did not replace her introspective side. Fellow students found an irresistible simplicity and open-heartedness about her. She seemed genuinely interested in making new friends, questioning them gently about their past lives and families. Yet at the same time she did not fully reciprocate such confidences. She enjoyed listening, and this in itself provided an excuse to remain quiet. Except perhaps to Miriam, Chana remained unrevealed.

She continued to find her real outlets in writing, although the hectic tumult of Nahalal sometimes made her long for the privacy and more leisurely pace of her former life. She poured out her uncensored feelings and critical evaluations of her new life into her diaries, while her letters home had to be always cheerful and reassuring. Above all, she did not want her mother to worry about her. Chana still felt tremendous guilt at having left her mother alone. She knew that time was running out for her family and friends in Budapest; somehow they must try to follow Chana to Palestine. There was little practical help that she could offer, but she hoped that with her encouragement, others might be inspired to help themselves. So, in her letters home, she was careful to avoid negative statements that could discourage those she loved from making their escape—even though her own feelings were often in conflict.

Chana's ambivalent attitudes about Eretz crystallized gradually in daily episodes, such as the problems she had with a broom. Assigned to the cowsheds, she was bothered by a broken broom that was used to clean out the feeding troughs. At first, she noticed the awkwardness of having to employ this disabled implement; the observation soon gave way to a desire to mend it. She managed to obtain a piece of wire and a wooden pole that could serve as the new handle. She had the right idea but, as she had never had to do anything so practical in Budapest, the execution defeated her. However, Chana had always had the talent of enlisting other people's help. She took the broom down to the school workshop and one of he craftsmen there fixed it for her. "It's a work of art, the way you did this!" she thanked him, and she could hardly wait for her fellow workers the next morning. "Well, what do you think of the broom?" They agreed that it had been splendidly fixed. To Chana's mind, the broom at once became a symbol of how life could gradually be improved: "I spent that little bit of time on something that would help many people. One person just has to start something and another will step in and carry it to completion." By that afternoon, however, the handle on the renewed broom became loose again and by the following morning it had reverted to its previous state of semi-usefulness. She was forced to re-evaluate, in her diary, her metaphor of progress: "Can one really repair something broken down? Is it possible to renew the old? Is there no other solution except a new beginning?"

Although Chana felt satisfied most of the time with her decision to come to Nahalal, she was not blind to flaws in the system—or reluctant to suggest changes. When Chana's turn came to wash the kitchen floor before the evening meal, she thought it made no sense to have it trampled by three hundred feet fresh from the fields. Rather than complain or argue, Chana quietly decided to defy the rule. She simply did not wash the floor the first evening until after supper. Fortunately, the administration had high regard for initiative and saw the wisdom of changing the rule instead of admonishing Chana.

Pnina describes Chana as a leader, a frequent champion of causes on behalf of other students: "When other girls were helpless, she would shout: 'Girls, come on, let's have a meeting!' " Then she chaired the meeting, helped formulate a strategy, and led a delegation to the principal. She believed that conflicts could be resolved through reasoning. Typical was her attitude toward Chana, the principal. On a Friday evening, when she was using her free time to write one of her lengthy letters home, the older Chana dropped by for a chat. She thought that Chana should not be using her typewriter, since it might bother some of the religious girls. Chana countered that she was writing home, and that the typewriter was not being used for work, which would be the Orthodox objection. It was really the equivalent of having a conversation with her mother, and so should offend no one. The principal yielded and gave her permission, provided nobody complained. After the principal left, Chana continued her letter with this remark: "Chana is a very interesting woman, multifaceted, and a complete dictator. Most of the girls respect her, but very few—or maybe none—like her. Personally I haven't had any clashes with her, I think she even likes me, although you can't tell with her. She's a fantastic diplomat, an excellent organizer, but they say she hasn't got much heart."

The two Chanas had somewhat similar personalities, which explains their mutual respect. Although the younger Chana wanted to be liked, it is obvious from her assessment of the older woman that she did not think popularity was essential in winning respect. Being a good organizer or diplomat was far more important, when it came to leadership, than being soft-hearted. To Miriam, who knew her best during this period, Chana already manifested all the qualities of the born leader.

Yet under her cheerful demeanor Chana kept up a constant flow of reflection, inner debate, and self-review. For example, her first diary entry after arriving in Palestine reveals mixed emotions. It should have been a moment of unalloyed triumph and joy; after all, she had just achieved the greatest dream in her life against formidable odds. But her tone is subdued, poignant:

> Yesterday, on the eve of Yom Kippur, I felt very fragile, in spirit, that is. I drew up an account of what was left behind and what awaits me here and I wasn't sure if it'll be worth it. For a moment, I couldn't see the goal. But I also let myself go deliberately; it was good to dissolve all the tension, this constant vigilance, it was good to cry for once. Even through the tears I could feel that I had chosen well, that my life's goal lies here. I might also say, this is my vocation. I want my stay here to be the fulfillment of a vocation, and not a form of vegetating. I think everybody here is on a similar mission.

It was becoming apparent that two different personalities were developing within Chana Szenes. There was the helpful, cheerful, and outgoing Chana, who seemed totally dedicated to her ideals, her studies, and her new life. And there was another, hidden person, who was introverted, reserved, riddled with doubts, fears, and guilts that she revealed only in her diaries. As the months and years passed, filled with frantic activity, these two Chanas would grow farther and farther apart, pulling in opposite directions, until they came together again, when she chose the mission that would fulfill—and end—her life.

FOUR

BOOTS

In November 1939, the warm weather was giving way to the rainy season, and Chana badly needed boots. She had sent a desperate letter to her mother less than a month after her arrival, asking for a calf-length pair. Although the official Directory and Yearbook for Palestine, an archetype of our Yellow Pages, records several dozens of boot- and shoemakers in Haifa, Chana claimed she had no faith in native skills: "I'd rather pay twenty piasters in customs duty than three times or more for poorly made boots." The desire for these boots obsessed her, or at least she used it as a running gag in her letters.

At noon I got a notice that a parcel had arrived, and I thought it must be the boots. I rushed to the post office this afternoon, and they said that I'd have to pay five piasters (there are one hundred piasters to the pound). I thought, well, it'll be worth it for the boots, so I paid. Then they bring out this parcel with no commercial value but with the word 'present' written on it just to be sure. At once I suspected the worst, and opening it, I saw this very beautiful scarf. I have no idea what I am going to do with it; on the other hand, five piasters is a lot of money. I almost didn't accept the parcel, but I changed my mind, and the girls here say that it is indeed a very beautiful scarf, which consoled me somewhat. At any rate, please thank Aunt Ilonka for me. I know she meant well and as I said the scarf is very lovely, and I'll put it away and there may even come an opportunity to use it.

Chana wrote such long chatty letters to her mother every week—rarely less than four closely typed large pages, and often more. Written in a breezy, deliberately cheerful style, they were filled with detailed answers to her mother's practical questions and worries, discussing her new life and asking about relatives and friends back home. Perhaps Chana sensed that it would be good for her mother to be getting the boots for her, that it provided a common term of reference for two lives that were inexorably drifting apart each day; it was another way of keeping contact over the vast distance.

If there was one person in whom Chana could confide honestly, it was her brother, Gyuri, thousands of miles away in Lyons. Their warm and protective relationship was heightened both by feelings of helplessness about the war looming over Europe and by anxiety about having left their mother alone in a country that was moving rapdily toward fascism and an alliance with Germany. Chana voiced one of her major fears in the earliest letter that she wrote expressly to Gyuri, in October 1939: "I only beg you one thing, my Gyurka, and I'm asking this on Mummy's behalf as well, because we discussed it before I left: Do not enlist in the army. Neither of us, I must confess, would have a moment's quiet if you enlisted."

She was also concerned that he might be lonely in France. Gyuri must have mentioned that he was not getting on with the Gouchats, the French family with whom Mrs. Szenes had arranged that he should board. Since one reason that Gyuri had left home was to become independent, even this tenuous family connection must have represented a sort of parental constraint. Chana was characteristically tactful: "You must understand why mother trusts the Gouchats; it's the only family she knows there, and it was a great comfort to her to know that they were there when she did not hear from you for so long. I gather from your letter that such trust was undeserved. But I hope you didn't break with them completely."

In her letters Chana often behaved as the elder sibling. She instructed Gyuri on how to make his *aliyah,* which she thought would be easier from France than if he were to return to Hungary. In another letter, she suggested that he would find a job faster in Eretz if he finished his training in textiles first, though "largely for selfish reasons" she confessed she was impatient to see him as soon as possible. She had already started exploring job opportunities for him with the director of a textile factory in Kfar Ata.

But Gyuri provided important support for Chana as well. Just as she encouraged him to tell her the "unvarnished truth—even if you dress things up for Mother, making a joke out of everything," so she revealed to him both sides of her new soil-bound existence:

> You know, when you start home after work with a hoe or spade over your shoulder, and you look over the Emek, knowing that this is Jewish soil, that thirty years ago it was one terrible swamp and yet now it's the most beautiful and fertile region of the country—it gives you a very, very good feeling. But I have to be honest. This kind of work isn't all that romantic. When I'm wielding a hoe or a broom, or

washing dishes or spreading manure, I must confess that sometimes it occurs to me that I might be better employed—but I'm not expressing this very well, because I can now really see that such tasks are not all that simple, that expertise is involved in everything, and above all, I can see how essential it all is—but perhaps something else, you understand, my Gyurka, what I'm thinking; well, perhaps, in a word, that I might be doing better at something else.

The awkward, almost inarticulate syntax of the last sentence clearly reveals Chana's inner struggle between her idealization of physical labor (which many intellectuals since Tolstoy had propounded) and her continuing need to find work that was mentally stimulating. Whenever Chana was advised by her mother and friends that she should be attending Hebrew University so that she would have higher skills to give to Eretz Israel, she always defended her decision clearly: someone had to grow food for the workers who would build the universities. She chose Palestine because she wanted to be useful. She could not dictate *how* she could be useful; that agenda would be set by the needs of Eretz Israel. Farmers and builders were in greater demand than dreamers or even teachers—although she wrote encouragingly to her cousin Évi Sas, who wanted to emigrate to Eretz and work as a nursery teacher. But for herself, Chana remained firm. When her mother in a letter relayed the opinion of another relative with whom she was in obvious agreement, Chana replied staunchly: "I understand Aunt Manci's viewpoint entirely, but I still think my decision is correct. I don't know precisely what I'll be doing in five or ten years, but I do know that I'm starting out from a very good place. I wouldn't have a better chance anywhere else to learn the language or get to know life and work in this country. And I do believe, quite apart from all this, that I will find my place in agriculture."

It is hard to say, of course, whether Chana would indeed have remained an agricultural worker all her life. In her diary she sounds much less certain than in her letters. Only a few days after refuting her mother and Aunt Manci, she told her diary that in the long term she envisioned some form of teaching as the only vocation for her. She certainly loved children and all her tutoring in Budapest and now in Nahalal testified to her inclination.

Yet despite her comforting words to Évi, Chana had reasons for not wishing to pursue a teaching career in Eretz. For one thing, she could have remained in Hungary as a teacher, and she wanted to distance herself in every way from the land she had left behind. Second, physical labor would certainly be different, and the challenge of its novelty and obvious difficulty appealed to her greatly. And there was still another consideration, which Chana learned only once she arrived in Eretz, the same one that another immigrant—an ex-teacher from Milwaukee—had found a generation earlier. As Golda Meir writes in her autobiography, "Teaching . . . was regarded by most of the people we met in Tel Aviv then [1921] as being too intellectual an occupation for a would-be pioneer, and I had to keep explaining that it was only temporary and that I had not come to Palestine in order to spread American culture."

Even as she defended to her family and friends the mundane chores that filled her days, Chana was frank in admitting to herself, "I'm working in the laundry, it's simple work, and I have to be honest and admit that it has very little educational value. I've learned a bit about washing and ironing, too." A few months later the frustration had shifted from the work to herself and new doubts crept in:

> I've been working almost two months in the kitchen, for the past two weeks as cook. I don't have much time to describe the work, nor is it that important to do it right now at half past four in the morning. It's more interesting for me to observe myself a little while doing this work. I am amazingly clumsy and slow. I'm a little astonished, because in other things I don't seem to be so hopeless, and I've never thought of myself as especially stupid. But during the past two weeks I've really surprised myself sometimes at my lack of intelligence in doing this work, not to mention my clumsiness. In this connection several things occurred to me. Am I making a mistake in neglecting the gifts that I have, and by choosing a field where I will probably not make my mark, or even be useless? . . . The work itself is often quite heavy and exhausting, all this washing and cleaning, and it often occurs to me that with all this energy . . . I think probably everybody goes through these feelings, changing either voluntarily or by force of circumstances from intellectual work to physical and more mechanical labor. Perhaps it's even harder if one choses to change, because one is responsible to oneself.

One can hear the two Chanas arguing, trying to close the gap between the ideal and the reality. The basic question was frightening: could she have been wrong? But the idealistic Chana could always find an answer. "Maybe, because I am so hopeless at it, this work is very good for me. Maybe I will learn some cleanliness and tidiness, which I must confess are not my forte." Still, to Gyuri she expressed the hope that things would change: "I know that these purely automatic chores are assigned only in the very beginning, and later the work will get more interesting. And these tasks do help one to get to know real life out here and to have one's perspectives and values transformed."

Transformation of values aside, November twenty-fifth was a red-letter day. The long-awaited boots finally arrived. Chana was quick to thank her mother, with enthusiasm unmarred by self-doubts or ideological ambivalence: "Today's mail brought fourfold joy: your letters from the ninth and thirteenth, a card from Grandmother, and the parcel all arrived at the same time. I paid only six piasters for the parcel. I was totally knocked out by the parcel: the boots are gorgeous, the size just excellent, and the quality also the best. Thank you very much for the enclosed first-aid package, I've already eaten some—it's yummy!"

FIVE

POETRY

In letters home, Chana employed her somewhat adolescent Budapest slang to maintain her relationships there on familiar and reassuring ground. The effortless outpouring of details in her accustomed vocabulary also gave Chana a respite from her constant struggle to master a new language with which she could express complicated new thoughts.

For several months after her arrival she stopped writing poetry. She was buried under an avalanche of experiences and had no room to absorb them. Even brief poems take a great deal of time to perfect, and Chana was too sophisticated now to pour out her feelings in unselfconscious disarray. For a poet to lose her language is a form of amputation, and Chana continued to feel the memories of writing fluently as sensations in a phantom limb.

The long letters written to Mrs. Szenes, Gyuri, or Évi give the raw data of her new life; the brief entries in her diary show a growing yearning for time and privacy to analyze and transform the material into feelings. After a hard day in the orchard, the kitchen, or the dairy, after she had finished her homework and the long letters home, it was hard to sit in a room filled with chattering girls and try to reflect, to compose her poetry, especially when she still felt herself an infant in Hebrew. "Simple words and phrases can only express simple thoughts," she remarked once in frustration. She wanted simplicity—but a simplicity that would convey the complex feelings and thoughts of an adult, not those of the child she had long left behind.

From about the age of seven Anikó had begun to develop a craft of making poems, becoming increasingly absorbed in the sophisticated rhythms and images of Hungarian, a language passionately in love with poetry. For eighteen years she moved through streets, restaurants, and cafés named after famous poets. Nobody growing up in Budapest, least of all the daughter of a well-known writer, could plead naiveté about the act of committing pen to paper.

Her first poems appeared in the homemade *Szenes Gazette* that Gyuri and Anikó "published" irregularly as children; issues came out whenever their mother found the time to type them. In May 1930 the *Esti Kúrir* (the *Evening Courier*) carried on its theater page a few sad lines about her father under the headline "Béla Szenes's Daughter Writes Poem." Anikó was then eight years old. In her teens she won a number of prizes for poems and translations. Despite the awards and the praise heaped upon her by teachers and family, the teenager's diary contains many expressions of self-doubt—some coy and some serious. A child born into a literary family bears special burdens. Anikó could never be sure if her poems were praised only from politeness to her mother or in deference to her father's memory. For Anikó, her deep admiration for Béla—who had achieved so much at such an early age—brought forth a natural conflict between wishing to prove herself worthy of his name and memory and fearing that she could never live up to his example.

After a literary friend of her mother's gave her an exceptionally warm response, Anikó was urged to take her poems to Piroska Reichardt, an editor of the most famous literary magazine of the period, called *Nyugat (The West)*. A week after her seventeenth birthday, she went to see Reichardt and described the visit in her diary:

> I've long been wanting to get a professional opinion and I think that's what I got from P.R. She greeted me with the statement that my poems had surprised her; she thinks I am talented! She actually said that my talent is above average and she believes that I will carry on writing, though not necessarily poetry, because she did not find enough lyricism in these verses. Then she told me the faults: They are too long, the content compromised for the sake of form, and some expressions are still childish. But the whole critique assumed that I had talent. It made me terribly happy, because after all this is how one gains confidence.

During this period Anikó was experimenting with almost every literary form. She wrote, aside from school requirements, a number of serious essays, many of which were descriptive travel pieces following one of her vacations abroad. Other essays had a more philosophical tone. She enjoyed reading classic novels and thought about writing fiction when she became older. She tried her hand at dramatic and satirical sketches, again sharing her father's bent. While her poetry continued to be serious and melancholy, some of her skits, written for parties and special occasions, expressed the lighter side of her nature. One clever sketch, written when she was fifteen, was called "A Marriage Proposal in 2036." It describes a boy and a girl who have just been to Mars on a date. Interestingly, it is the girl who surprises the boy by proposing to him. Unfortunately, it received mixed reviews when Anikó read it to her family.

"Judging by the stony silence following my reading I could see that they did not like it at all. My face must have been very red—I felt it burning—but I think I behaved pretty well. Now I feel nervous about reading it in class tomorrow, and I fear it won't go over well there either."

Whatever reception her work received, from Anikó's early childhood to Chana's final days, the need to write poetry remained constant. Chana's aliyah dealt a decisive blow to Anikó, the fledgling Hungarian poet, but her Zionist commitment was paramount. From shortly after her arrival in Palestine, only the letters home and occasional passages in her diary were still in Hungarian. Otherwise, Chana struggled continually to express in her adopted tongue the subtle complexities of her thoughts, which she knew to be the essence of poetry. Technically she first had to learn a new prosody, a poetic vocabulary, almost a new craft. She had to find out which images were fresh and which were worn. Just as she stood on the threshold of adulthood, making momentous discoveries, Chana suddenly found herself learning to express herself in what amounted to baby talk. After six months in the Land, she despaired of ever writing in Hebrew. She noted "without comment" these four lines that came to her while walking in the fields:

> *Our people plow the black soil*
> *Their arms harvest the golden sheaves,*
> *By the time the corn covers the ground,*
> *Our faces are glistening with its gold.*

The words are from her everyday life, but the thought belongs to the propaganda of the soil that brought her to Zion. There is nothing of Chana herself in those lines; anyone could have written them. They show nothing of the power and originality of her later poems, some of which have been set to music and are known and loved by every Israeli.

Though she could not yet shape Hebrew with the same skill she had in Hungarian, though numbing chores and studies made her weary beyond thinking, the poet remained alive, if dormant, inside Chana the pioneer. Passages in the diary show how she occasionally managed to transmute the dreary routine of her day into poetic metaphor. One day she was arranging grapefruits in the storage shed, putting the whole ones in the bottom, while the bruised and imperfect fruits were placed gently on top. The thought came to her that "this is God's order for our people. He placed the strong ones at the bottom, so they could withstand the burdens involved in building a new country." She began to imagine a different and a better world where only wholesome fruit existed, abolishing the need for distinctions between bottom and top. She transformed the shed into a single wide shelf, where all fruit was arranged on the same level. More poetry went into these utopian prose fancies than into the verses she was trying to write at the time.

Even her botany classes offered her provocative themes to explore. Botany itself bored her, because she had covered most of the same ground in Hungary. But in one lecture, the teacher described some cells as pioneers: they penetrated the soil and perished in the process, but in their destruction, the ground was prepared for the real roots. The allegorical possibilities captured Chana's interest.

"When we look into the faces of farmers here in Nahalal," she wrote in her diary that night, "how old they look, despite their young age. We see the ravages of their fight with the soil. They are like the cells that died in penetrating the ground, thereby helping all other plants to take root. Is our generation still like those pioneer cells? Is that the fate of all tillers of the soil? I feel that these questions are more interesting than the whole subject of botany." And water plants, which feed higher organisms in the food chain, led Chana to ask herself, "Is it our vocation to serve as material for some higher purpose in nature? If a greater law exists, at least we will not feel that everything we do is self-serving. Perhaps that is what raises man above beast."

Her hungry mind was fed by everything she did. Gathering hay after the harvest, she was torn again by the dialectic of her choices: "I think I'm fulfilling my goal. My goals are doubtless fine and correct. But should one be permitted to long for something distant and neglect what is close at hand? Each person must seek her own path and vocation, even if the whole world and everything is in turmoil!—No, no, I can't seek explanations and justifications. 'Yes' and 'no' are at war inside me; I am tossed on a sea of contradictions."

Still, the act of analysis, of observing herself, usually produced calm. By day the pioneer labored, and at night the poet reflected.

"Green covers the whole field, the harvester harvests it, the plants fall to the ground and there is nobody left to lift them up. Would you like to save the life that has fallen from the scorching fire of the sun, from the blowing wind? Gather them into a single large heap. Whatever is left out, leave to the wind. That is how it will be with our people, Israel, after the harvest."

SIX

THE BOY QUESTION

At the age of nineteen Chana had yet to experience her first real kiss, although she had had plenty of offers. In her second year at Nahalal, she visited a neighboring kibbutz overnight and a young man, Moshe, whom she had met before, came to see her in the evening. He confessed his love for her. Sensing her reserve, perhaps, he went on to suggest that they be like brother and sister to each other. When he tried to give her a brotherly kiss on the cheek, she refused. He wondered aloud whether there was any point in his pursuing a relationship with her. She told him exactly what she felt: She simply did not care that deeply for him. When she tried to shake hands, he bent down and kissed her hand.

"When he left, I felt something pressing on my heart. I was thinking: Isn't it stupid of me to be so terribly afraid of life? Could I not have granted him—and myself—that kiss? Just a kiss, hardly meaningful at all. And yet I couldn't. I am keeping back this kiss, the first one, for someone special, the real one."

Chana's yearning for romance was of a piece with her habitual idealism. Still, her behavior must have seemed odd even for a well-brought-up young lady in those days. It was especially incongruous given the more casual mores and informal atmosphere of the village, not to mention the camaraderie and unavoidable intimacies of the kibbutz. After this particular young man retreated in unrecorded confusion, Chana's thoughts turned to her distant mother, the perfect chaperone at Budapest balls and parties: "She would be happy knowing that in any situation I behave just as if she was sitting right next to me."

Chana had the usual desires and she had every intention of finding the right man to love. She was looking forward to having children. However, when she contemplated bringing up her future children, she somehow neglected to consider the reality of conceiving them. The "boy-question," as Chana sometimes called it, crops up many times in her diary and letters.

At first she joked about it, wondering why her diary did not contain more soulful sighs and silly daydreams about boys. Her letters from Nahalal reported regularly about various young men's interest in her, but these mentions were perfunctory. As time went on, the diary entries grew more serious, indicating that the "boy-question" troubled Chana more and more. She could no longer dismiss the subject with a joke and a shrug, as saucy Anikó had years ago in Budapest.

From the time she was a fifteen-year-old schoolgirl, Anikó had attracted a number of boys. While she was never considered beautiful, she was lively, witty, and intelligent. Despite an underlying seriousness, she could be a charming and lighthearted companion. She went to the usual parties, and sometimes danced through half the night. Various boys, usually Gyuri's classmates, would appear from time to time at Mrs. Szenes's little house with awkwardly held bouquets, asking her out. She was sixteen when some of them began to propose marriage. At first, the proposals were flattering and Anikó responded with good humor, but when some boys persisted— no doubt in a proper and well-behaved manner—she found their advances tiresome.

In her diary, at least, Anikó judged boys by their intellects. She liked being with them only when they were good conversationalists. She enjoyed going for long walks, but whenever a boy became too serious—as often happened—she would acknowledge the compliment and quickly retreat. She seemed perpetually disappointed that passion should interfere with friendship. A typical entry in her diary at sixteen reads:

> This afternoon went for a walk with P. and we discussed things that are pure diary-stuff. After some tactful introductory remarks he let me know that he loves me. I listened with sweet innocence, though it wasn't a big surprise because we were at the movies yesterday with two other boys, and he was giving me those meaningful looks in the dark. So his declaration didn't surprise me one bit. I guessed something was up when he wanted to spend time with me again today, and insisted on going for a walk. I was nice to him back, even if I didn't say that I loved him, which might have been a lie. But I'm glad because it was the first time that such a declaration actually pleased me. (I won't say I minded them before, but there had not been any mutual feelings.)

The novelty of such proposals wore off quickly, and by the following year, one detects a firmer note.

> I should mention the episode with Dénes. The other day I got a letter from him, in which he confesses that he has been in love with

me for years. He presents his case: his school achievements were purely for me and he thinks he might do still more—because of me. He begs me to give him a yes or a no. I was totally astonished at his letter. I never considered D. such an idealist who would quietly struggle, let alone suffer (he claims to have suffered, too), without trying a more direct approach. I was very uncomfortable with all this, but replied at once, because if what he wrote is true, then he is taking it very seriously, and I didn't want him up in the air. Quite nicely, but very firmly, I said no. Actually, he's quite a decent guy, but he has some traits that place him completely outside any consideration.

A couple of weeks earlier she reported mischievously, and only half-facetiously, that a Gypsy girl had read her palm: she was to marry at eighteen somebody with an automobile; he wouldn't be really rich, but they would be happy together with their baby son. As for the past, the dark-eyed Gypsy girl guessed that she had been in love twice. Anikó commented, with characteristic preference for analysis over romance: "That might be true, except that I don't think either time it was real love."

After she became a Zionist, Anikó met many like-minded young men in the various youth organizations, but the pursuit of their common ideals tended to sublimate other emotions. She came to regard romantic involvements as frivolous compared to the giant tasks of learning Hebrew and finding her way to Palestine. An increasing sense of her Jewish identity, a result of both her Zionism and the growth of anti-Semitism around her, also affected her relationships. She mentions a young man visiting Budapest from Transylvania, the Romanian province that belonged to Hungary until its defeat in the First World War. After returning to Kolozsvár (now Cluj) he wrote her a few letters, which were very warm in contrast to the coolness of her replies. In the middle of the public debates over anti-Jewish legislation in 1938 he wrote that he finally understood the reason for her lack of enthusiasm: she must be afraid that he, as a Christian, might have a low opinion of her, because she was Jewish; but she should rest assured that he was capable of making distinctions between Jews and Jews. "When I read this," Anikó told her diary, "I sat down at once and replied that he apparently could not imagine a Jewish girl having any self-respect; that I would not want to be considered an exception, but that he should consider those Jews whom he liked along with the rest of the race. In other words, he got what he deserved and with this I concluded the correspondence."

Although she regarded her friendships within the Zionist movement in purely comradely terms, some of the boys clearly had more in mind. A couple of youths who knew her in the Maccabean Society continued their interest in Chana after she left them on the platform waving to her departing train. One, a scion of the wealthy Tischler family, came to see Mrs. Szenes in the autumn of 1939, saying that he was thinking of making his aliyah, but first wanted to make sure that her daughter's affections were still free. Mrs. Szenes would not presume to vouch for Anikó's feelings and asked only whether the boy thought that she cared enough for him. He replied, "I'm sure we would have a wonderful life together." Chana records in December that she had indeed received in the mail two proposals for marriage. "I didn't have to think for one moment what to reply." Her customary sense of humor and self-mockery were mixed with a new seriousness. She lived now in an adult world, which was on the brink of disaster. There was no room or time for romance. Or so she told herself.

Nahalal could not have been more different from the ballrooms and tea parties of prewar Budapest. The boys here were simple and unsophisticated; it was rare, especially in the beginning, for Chana to meet anybody in the village with whom she could have an intellectual conversation. These boys were real shepherds, not those of literary Arcadia. Chana's own expectations, that lightning would strike her when her true love appeared, precluded her from giving anybody a chance to develop a gradual and deeper relationship. A few months following the mail-order proposals from Budapest, Chana mentioned the "boy-problem" again in her diary, trying to analyze why she had abruptly broken off with five or six boys who had shown interest in her.

"I'd love to be loved," she quoted a song, "and I would really like to love someone. That's why the moment I meet somebody new, immediately I try to size up whether he is the 'real thing.' When I find that he isn't, I'd rather break it off completely, because I don't want superficial courting or some slight friendship. I feel I need a serious friend, well, let's call it by the real name—lover—or nothing."

This all-or-nothing attitude was hardly likely to help her find love. Just as she demanded the highest standards for herself, she was unduly critical of any candidate for her affections. Too much was at stake for her, she felt; in her emotional immaturity she did not realize that it was she who had raised the stakes too high. In going to a concert at a nearby kibbutz she described looking at the faces: "Perhaps *he* is here among them, the one I seek, and we pass each other. Or maybe *he* is so far away that we won't meet. But I am too optimistic ever to believe that."

Boys from the village and its neighborhood often came to the school to talk and invited the girls for walks. "At first I went quite gladly, but later I realized it was pointless," Chana wrote with a mysterious finality. She had no objection to walking and talking, but she claimed that the boys would not be satisfied with that. In principle, she certainly seemed to be open to meeting young men, and began to spend time with an emigré Hungarian, Lajos Friedman, whose family owned a factory. Chana's first mention of him occurs in the midst of reciting her plans to visit Jerusalem for a few days. "A certain person" there apparently is anxious to see her, one who "has been very demonstrably sweet in letting me know that he is thinking of me." Lajos had visited Nahalal in his shiny new car and mutual friends had introduced them. From the start they impressed each other. The "demonstrable sweetness" followed literally with the huge box of chocolates he sent her after their first meeting. It was the obvious way to win the heart of a girl living in a boarding school, and Chana was pleased. Still, she told her diary, "I've heard also from others that he really likes me. I don't know him very well and I don't want to prejudge, but deep in my heart I can already hear the word no. Yet, I'd so much like finally to be able to feel yes."

Despite Chana's customary forebodings, the intermittent friendship with Lajos continued with mutual visits between Nahalal and Jerusalem. Soon he proposed and in early 1941 Chana felt the matter serious enough to write her mother at length about it. She dwelled mainly on the differences in their philosophies and social situations: he was a young capitalist, she a socialist. He liked a fast and sophisticated city life; she was thinking of devoting her talents to raising chickens in the country. She was interested in things of the mind and the spirit, and she thought him weaker than herself. But she was also worldly enough to consider the more conventional criteria that have ruled the institution of marriage for thousands of years. His wealth could provide a carefree future for them both: "Sometimes I should bear more responsibility toward myself and take such things into account." However, she immediately returned to the "debit" column, for she could not see herself living on money gained through the exploitation of others. Most of all, it bothered her that after fifteen years in Eretz, Lajos still could not speak Hebrew properly. It may have been his parents' fault, but it showed a less serious commitment to Zion than her own.

Mrs. Szenes read this analysis correctly: Chana wanted to be talked out of marriage. She urged her daughter to wait until she found someone she really loved and admired. This, she felt, was more important than ideological differences or preference of lifestyle; after all, it was too early to know whether Chana might not move back into a city later in life.

Several weeks before this advice reached her, Chana had already made her decision. What she hated most about saying no was the pain she caused Lajos, and for the first time she, too, cared deeply enough to feel hurt. She set the jewel of her pain into four simple lines of poetry addressed to "a good friend":

> *I wounded him. I hardly noticed*
> *That I too was wounded.*
> *The arrow was tipped at both ends.*
> *Now there is a scar.*

Lajos had been debonair and fun, but ultimately, it was the past they shared and not the future. He reminded Chana of the values and the language she had left behind in Budapest. In the new land she wanted to find a new kind of man. Yet she seemed reluctant to take advantage of the relative freedom of Nahalal after the highly regulated life she had led under her mother's loving supervision. Even though the school was an all-female institution, the girls were allowed to roam freely in their leisure time. They had many parties to which young men from the village were invited, and they often walked or hitch-hiked to neighboring settlements. This relaxed atmosphere—filled with young people working hard and playing hard, all fired by a common cause—was conducive to the forming of easy attachments, even on an experimental basis. It was the exact opposite of the rigid Central European world where men still kissed ladies' hands and where young girls were chaperoned everywhere. Here, Chana was not only maturing fast, but lived close to nature—literally with the birds and the bees; milking cows became one of her favorite occupations. She gradually learned about alternative social systems. The kibbutz, like so many utopian experiments, sanctioned an utterly different family structure; some had the reputation of encouraging free love—a concept that would have shocked Mrs. Szenes.

Gyuri, too, had heard about "women being easy in Eretz" and playfully asked his sister to comment. "I can't say much about that," she replied with the utmost seriousness, "but I think the customs here are different. In some ways the girls are more honest and simple—there's less fuss for instance about marriage—yet I don't believe ultimately that they are any 'easier.' If anything, morals are stricter in the kibbutz." Or so she preferred to think, warding off even a "brotherly" kiss.

As her second spring in Palestine approached, Chana described herself as an empty pot, then a pot with holes in it. All the fresh experiences and new knowledge were pouring into her, then seeping away. She reached her hands out, but they could not grasp water. She needed people who would share her thoughts and feelings. Upon reflection, she admitted that it was not people in general that she needed, but rather one person, one man. And that could not be just any man. The old worry surfaced: perhaps she was incapable of such a relationship. "Why am I so alone?" she asked, close to despair.

Ultimately, the "boy-question" had less to do with opportunity or morality than with Chana's own psychology. Her search for a male ideal transcended the usual teenage romanticism and probably had its roots in the early loss of her father. Her love for Béla was sacred, especially as her last memories of him belonged to a time when she was only five years old. Chana never experienced the difficulties of adolescent rebellion with her father. Nor was he there to approve or disapprove of these male contenders for her affections, and his absence made him all the more powerful. Chana herself could not help but measure each boy against the ideal of her father. No man, and certainly no callow boy, could possibly compete with Béla, for he was not just her daddy, a benevolent giant frozen in time: he was still alive in his much-revered books and plays, which gave his children great delight and reflected glory.

Even if a man like Béla existed, she was unlikely to find him in Nahalal. Social conditions attracted a completely different kind of pioneer to Palestine than men of Béla's urbane gentility, and even if such people came as immigrants, they were forced to undergo a complete change. Chana was also the product of the rigidly class-conscious society in which she had grown up. Most of the young men around her in Palestine would have been considered ineligible as possible marriage partners in Budapest. She could not wholly abandon her former values and she was not the kind of rebel to marry someone for the sake of rebellion.

Most of all, however, Chana feared a conflict between marriage and pursuit of her own dreams. She realized early that her independence of thought and action might well be threatened by a conventional marriage. When Chana became a Zionist, she started to define her goals in political and social terms, not by the pursuit of personal happiness. These were goals she would have to achieve by herself or with comrades, not with a husband—although she longed to share them with the undefined "right one." Unfortunately, she seemed to attract mostly young men who were interested in her strength of character and will; such a person would have been a burden, not a helpmate. On the other hand, if she were to meet someone who could sweep her off her feet, a dominant personality might inhibit her own freedom.

Chana's dilemma about men grew and she withdrew more and more into an emotional shell inhabited by Béla and Gyuri, and on her safe, defined relationship with her brother she focused the love and caring she could not allow herself to feel for other men. As time went on, and the dangers around him increased, Chana's longing for Gyuri became more acute. In September 1940, nearing the anniversary of her arrival in Palestine, she mentioned receiving visits from two boys.

"I'd be happy to exchange both of them for just one—who is to my liking. And I'd give them all away, even that special one, for my brother . . . In the evening sometimes the thought bursts upon me: this can't go on! It has been two years since I saw him, and I'm so worried that when we meet again we might be strangers."

SEVEN

FAMILY REUNION

Gyuri was also eighteen when he left Hungary, upon graduation from high school. His departure in 1938 was different from Anikó's in that he intended to return to Budapest when he finished his studies in Lyons. Studying abroad, especially in the more sophisticated cities of the West, had an honorable tradition among Hungarians. The only remarkable aspect of Gyuri's studies was the subject matter—textiles. He had not the slightest interest or background in the manufacturing or design of textiles; the idea came about as a result of discussions Mrs. Szenes held with relatives and friends. She was strongly advised that Gyuri must learn a practical and internationally recognized profession in facing an uncertain world. Gyuri had of course been consulted about his future, but like many eighteen-year-olds, he had no clear alternative of his own to propose. He was sensible enough to know that he would need to find a way of supporting himself. The attraction of this plan lay in its promise of foreign adventure and the independence it would give him.

In the year of his graduation, existing laws, which restricted the number of Jewish students attending Hungarian universities (the so-called *numerus clausus*), were further tightened. As a male citizen, Gyuri was affected more immediately by discriminatory laws. Jews were excluded from the regular defense forces; they were conscripted instead into forced labor battalions, which were organized when Hungary joined the war. The battalions, consisting of unarmed men, were thrown into the front and forced to dig trenches and perform other menial tasks amidst appalling physical conditions, ostensibly proving their patriotism through such service. This was the prospect facing Gyuri if he had decided to remain in Hungary.

A highly intelligent, well-informed, and above all pragmatic young man, Gyuri watched several of his non-Jewish classmates yielding to the growing influence of the new Germany and joining right-wing organizations. The Arrow Cross party, which used a double-pointed cross instead of the swastika as its symbol, had grown rapidly since its founding in 1935. A couple of Gyuri's schoolmates had joined this Fascist organization and he made a point of asking them, before he left, to watch out for his sister and mother. Anikó was skeptical of her assigned guardians.

Gyuri's exemption from military service proved a boon; it left him free to leave home, which he was anxious to do. Although he dearly loved his mother and sister, he felt hindered from launching his own independent life by too much love and attention. He had spent his adolescence in a household filled with females. His mother and grandmother were widows, sad and serious much of the time. Anikó was an agreeable companion, but she was a younger sister, caught up in her own world. There were various uncles and friends of the family, but none of them close enough to be a substitute father to the young man.

With each passing year, Béla grew more wonderful in Gyuri's memory. He had been an inexhaustible fountain of stories, poems, and jokes for his children. Two published collections, called *Gyurika,* contained nonsense poems, tales, and sketches that he wrote and dedicated to his son. Gyuri was still too young to appreciate these public proofs of his father's love. He prized more his memories of Béla's down-to-earth kindness and humor. There was the time when Gyuri was five or six:

> I was on a walk with our governess in a rural, outlying area of Buda. We came to a large meadow where a young boy of about my age was herding his goats. He was barefoot and in rags, and I wore my city finery, but we quickly became friends. When it was time to go home I said to him: "There's a children's party at our house next Tuesday afternoon, with lots of cakes, hot chocolate, and ice cream. Why don't you come and we can meet again?" We agreed and I went home with my governess. The following Tuesday, we were in the middle of the party, when the caretaker rushed in to tell my father: "A ragged little urchin is waiting outside the garden gate with twenty or thirty goats, claiming that Master Gyuri has invited him to the tea party." To father's question I replied that I had indeed invited the little boy, who was very nice but had never had *torta* in his life. My father and I then went out to the gate, taking a couple of slices of cake for the boy, and my father told the shepherd boy: "Look, I'm sorry but you can't come in with all these goats; come back without them some other day to play with Gyuri." My mother was upset, afraid that I'd fall into bad company, but father told her: "I'm glad our son has such a good heart."

Anikó may have taken after Béla professionally, but Gyuri inherited his father's humor and sunny disposition. An outgoing young man, Gyuri loved sports: swimming, soccer, and tennis. He excelled especially in Ping-Pong, which is respected almost as highly in Hungary as in China, and his skill in this recreation was to prove useful later. Gyuri also had a serious side: He loved literature and classical music. He shared with Anikó a keen interest in world affairs, though his outlook was more detached and secular, hers more poetic and mystical.

When Gyuri left for Milan in early July, Anikó had gone to stay with friends at Lake Balaton, a favorite summer resort in Hungary. She had said goodbye to him once already, but as his train to Milan was passing through Lelle on the Balaton, she had a second chance to see "the old man" off. They had been trained from childhood to control their emotions; their farewell conversation revolved around his tennis racket, her suntan, Italian lessons, and her memories of the swimming pool in Milan, which she had visited exactly a year before.

Actually, Anikó was happy to see Gyuri seizing the opportunity to leave home. She was mostly concerned about their mother and how distressed she would be at losing her son. In this constrained poem, called "Farewell," Anikó tried to express her mother's and her own emotions at Gyuri's departure:

> *You left. We waved a long time.*
> *Porters clattered in the background.*
> *We watched and you disappeared.*
>
> *Life led you. You were happy.*
> *Maybe your heart had songs within.*
> *Our tears were well hidden.*
>
> *Wordless we went home*
> *Watching the sky, pale and blue,*
> *And our soul, unseen, is secretly*
> *Waving still to you.*

Opportunities for study did not materialize in Milan, and after a few weeks, through further arrangements made by his mother and her friend Edith Singer, Gyuri moved to Lyons, where he would remain for the next four years. Though smaller than Budapest in population, this cosmopolitan city in southeastern France is actually older than Paris. For two thousand years it has been important for trading and commerce, for five hundred it has been a center for silk-manufacturing and textiles. Given that Gyuri planned to go into textiles, Lyons was the logical place to study.

Gyuri started his life in the French city by following his mother's instructions and boarding with the Gouchat family. When this proved not to his liking, he found somewhere else to stay, arranged with restaurants to send meals to his room, and struck out on his new life with gusto. L'Ecole de Tissage, the school he attended, had the highest academic standards and an excellent reputation. Gyuri, whose knowledge of French and of textiles was equally minimal, settled into a routine of hard work. Fortunately, he possessed great natural gifts as a linguist, and in a few months he was completely fluent. He sometimes wrote to his mother and sister in French to show off his progress.

If he was not dedicated to the idea of spending his life in textiles, he quickly grew interested in the subject and became very good at it, rising to the top of his class his second year and graduating with a certificate of merit, only three of which were awarded. The chemical industry in Lyons continually developed new man-made materials for silk substitutes, and the school was in the forefront of experimenting with rayon and other fabrics. Besides enjoying the technical aspects of his new subjects, Gyuri also found creative outlets in design. He was gratified at having one of his submissions to a schoolwide competition chosen among the top three and used for an actual design.

The hours of study were long, especially in his first year, but Gyuri developed a great deal of self-discipline. He began every morning with ten minutes of physical exercise, and after school he pursued other sports. He soon joined a Ping-Pong club, and won various prizes. From his first prize money of twenty-four francs, he had photographs made of himself for his mother and sister. He also bought a bicycle, both for getting around the city and to make excursions to neighboring towns. After his first-year exams, he took a two-week cycling tour of several hundred miles.

Gyuri had been away from home less than a year when, during Anikó's ten-day Easter break in 1939, she and Mrs. Szenes came to visit him. The happy reunion was celebrated with Hungarian delicacies, such as salami and goose-liver paté; the pièce de résistance was a chocolate cream cake that Mrs. Szenes had baked herself and wrapped in foil for the long train journey. She now insisted on cutting it: inside the cake was a five-hundred-Swiss-franc note that she had folded and hid carefully in grease-resistant paper. Because of Hungary's worsening economy, there was a ban on the export of hard currency from the country. Gyuri's tuition and living expenses were subsidized by Jewish philanthropy from America, but life was expensive in Lyons and Gyuri was not adept at managing his funds.

In honor of his mother, though, he had tidied his room. Only later, when she happened to open one of the closets, did all the hidden laundry and shoes come tumbling out. While Gyuri attended classes, Mrs. Szenes and Anikó helped put his room and clothes into order, and even managed some sightseeing. In the evening they talked. Anikó was excited to discover that Gyuri too espoused the cause of Zionism. After he finished his training in the textile trade, he hoped to put his knowledge to use in a country he could call his own. Despite his sunny and outgoing nature, Gyuri did not feel at home in France. Occasionally he felt homesick and lonely, as any young man would his first time abroad. And during the year he had been away the political situation in Hungary had deteriorated. He could not imagine his future in either country.

As Mrs. Szenes listened to her two children passionately discussing Zionist issues and problems, she felt left out. It had all happened so fast. When Gyuri left, only nine months before, both her children were ordinary Hungarian teenagers who happened to be Jewish. Neither of them could have imagined their future outside Hungary. Then in late October 1938, Anikó first revealed to her mother that she had become a Zionist. The following March, just before this visit to Lyons, she had composed and sent off her Hebrew application to Nahalal. And now, in April, Gyuri too was planning to leave Europe.

Kató Szenes wanted only to see her children happy and fulfilled in a place where their talents could blossom. She knew that their opportunities in Hungary were diminishing, but she hoped, as did most Hungarian Jews, that all this madness would soon end. Losing her children to such a distant and dangerous land as Palestine made her heart heavy. She stood silently by when Anikó shouted goodbye to Gyuri from the train: "Next year in Jerusalem!" He waved back happily from the platform. It was the last time the three of them would ever be together.

EIGHT

FALL OF FRANCE

Gyuri's route to Zionism was different from Anikó's. His final years in Budapest had made him aware of the dark future that awaited Jewish youth there; hearing Anikó's tremendous determination to leave Hungary inspired him. But his decision was based too on his own observations in France. Here in the cradle of the revolution that declared equality and fraternity to all, he felt a constant and subtle discrimination, not because he was a foreigner, but because he was a Jew. No matter how successful he was in his exams, his designs, or his Ping-Pong, or how helpful he was to fellow students, he felt that his achievements were attributed not to ability, nor to hard work and determination, but to the fact that he was a Jew, as if this somehow had given him an unfair advantage.

The experience of anti-Semitism had an immediate effect on a young man who was trying to determine what to do with his life and where to do it. France had seemed much more civilized than Hungary. She had stood for many of the most cherished values of mankind, she had given refuge to many idealists and fighters for good causes. Yet Gyuri could no more see his future in France than he could see it in Hungary. His disappointment was profound, even if it did not affect his mood on the surface. He worked just as hard and seemed to enjoy life as much as before. But his mind began to explore the possibility of a journey that would lead him to Zion.

Gyuri was not alone in his disillusionment. Many Frenchmen saw dangers of internal fascism in the gradual decline of liberalism, which had been a French tradition for a hundred and fifty years. But they could not imagine that it would be dictated so swiftly and brutally by Germany, their greatest external enemy, which had already invaded their country twice in less than a century. Yet all the signs were there and what happened in France since the Revolution illuminates the vicissitudes of European Jewry as a whole.

As in most Christian countries, where the Church had taught that the

Jews had been responsible for killing Christ, there has long been a primitive and atavistic anti-Semitism in France. There were no ghettoes as in the German and Italian city-states, but Jews were isolated and many of them were forced into occupations forbidden to Christians, such as money-lending, which emphasized their apartness.

The enlightenment of the late eighteenth century saw the degraded condition of the Jews as a symbol of larger social inequities. The French Revolution put an end to the medieval power and religious intolerance of the Catholic church, but the first to be enfranchised were the Protestants. Despite the universal declaration of the Rights of Man, the Jews were not to benefit immediately from the new constitution. About three quarters of the forty thousand Jews living in France were settled in the provinces of Alsace and Lorraine, despised as usurers. Another few thousand Jews were scattered around Avignon and throughout Provence, mostly Sephardic Jews who escaped from Spain in 1492 when Ferdinand and Isabella not only dispatched Columbus to find the Indies, but also expelled the entire flourishing Jewish community from their kingdom. The Sephardim were prosperous and well established, and they claimed that they were in fact French and completely divorced from the Ashkenazi Jews of Alsace. Their arguments accepted, they were granted active citizenship in January 1790, a year and a half before all Jews gained full citizenship. But it was Napoleon Bonaparte who first offered Jews a partnership in a modern secular state. He was much more than a hero to Jews. Both before and after he became emperor, Napoleon was responsible for a number of symbolic and substantive gestures that would change forever the position of Jews in Europe. While still a Republican, he abolished the Jewish ghetto of Venice in 1797, that of Mainz the following year. When he became emperor he tore down the walls of the ancient ghettoes of Rome and Frankfurt, granting the Jews of Hamburg and the North German states full civil rights. During his Syrian campaign in 1799 (almost a century before Herzl), Bonaparte had invited all the Jews of Asia and Africa to help him re-establish ancient Jerusalem as the capital of a new Jewish homeland. No doubt his motives were self-interested rather than ideological. As a strategist, he saw Jerusalem as a base from which to attack Constantinople, and from there follow the historic Turkish routes to Vienna, the Crimea, and the rest of Russia. The British navy and Nelson may have frustrated him, but the symbolic value of Jerusalem was not lost on him.

Although his grand designs ended in failure, Napoleon's attitude toward the Jews permanently changed their image, if not always their status, in Christian Europe. During the nineteenth century they came to play an increasingly important part in the rise of the middle and professional classes. They prospered and made contributions to French culture, politics, business, and science quite out of proportion to their numbers, which were under one hundred thousand. This population was to double as a result of pogroms and expulsions of Jews from Russia that began with the May Laws of 1882. Many of these immigrant Jews settled in urban slums, which became to Paris what the Lower East Side was to New York, creating similar divisions between the Jewish establishment and an immigrant underclass. Their presence inevitably brought new tensions.

Following the humiliating defeat of 1871 at the hand of a newly unified and autocratic Germany, democracy and liberalism in France came under increasing attack. Nationalism and racial purity were loudly touted as the cure for the bankrupt ideologies of liberalism. The fin de siècle trial of Captain Alfred Dreyfus, falsely accused and convicted of treason, was a watershed in the polarization that was to destroy the fragile fabric of Western European society during the next century. Liberals thought that their cause was vindicated when Dreyfus was brought back from Devil's Island. But there were some far-sighted people who realized that Zola's famous accusation against the persecutors of Dreyfus was in fact aimed at the whole system. Theodor Herzl, living in Paris, also saw Dreyfus as a symptom of the anti-Semitic disease for which the cure would be Zionism, not liberalism.

At first France seemed to emerge as one of the victors of the First World War, in which she lost two million of her young men. French policy after the war was to prevent Germany, which had almost twice her population and the largest territory in Europe, from rising from its ashes. But when France tried to keep control of the Rhineland, she was opposed at the conference table by her former Anglo-American allies, who insisted on a demilitarized Rhineland under German sovereignty. In turn, Great Britain and the United States were willing to guarantee France's security. However, President Woodrow Wilson, proclaimed as the savior of Europe, failed to persuade the United States Senate at home to ratify the Treaty of Versailles. American inaction prompted Britain to renounce her own part of the guarantee. So France ended up without the Rhineland and with no security guarantees from her former allies.

War reparations became another sore point. After Germany defeated France in 1871, she exacted a lump sum as punitive damages. Now it was France's turn, and she wanted Germany to pay the actual cost of reconstruction until it was completed. These vast and undefined sums would be stretched out at least until 1940, and by some estimates 1960. The French hoped, somewhat wildly, that German reparations could replace the unpopular income tax that had been introduced to finance the war.

Germany deeply resented the payments; she also claimed insolvency in the economic crisis that followed the collapse of her currency. Britain actually supported the German request for a moratorium on payments, and called a conference to discuss the matter. Fearing the rekindling of the prewar alliance between Britain and Germany, the French government declared Germany to be in default and occupied the Ruhr, which upset both the British and the Americans; only Mussolini approved. It also angered the German workers of the Ruhr, the country's industrial base. They stopped working and Germany became even less able to pay her debts.

The next decade produced various treaties and conferences but little to reassure France. The economic crisis of 1930 forced Germany to stop further reparations payments, which did not prevent Hitler and his National Socialist party from using Germany's humiliation as an excuse for rearmament. France watched with alarm the military resurgence of Germany, but could not get the attention of the appeasement-minded British or isolationist Americans. She then tried to forge new alliances with Italy, Poland, and some Balkan countries that had benefited from the Treaty of Versailles, and even signed an agreement with the Soviet Union.

Then came Mussolini's invasion of Ethiopia, followed by Hitler's repossession of the Rhineland in March 1936. The French government heeded British advice to do nothing, thus losing the opportunity to strike back at a Germany that was still relatively weak. Hitler took this inaction as permission for further aggression. The last gesture of French liberalism came in 1936, when the Chamber of Deputies elected Léon Blum, a Socialist and a Jew, to head a left-wing coalition of the Front Populaire. In his brief year as premier, Blum initiated the forty-hour work week, paid holidays, and a whirlwind of social reforms that were essential to prevent the radical right from seizing power. But he neglected foreign policy, and in particular failed to win cabinet backing for the democratic side in the Spanish Civil War. By the time his successor began to address the Fascist threat, it was late. Austria had welcomed Hitler, and Prime Minister Neville Chamberlain had handed him Czechoslovakia while pressuring France to abandon their treaty of mutual defense. There was a last-ditch attempt to strengthen the alliance with the Soviet Union, but this was forestalled by Hitler, who made his own pact with Stalin and set the stage for the dismemberment of Poland.

Although Britain and France finally declared war on Nazi Germany two days after the attack on Poland, this was anything but a joint action. Many in the French government urged capitulation as preferable to another bloody war. And even those who opted to fight felt, with some justification, that with the British as friends, France did not need any enemies. Hitler exploited the wavering resolve of these uneasy allies and felt safe to continue his aggression.

By March 1940, Mrs. Szenes was sufficiently concerned about Gyuri to visit him in Lyons. Conditions in France had worsened considerably during that year. Every night there was a blackout; food was more severely rationed than in Budapest. Hungary had not entered the war, so Kató obtained a visa without trouble. The whole trip was hastily planned. She had sent Gyuri a telegram but he did not receive it. When she arrived, he was in Paris playing in a Ping-Pong tournament. He was greatly surprised to see his mother waiting in his room upon his return.

They spent most of Kató's visit discussing Gyuri's future and trying to second-guess the outcome of the war that was coming closer. If the Germans did occupy France, where and how would Gyuri flee? He might be safer in Hungary, which had not yet joined the conflict. On the other hand, what would he do back at home? And what if the authorities drafted him into a forced-labor battalion?

They concluded that the best thing was for Gyuri to remain in Lyons and finish his studies. Meanwhile Anikó was sure to obtain a certificate that could get him to Palestine. If he did not return to Hungary he might be technically considered a deserter, but that was preferable to fighting on the German side and perhaps being killed. At any rate, Gyuri planned to emigrate and had no intention of returning to Hungary. The final question was how Mrs. Szenes would arrange to join him and Anikó in Eretz Israel. There were many questions to which there seemed to be no answers.

Mrs. Szenes returned to Budapest at the end of March. Two weeks later Hungary officially entered the war, joining Hitler's attack on Yugoslavia. She was immediately rewarded with the recovery of some southern territories in the so-called Délvidék, which had been Hungarian until twenty years before. Pro-German sentiment was growing in Budapest with each new triumph by the Third Reich.

On May 10, 1940, Hitler carried his blitzkrieg into Holland and Belgium, smashing through France's defenses near Sedan. In a panic, the French government appealed to Britain and America for help. Neville Chamberlain, still the prime minister, hesitated to commit British air power to the defense of Paris. The United States would maintain its neutrality for another eighteen months; President Roosevelt offered words of moral encouragement.

In the beginning of June it looked as if nothing would stop the Nazi takeover of Western Europe. After the subjugation of the Low Countries, the evacuation of British troops from Dunkirk was completed on June fourth. On the ninth Norway surrendered, and the Germans stood at the gates of Paris. By this time Winston Churchill had finally taken over the reins of a coalition government in Britain, but it was too late to save France. On June tenth Paris was abandoned, despite personal appeals from Churchill, who even suggested merging Britain and France into one country to fight against Hitler. On June fourteenth the supposedly impregnable Maginot Line was breached by the full onslaught of the Wehrmacht. Seven days later, on June twenty-first, Marshal Pétain submitted to German terms and signed an armistice in the same railroad car in which General Foch had dictated terms to the Germans in 1918.

For several tense weeks, both Mrs. Szenes in Budapest and Chana in Nahalal waited in vain for news of Gyuri.

NINE

TROUBLE IN PALESTINE

As a child Anikó had been keenly aware of international politics. Her diaries from age thirteen on are full of references to current events: Mussolini's invasion of Ethiopia in 1935, Hitler's takeover of neighboring Austria in 1938, soon to be followed by the dismemberment of Czechoslovakia, and the brief rejoicing in Hungary over the recovered territories.

Now, Chana's concern was intense and personal, but it was difficult to keep abreast of world events in the pastoral, almost backward atmosphere of Nahalal. The first few months after her arrival were relatively quiet, but Palestine was still under British rule, while Hungary was now an ally of Germany. Chana listened to short wave radio at night, but mostly what she heard was propaganda. It was hard to decide what was true, and letters were no more helpful than radio reports. The Szenes family knew better than to discuss politics in their correspondence. Only in the most general way did they ever allude to domestic conditions or such major events as the fall of France. Despite their caution, letters were sometimes returned, and occasional passages heavily expunged in black testified to the military censors' vigilance.

Quite apart from the conflagration that was spreading from Europe to engulf the rest of the world, Palestine was facing conflicts of its own. Chana had arrived at a critical time when the triangle of tension between Jews and Arabs, and increasingly between the Jews and the British, was reaching its breaking point, and within a few months, the island of Britain had to make her lonely last stand for her most cherished values and declining empire.

The pastoral peace that Chana felt upon reaching the shores of Palestine was shattered in the early days of 1940, when the provisions of the British government's White Paper went into effect, essentially repealing the Balfour Declaration. In 1920 the League of Nations had given Great Britain the mandate to administer Palestine until some plan could be worked out for the establishment of a Jewish homeland. The principle providing for such a homeland had been enunciated in November 1917, after two decades of intense lobbying begun by Herzl himself and ably carried forward by Chaim Weizmann and others. Although members of the British government were sympathetic to the Jewish question, what actually motivated the highly ambiguous Balfour resolution was the need to win the war with American and Jewish help. Arthur Balfour, British foreign secretary, communicated this one-sentence resolution by the British War Cabinet to Lord Rothschild, a leading figure of the British Jewish community, and it became the cornerstone of British policy for the next two decades:

> His Majesty's Government views with favour the establishment in Palestine of a national home for the Jewish People, and will use their best endeavours to facilitate the achievement of this object, it being clearly understood that nothing shall be done which may prejudice the civil and religious rights of the existing non-Jewish communities in Palestine, or the rights and political status enjoyed by Jews in any other country.

The declaration did not itself create a Jewish homeland. There were deep divisions in the Jewish communities of Europe and America, even among Zionists, over whether Palestine was a suitable place to build the Jewish state. Weizmann, who had developed friendly relations with Arab chieftains, such as the Hashemite Faisal, was optimistically expecting the Mandate government to offer the influx of Jewish immigrants unused crown lands to create new settlements. This never materialized, and every acre of swamp and useless desert land had to be bought at fantastically inflated prices from Arab landlords, who at first welcomed this unexpected bonanza. And while individual Arabs may have been friendly enough to the newcomers, there were frequent and cataclysmic fights among the Arabs themselves. Prince Ibn Saud wiped out the Hashemite army and proceeded to carve out the kingdom of Arabia. Prince Faisal meanwhile tried to take possession of Syria, which the British (or at least T. E. Lawrence) had promised him for supporting the Allied cause during the war. The French—who were entrusted by the League of Nations with a Mandate to administer Syria and went ahead with the creation of an artificial state that came to be known as The Lebanon—did not want to deal with an Arab ruler and expelled Faisal. Arab resentment against the French immediately spilled over into Palestine and spelled the end of any cooperation with British plans to allow Jews to return to their ancient homeland. Caught in the raids between roaming Arab bands, five Jewish settlements in the northern Galilee near the border with Syria became subject to vicious attacks. Acts of violence escalated on all sides. Riots ensued. To make matters worse, when the grand mufti of Jerusalem died, the British high commissioner for Palestine appointed as his successor Haj Amin el-Husseini, a Moslem fanatic who agitated ceaselessly for the extermination of all Jewish settlers. His anti-British and anti-Semitic views naturally brought him to the attention of Adolf Hitler.

But the great powers had not finished with the map of the Near East. To keep Faisal's elder brother Abdullah content and to prevent him from marching on to Damascus, Winston Churchill—attended by Colonel Lawrence of Arabia—carved Transjordan out of the Palestine Mandate. Just ten thousand of the original forty-five thousand square miles of the promised Jewish homeland were left. Thus Jordan was born, and the main elements of today's Middle Eastern conflict, with its principal antagonists, were in place.

The main source of discord between Arabs and Jews came from Jewish immigration, the logical consequence of the Balfour Declaration. But the declaration had vaguely promised a homeland, not specifically an independent Jewish state. By July 1922, when the Mandate was finally ratified by the League of Nations, the British had already retreated under Arab pressure from allowing the possibility of Palestine's eventually becoming Jewish. They set an immigration quota of 16,500 Jewish pioneers a year (instead of the 80,000 Weizmann had envisioned), which would keep the Jews a permanent minority in their alleged homeland. Despite these and other difficulties, Jews were arriving in increasing numbers. In the five years following the First World War, known as the Third Aliyah, the Jewish population of Palestine doubled, surpassing 100,000 for the first time in nineteen centuries.

In 1924 the United States introduced quotas to stem the flow of undesirable immigrants. The legislation was aimed mainly against Asians, but it also affected the villages of Eastern Europe, where millions were yearning for the land of the free. The Fourth Aliyah diverted a number of these to Palestine and in 1925, more than 34,000 Jews made their ascent to Zion. The influx tapered off thereafter, because the Mandate with its undeveloped, colonial economy could not absorb all the newcomers.

But when the Nazis came to power in Germany at the beginning of 1933, immigration to Palestine resumed with a renewed urgency. This Fifth (or so-called "Hitler") Aliyah would bring tens of thousands, including Chana, to the Land. In 1935, the year of the Nuremberg Laws—which stripped German Jews of their citizenship and deprived them of their livelihood—a record 61,854 people managed to reach the shores of Eretz Israel.

For a while the Arab majority more or less acquiesced in this influx, which greatly boosted the economy of Palestine. Arabs sold land to the settlers at inflated prices and continued to provide needed workers, goods, and services. But as the Jewish population grew rapidly, so did unemployment and the competition for commerce, for land, and for shelter. The Arab riots of the early twenties resumed, but this time the Jews were also becoming militant.

Meanwhile in the rest of the world, the Great Depression and nationalistic movements combined to fan the flames of anti-Semitism, raising the specter of a tidal wave of Jewish refugees. The 1924 immigration act had set an annual quota of 26,000 German nationals who could be admitted to the United States. Most of the slots went unfilled because the United States government required police certificates (it still does) and military records, which Jews fleeing Nazi Germany obviously could not obtain. In the year Hitler came to power, only 6 percent of the global quota for immigrants into the United States was filled. During the next four years the United States admitted 55,000 immigrants, out of a possible 600,000. In the same period, 160,000 Jews were absorbed into tiny and backward Palestine, causing increasing tension and violence.

The mid-1930s saw the rise of the Haganah, a full-fledged defense force against Arab attacks, and the Irgun Zvai Leumi ("National Military Organization"), a counter-terrorist organization founded by Vladimir Jabotinsky and later led by Menachem Begin. The British reaction to the new rounds of violence was characteristic. They set up a commission under Lord Peel, which after two years of hearings, yielded the insight that the one million Arabs and the four hundred thousand Jews could not live peaceably together. The commission suggested a partition of Palestine, a plan that formed the basis of the United Nations resolution that created Israel ten years later. The proposal alone created a surge of violence and terrorism that exceeded the bloodshed of earlier years. During the three years before Chana arrived in Palestine, some five thousand people— British, Jews, and Arabs—were assassinated, murdered, or hanged.

The immigration of Jewish refugees to Palestine, Western Europe, and the United States had been successfully blocked through creative bureaucratic measures; all that remained now was to show a semblance of concern. So in 1938 the Evian Conference was convened to discuss what to do with Jewish refugees.

At Evian, a pleasant and quiet spa on the French side of Lake Geneva, the British diplomats simply ruled the subject of Palestine out of order. The White Paper had, after all, proposed the best solutions, and an international conference was not the proper forum to discuss British policy. A wide assortment of groups, including the Quakers and the United States Congress, tried in vain to move President Roosevelt to save 20,000 homeless Jewish children, but the only substantial offer to help the refugees came from the tiny Dominican Republic. Evian confirmed to Hitler and

Goebbels that there was no point in expelling the Jews, since nobody else wanted them either. Another solution to "the Jewish problem" would have to be found.

By 1939 the British government was expressing concern that the Arabs, who were already openly sympathetic to Hitler, might join the Axis alliance formed by the Fascist states, or that the frequent riots might spread from Palestine to neighboring Egypt, endanger British control of the Suez Canal, and block the vital route to India. So Chamberlain issued another White Paper on May 17, 1939, in effect renouncing the Balfour Declaration altogether. The partition plan was abandoned at the urging of the Arabs as too generous; in future, slightly more than 5 percent of the original Mandate area would be available for purchase by Jewish settlers, and even that would require special permission from the British high commissioner. The White Paper promised an independent Palestinian state within ten years— for Arabs. Jewish immigration was to be limited to 10,000 a year for five years. As for the pressing refugee problem, His Majesty's government was prepared to admit 25,000 people into Palestine immediately, as a one-time humanitarian gesture. After five years, when this total of 75,000 Jews had been admitted, Palestine would be closed to Jewish immigration. Forever.

The White Paper was rejected by all sides. The World Zionist Congress launched a vociferous campaign of protest and President Roosevelt called it "unwise." Even the Arabs opposed the new plan, because to them the new quota of 75,000 constituted that many superfluous Jews. Every Jew was affected by the White Paper, as it went into effect at the beginning of 1940.

The Szenes family felt the blow directly. Within the foreseeable future, only 50,000 certificates of immigration would be issued for millions of potential applicants. Gyuri and Kató could not expect to be anywhere near the top of a waiting list, as they were not in countries under direct occupation. Young Zionists with strong bodies would naturally be given preference. The prospect was particularly bleak for Mrs. Szenes, who had never given serious thought to emigration. Gyuri had a slightly better chance of getting a certificate; France was still allied with Great Britain and his youth and training would make him valuable.

Chana encountered formidable obstacles when she tried to find out about procedures for Gyori's immigration. However, she also gained useful insight into the internal politics of the Mandate and its complex bureaucracies. One casualty of this experience was her long-cherished enthusiasm for the British. She had grown up with an admiration for English culture and language that was not unusual among Hungarian intellectuals. Gyuri and Anikó had attended the English elementary school in Buda that had been founded by Judith Schanda, one of Kató's oldest friends who later played an important role in her life. Soon after Chana arrived in Palestine, however, she realized that it was difficult to remain both an Anglophile and a Zionist. The war that finally erupted between Germany, which wanted to expel the Jews, and Great Britain, which did not want to receive them, forced the Jewish community of Eretz Israel into a hopeless predicament. The dilemma was defined by David Ben-Gurion, chairman of the Zionist Executive in Palestine: "We shall fight the war as if there were no White Paper and we shall fight the White Paper as if there were no war." This schizophrenic attitude grew sharper as the Jewish catastrophe ripened both in Europe and in Palestine; one of its direct results would be the strange mission of Jewish paratroopers wearing British uniforms.

TEN

SEEING SIGHTS

As Chana learned about the recent history and political turmoil of her new country, her desire grew to explore it. The rigorous school routine would have been hard to bear if it had not been broken by frequent excursions. The girls visited the moshav regularly, of course, and Chana was particularly fond of attending the private concerts at the Nahalal doctor's house on Sunday evenings. She tried to go there each week, although sometimes her assignment in the dairy or the kitchen prevented it.

Most exciting, however, were the longer trips, which could only be taken on weekends or holidays. Chana used her first break, during Chanukah 1939, to explore Haifa, which she had seen for just two brief days when she first arrived. The holidays enabled her to leave school on Friday morning, so she caught a 7:00 A.M. bus and arrived at the Kraus family's apartment an hour later. Imre and Ilonka Kraus were immigrants from Hungary to whom Mrs. Szenes had written, hoping that they would keep an eye on her daughter. They had kindly invited Chana to visit whenever she was able.

Chana had happily packed her overnight bag with some of the elegant European clothes she had not worn since September. As soon as she arrived, there was a Chanukah celebration for the Krauses' little daughter, Zsuzsa. After the party, Chana spent the rest of the morning shopping in Haifa and doing errands for her friends back at school. She observed life in the city with a certain sense of detachment, feeling somewhat overdressed in her cosmopolitan clothes from Budapest.

After lunch, the Kraus family took her on a sightseeing tour of Mount Carmel, the steep and massive rock-mountain that dominates Haifa. Chana was impressed by the modern houses and roads, and enchanted by the beauty of the Carmel, whose villas brought back memories of her home in Buda. She was overwhelmed by the subtropical flora blooming in the middle of winter, and drank in the panoramic view of the Mediterranean stretching from the busy seaport below toward Akko and The Lebanon. As Chana absorbed the sights and the exotic scents, she could have no inkling that for long decades Mount Carmel would be home to her mother and brother.

That evening the Krauses took her to a party at the home of some Hungarian friends. The people were friendly and welcoming, and Chana had a wonderful time until 3:00 A.M. She found that, despite fatigue caused by hard work, everybody was in high spirits, mixing songs and dances in Hungarian and Hebrew. Next morning she slept late, and the Shabbat was spent talking with two Hungarian boys whose relatives she knew at home. Leo Bergmann, a relative of her Uncle Pali in Dombovár, had written to Chana suggesting that they should meet; she found him quite pleasant, but in her report to her cousin Évi she hastened to add that she felt nothing special for him.

Then some friends from the previous evening's party dropped by to continue unfinished conversations, and that evening they all went to another party, this time dominated by Russian and Polish immigrants who worked in the Rutenberg factory with Imre Kraus. Because of the mixture of languages, the conversation was mainly in Hebrew, but the songs included some soulful Russian tunes. This party was mostly for young couples, however, and Chana was ready to go home by one o'clock.

Sunday morning she completed more errands, buying toiletries, first aid items, and photographic supplies. She was particularly pleased with herself for exchanging something she had bought and never used; the eighteen piasters she got back paid for all her new acquisitions. Chana was always careful with money and did not like to spend it on herself. In the afternoon she met Leo Bergmann again: "He happened to have time and I didn't have anything else scheduled," she wrote Évi, and that was as much enthusiasm as she could muster about Leo. By Sunday evening she was back in Nahalal, exhausted but refreshed.

In contrast to this worldly excursion to Haifa, with all its connections to her Hungarian past, Chana's trip the following April showed her new vistas. With her two roommates, Miriam and Pnina, she decided to hitch a ride eastward on the main road between Haifa and the Sea of Galilee, to Tiberias. In those days there were few cars, and real pioneers did not own them; that was why Lajos Friedman had made such an impression. After a fairly lengthy wait by the roadside, they finally managed to flag down a shiny automobile driven by an Englishman from Haifa.

Chana was an excellent travel writer, with a fine eye for detail. Above all, she was an enthusiastic tourist. Now, as the car followed the ancient, winding road, she wished she had the powers of an Impressionist painter to record the passing daubs of color, the miniature houses with flowering orchards and tiny gardens that greeted them at each turn. The girls barely had time to exchange delighted looks as the scenes kept changing, each more beautiful than the last. Early on they passed Nazareth on its lofty perch. Chana could catch only a few glimpses of historic Nazareth, with its "blinding white monasteries, churches, old stone houses, Arabs, monks, nuns." After about half an hour, the serpentine road through the ancient hill country began to curve upward; the knolls seemed to crowd in on them, in preparation for the breathtaking view of the entire Galil, with the lake's blue patch far below them. Opposite, the heights of Golan rose toward the sky, embracing the body of water called in Hebrew *Yam Kinneret.* The car began its headlong plunge down the hairpin turns. Suddenly the hillsides became greener, tamed with olive groves and vineyards and cypresses. Enthralled, they saw their destination below: the whitewashed town of Tiberias next to the sea. Chana was in love with the landscape, finding fresh confirmation in each new sight for the love she felt for Eretz as a whole.

The Englishman let them off in the middle of Tiberias. He had said very little during the entire trip, but he did promise to pick them up in the same spot in the afternoon and to take them back to Nahalal. The first thing the girls wanted after the hot journey was to wade into the water. Hunger took precedence, however; they picnicked in a park near the waterfront, supplementing the dry Hungarian salami that Mrs. Szenes had included in her latest parcel with some freshly bought bread and oranges. Chana carefully noted for her mother that the entire lunch did not cost more than a piaster. After their repast, the girls noticed an older gentleman who looked like a policeman, and they asked him what to see in town and whether it was safe to go into the Arab quarter. The man kindly offered to show them the sights.

The pungent smells from the ramshackle buildings mixed with those of commerce in the winding alleys. Popular English songs blared from a café, competing with the Arabic music in the shops. The eager young tourists were impressed by the diversity of cultures and races. They saw exotic pilgrims with white long beards, European Jews rubbing shoulders with Arab vendors—some wearing their own distinctive dress, others a mixture of West and East that reflected the character of the whole town. Their guide took them to the Oriental Jewish quarter. Outwardly this district looked a little more modern but not much tidier than the Arab quarter. Sephardic Jews, returning to Palestine from Arab countries, now wore European clothes, but to confuse matters further, spoke Arabic. They knew Hebrew, like Jews throughout the Diaspora, only as the language of liturgy.

Chana was fascinated by the furnishing of their synagogue, which was a square hall. The walls all around were lined with benches, and colorful cushions piled high on them helped to create an atmosphere of Oriental luxury and comfort. She admired the ornately carved Torah cabinet and remarked on the absence of a women's gallery; only men attended services.

They would have liked to spend more time exploring the other sights of Tiberias, but it was getting late and they began thinking about getting back. While they were vainly hoping for the Englishman to return to the public park, Chana made friends with the children who were playing there. She was always happy in the company of small children and the thought came to her again that she should choose a vocation that would include children.

By three o'clock they had to accept that their chauffeur was not returning for them. There would be no bus after sundown or the next day because of the Shabbat. It was possible that they would not get back to Nahalal until some time on Sunday, when they would have to face the consequences of missing classes—not to mention the expense of paying for a hotel and the extra meals. Unlike her two companions, Chana's attitude was one of joyous optimism. She sat in the shade by the roadside on top of somebody's mailbox and sang, oblivious to their growing depression. After about an hour a car appeared in the bend; Miriam and Pnina, pretending to be in dire distress, waved their arms to attract the young driver's attention. He was startled by the pair of boisterous young women piling into the back seat, while Chana leaped from her roadside ambush into the passenger seat, almost crushing a beautiful new hat, which he barely rescued with one hand, while with the other he quickly tried to close the door against other surprise guests. They reassured him that there were no more than three, and proceeded in renewed high spirits back home to the Emek.

Chana's description of this trip in a letter to her mother bubbled with such vitality that she laughingly excused herself for the lengthy travelogue: "I always skip in travel books those lengthy passages about the scenery; so I should not inflict on others what I wouldn't wish on myself. And I should be especially sparing of my own mother." She also had to consider the British censor, who disliked long letters written in exotic languages like Hungarian, with such rich opportunities for hidden meanings. But she decided to ignore the censor for once rather than cut short her lively narrative. The freshness of her experience with this rich and varied landscape meant much to her, and she needed to share it with her mother.

Although she delighted in being a tourist, many of Chana's trips had a practical purpose. In early May 1940 she visited both Jerusalem and Tel Aviv, trying to straighten out the complicated immigration procedures for Gyuri, to secure his passage by boat, and to explore job possibilities in textiles. With Hitler poised to strike at France, Chana felt a desperate sense of urgency, and her impressions of the Holy City are brief. Still, the overwhelming encounter with the citadel of Zion made her eloquent with delight.

"Oh, it's impossible to write enough to convey it to the imagination. From every facet it is different, each of its quarters is another world. Next to the Old City, frozen in the centuries, stand the modern buildings of the new center, and not far from there is the Jewish Quarter; elsewhere there are fabled villas and gardens, convents, the churches of every faith and all peoples, each with distinctive faces and dresses; there is no end to all the colors.''

In Jerusalem she stayed with Dr. Fekete, a professor of mathematics at Hebrew University, who had been a friend of the Szenes family before he emigrated from Hungary. He was one of the few contacts Chana had when she decided to make her aliyah, and he and his wife were generous with advice and support. She asked him about Gyuri's chances of being accepted into Hebrew University. He was reasonably encouraging but urged her to obtain from Gyuri his graduation certificate and other supporting materials. Chana's efforts had already secured an immigration certificate for her brother, but it had to be used within six months. Moreover, the certificate was worthless without proof of employment, which was the reason for Chana's frantic efforts now. But skilled employment opportunities were limited at this time in Palestine and there was only one silk factory. Higher studies at Hebrew University, she reported to Gyuri, seemed an easier option.

During her stay in Jerusalem, she spent much of her time in the pleasant company of Lajos Friedman, the beau who had kept her intermittently supplied with chocolates. Chana met his family, who welcomed her like a daughter, and Lajos chauffeured her about the city in his impressive new automobile. An inveterate hitch-hiker, Chana insisted that they stop and offer rides to anyone and everyone along the roadside. Sharing such a luxury was for her the best way to enjoy it.

Between her errands on Gyuri's behalf, Lajos showed Chana the sights in and around Jerusalem—museums, the gardens of the King David Hotel, the Hadassah hospital, the Arab village of Bethlehem, and the agricultural school at Tapliot, a less impressive one than Nahalal. Lajos showed her his parents' factory and used his influence to arrange a visit to the Tnuva dairy plant, where Chana could observe how her own training might be put to professional use one day.

After three whirlwind days in Jerusalem, Chana hitch-hiked to Tel Aviv. She did not like this bustling city; perhaps it reminded her too much of the European lifestyle that she had left behind. She came to Tel Aviv not as a tourist but to find a publisher for her father's works. First she had to locate a translator who could do justice to the delicate verbal play and fragile style of Béla's writings. She could not get his plays produced, but her efforts led to a highly successful publication of *Csibi,* a children's classic Béla had originally written for her and Gyuri.

Chana spent two days in Tel Aviv fulfilling obligations to her mother and friends, with exhausting visits to Hungarian homes or rendezvous at Hungarian cafés, listening to gypsy music and eating Hungarian pastries.

She was irritated by the café atmosphere, where everybody spoke Hungarian as if Hebrew did not exist. Chana's idea of Zion was focused on building a new kind of life, as different as possible from the world she had left behind. The lazy café atmosphere of these city Jews seemed like a mirage in the desert, familiar yet unreal, and one that she no longer desired. Still, she tried to retain an outward pretense of polite interest when proud hosts displayed their objets d'art and silverware. She was instructed to make a thorough report to her family on everything she saw. After she had been forced to admire the apartment of a certain Gyuri, a distant relative through the Sas family in Dombovár, she wrote to her mother with unaccustomed venom: "Please write to Dombovár and tell them that Gyuri's apartment is very fine; they should post this fact on the doors of the synagogue, so that every good Jew will know it and can enjoy his Shabbat." She was relieved to return to the comparative austerity of Nahalal.

After an exhausting first year at school, Chana wanted to spend her first extended vacation as far as possible from the European city life. She talked to Miriam and they decided to explore the Galil more thoroughly. The two friends planned a low-budget two-week tour on the cheap, which meant staying at kibbutzim or with friends. They would see as many places as possible, enjoying the chance to deepen their knowledge of the land and its people. In just one year they would be graduating, eager to apply their new skills, but with no idea where and under what circumstances. The Galil was a good place to begin their future: the oldest and most famous of the Jewish settlements were there.

They began their trip at the end of exams in July 1940. By the end of the first day they reached Kefar Giladi, beginning a northern loop around the Sea of Galilee through the rocky landscape to the northernmost border of Palestine. Early next morning Chana climbed the impressive mountain opposite Kefar Giladi, to commune alone with the wind and the quiet. In the glory of a summer morning, it suddenly came to her why Moses had received the Torah on a mountaintop:

> Here you can see how small a human being is. And yet it feels safe because of the nearness of God. On a mountaintop the horizon opens up, in every sense of the word, and the order in the universe becomes clear. On a mountain you can believe, you *must* believe. On a mountain, the question is posed automatically: "Whom shall I send?"— "Send me, to serve that which is good and beautiful."—But will I be able to serve?

From Kefar Giladi they made the brief journey to the village of Dan, hidden amidst lush vegetation in the easternmost corner of upper Galilee. The Jordan River has its springs here; papyrus was one of the main crops.

Chana was enchanted by the springs themselves, called Tel-el-Kadi, which were near a primitive Arab railroad stop. She noticed how well the recent Jewish settlers of Dan got on with their Arab neighbors, even across the border with Syria. They were not aggressive in their vigilance; while not neglecting their defense, they derived their sense of safety largely from having friendly relations with their neighbors.

Just south of Dan they inspected the new settlements of Dafna and Shear Yashuv, whose young members were still in the early phases of body-breaking labor, freeing the soil from the ancient rocks and stones. With her growing expertise, Chana assessed their chances of success: "The soil is good and they've got plenty of water . . . If there are no disturbances to hinder their development, there should be a good future ahead of them. They all have the requisite talent to build a good agricultural settlement." Here and at other kibbutzim Miriam and Chana kept meeting recent graduates from Nahalal, and Chana was pleased to see how well their training had adapted them to their work.

Their attention turned from agriculture to fishing: the two girls were enchanted by the scenery of Lake Hula. They visited Hulata, another young kibbutz along its shores, and took a boat trip to the sources of the River Jordan on the south end of the lake. It was a tropical paradise, with jungles of papyrus reeds, water lilies, and flamingos. In the warm summer night, the visitors watched the kibbutzniks setting their nets. The moonlit silence was disturbed only by the rhythmic splashing of the oars. Chana watched the dark outlines of these muscular young men as they plied the oars with such sureness amidst the muddy swamps, expertly casting their nets over the secret lairs of fish.

Next day the girls headed south, following the Jordan River and the shore of the Sea of Galilee to Ginnosar, where ancient villages on hilltops tried to ignore the brave new world being born in the fertile valley below. Everywhere they found genuine and overwhelming hospitality. They swam in the lakes, went riding and walking, and spent long evenings talking and singing. For Chana it was a happy two weeks, a sort of honeymoon with the land to which she had been long betrothed. She managed to push from her mind the worries of war, the imminent threat to Gyuri in a recently occupied France. And she thought of her mother with a mixture of anxiety and indulgent humor, trying to imagine her reaction if she could see her very-properly-brought-up daughter hitching a ride and sleeping outdoors or in whatever shelter the poor and struggling kibbutzim could find for visitors.

It was the rough and improvised nature of her vacation that appealed most to Chana. Apart from the pleasure and relaxation after months of studying and hard work, she met many wonderful new people. But most valuable to her was the opportunity to clarify her thinking about the future, something that was difficult during the demanding routine at the school. She summed it up for her mother: "First of all, I had a chance to get to know a little of the life out here. 2. I saw evidence that the school is really a good preparation for such life. 3. I am even more excited about the second year of studying and I've decided to specialize in poultry work."

The trip strengthened Chana's belief in her new country and in herself— and her belief that their futures would be joined: "I felt from every heart the beauty of youth, in song and laughter, in the strength and the will to see and feel everything that is beautiful and to take delight in it."

When Chana and Miriam returned to Nahalal, the reality of war crowded in on them. Although Palestine was not a major theater of war, stray bombings by German and Italian planes had begun. Haifa had already been bombed twice, and the second attack caused many casualties. There was a nightly blackout at Nahalal, and while the bombs fell over Haifa, the girls had to leave their bedrooms to seek safety in improvised shelters.

For most of her life Chana had heard people talk about the coming war. When she was fifteen she prayed in her diary that there would be no war and she still felt herself a pacifist. But now she had seen a land that was productive and peaceful, where tough young idealists were investing untold sweat and immeasurable hope, a land that was waiting for her to do the same. Fear of war had not prevented war. Desire for peace had not preserved the peace. She began to think that another way would have to be found.

ELEVEN

RESOLVING

It was Chana's second Yom Kippur in the land, October 11, 1940. But on this Day of Atonement her thoughts turned to the worsening international situation. The war was creeping closer to Greece and North Africa, but Eretz Israel was still a relatively peaceful haven.

In her diary she noted the irony that while Jews were confessing their sins on this Yom Kippur, their enemies, the real sinners, were busy killing, utterly unconcerned about their own guilt.

On Yom Kippur Chana wanted to confess her own sins of omission, to rid herself of the guilt that assailed her whenever she found time to reflect in her diary. "I sinned against my mother because I did not take all her needs into consideration in deciding to leave. I sinned against Eretz, by making superficial judgments and without studying in depth its problems. I sinned against some people by being insincere, pretending to be interested in them while I really felt indifferent. I sinned against myself by wasting my energies and talent, and by neglecting my own intellectual development."

But on the whole, the nineteen-year-old Chana was not displeased with her deeds of the last year: "In all my sins I was pursuing a single goal and my intentions were pure. If I did not succeed, if I lacked the strength, if I did not find the right path, the right form—I have my regrets, but little to be ashamed of."

As usual, Chana felt new energy from her spiritual stocktaking and faced the new school year full of resolutions and plans. As she had written to Kató, she decided to specialize in raising poultry. She enjoyed working in the orchards and in the dairy, but chickens had become her favorites. As was her habit, she applied herself enthusiastically to her chosen tasks, and she soon developed various strategies to determine which hens were the best layers, marking the appropriate apertures with crayons of different colors that would rub off on the new-laid egg. Chana could appreciate the humor of her latest preoccupation, imagining what people back home would say if they could see her. She even got Miriam to take photographs of her surrounded by chickens.

Chana saw her interest in poultry as part of a more distant goal. She dreamed of becoming an expert who would travel all over the country to instruct the new settlements about raising chickens. That way she could learn as much as possible about her country and its problems. Yet she knew well enough that Eretz Israel had a well-developed poultry industry already that did not really require her talents. So where was she needed most? How could she prepare herself best for the task?

For a recent and very young immigrant, Chana had a remarkably clear vision of the problems of political organization and management, of social and educational services, which were underdeveloped and fragile in the infant country. She saw how social and leadership skills, or the lack of them, would affect Eretz's future, and she realized that even in her limited sphere she had some impact on the people around her: "I notice sometimes how I can calm and reassure them and at other times fire them with enthusiasm. Is it right to leave these talents unexploited, hidden, unused?" What if she was deluding herself about the glory of doing manual labor? Was she not perhaps avoiding other work where her special talents were more needed?

For all her dedication to Nahalal and all it represented, at times Chana felt too close to the soil, literally sunk to her knees in the mud. On an idle Shabbat, restless with the day of rest, she dreamed of escaping from the prison of her workaday world, to be riding, flying across meadows with the wind on her face, she and the horse racing a gathering storm.

"I want this wind to break the chains of routine; I want to say words that are not heard day after day; I want to meet people one does not meet every day."

Her diary was more important than ever now, in keeping in touch with her secret self, organizing the chaotic thoughts and questions of the bustling week. She always came back to writing, her only way of understanding herself.

Whenever she could find the time, she read. She tried, through her reading, to nourish the more spiritual side of her nature. Although Chana had little use for the outward show of organized religion, she was deeply religious. She had no interest in the dead rituals of words repeated to the point of meaninglessness. A character in a novel, a simple poem or a walk in nature gave her more religious inspiration than all the wisdom to be found in holy books.

One book that moved her during this period was *Mother* by Sholem Asch. Reading it made Chana want to raise a statue to her own mother for letting her children go out into the world, when she could so easily have stopped them. If she really had great talent, Chana thought, she would be able to express all her love in a stanza, or else "not a thousand pages would suffice to create her portrait." She had written her first poem about Kató at the age of twelve:

> If the world offered a reward,
> A laurel for patience and love,
> One person alone would be worthy:
> Mother.
>
> Let there be thanks in your hearts
> And on your lips a prayer,
> Whenever you hear that loveliest word:
> Mother.

And now in the loneliness of her crowded life at Nahalal, she made one of her first attempts in Hebrew to describe her mother's quiet heroism, expressing her marvel at all mothers. That Mrs. Szenes could not have read it without a translation was to Chana a sad symbol of the chasm between them:

> Where did you learn to wipe the tears,
> To quietly bear the pain,
> To hide in your heart the cry, the hurt,
> The suffering and the complaint?
>
> Hear the wind!
> Its open maw
> Roars through hill and dale.
> See the ocean . . .
> The giant rocks,
> In anger and wrath it flails.
>
> Nature all arush, agush
> Breaks out of each form and fence:
> From where is this quiet in your hearts,
> Where have you learned your strength?

> *[Translated by Ruth Finer Mintz.]*

The beginning of 1941 found Chana recovering from jaundice. The sickness lasted only a few days, but now she was feeling pains in her chest again. She began to fear that she had inherited her father's defective heart. Death seemed too abstract to her nineteen-year-old mind. But what if the disease prevented her from pursuing her life's goals? What if she had to give up the idea of physical work? She worried but did not go to see the doctor: she did not want to hear any bad news.

The brief rainy season heralded the return of spring. Although Chana had regained her physical strength, inside she often felt empty and lost. She wondered why she felt alone, surrounded by so many people; yet she prized what little solitude she could find in her hectic existence. She had no private room at the school, so before going to bed she often took a solitary walk in the village to sort out her thoughts. One such walk is preserved in her diary:

> Tiny lights flicker from either side of the wide road. All around me the sounds of music, singing, talk, and laughter. Very far away I hear a dog barking. The houses grow distant, the stars nearer. Suddenly I am gripped by fear: Where is my life going? Will I be marching alone in the night, looking at the shining stars, thinking only that they are so close? What if I could not hear the songs, the laughter all around me, because I could not stop and go into one of these small houses? What must I choose: the feeble lights flickering through these nearby windows, or the blinding light of the distant stars? The worst feeling is that I might be tempted by the tiny lights: If I went into a tiny house, my soul would desire the heavenly bodies. I seem to be filled with discontent and doubt; I feel uncertain and distrustful. Sometimes I feel I've been sent for some specific task that isn't clear to me. After all, everybody has some goal in life. I feel a sense of responsibility for others, as if I owed them something. But there are other times when I feel that all this is silly. Why should one person's efforts count for much, and why mine?

Chana's sense of futility was reinforced by external events. By April 1941 Yugoslavia had fallen and the war had moved to Greece. The war in the Balkans cut off the land routes between Hungary and Palestine. Mail became sporadic. Chana's sense of isolation from her family and loved ones grew along with her feeling of helplessness. The British and the Germans were clashing in North Africa and neighboring Egypt; Palestine itself could be overrun. The Germans already spread propaganda to fan anti-Jewish and anti-British sentiment among the Arabs, leading to riots and armed clashes.

Like most of the half million Jews in Palestine, Chana felt divided about the war. There was no question about being anti-Nazi; no Jewish family was left untouched by persecution. But tensions were growing also with the British, who did not rescind or even modify the White Paper with the outbreak of war and in the face of increasing evidence of genocide. On the contrary, its provisions were enforced with increasing severity by the

Colonial Office in London, despite Jewish sabotage activities and polite protests from America. Even as the desperation of Jewish refugees and survivors in Europe intensified, the British policy of blocking their entry into Palestine was actually strengthened under the conditions of war. The Haganah found it more difficult to hire seaworthy transports for refugees in the ports of Southern Europe and Turkey, as both the Mediterranean and the Black Sea were becoming major theaters of war. In the five years just before the war some thirty-two clandestine ships had made about fifty voyages, bringing more than 21,600 illegal immigrants to Palestine. During the crucial period of 1940–1944, half that number of voyages took place, and seven of the twenty vessels were sunk. Of the millions waiting, only 16,456 refugees got through.

Every month, some fresh crisis gripped the Jewish community as another of these ships, crammed with human cargo, appeared off the shores of Eretz Israel. British agents in Europe tried to prevent first the sale, then the departure of the ships. When the ships sailed anyway, the Royal Navy shadowed them across the Mediterranean and then lay in wait at the edge of Palestine's territorial waters, while the Haganah pilots tried to evade the blockade. As soon as the refugee ships crossed the territorial limit, the British ships swung into action, trying to ram them. If that failed, the destroyers sometimes turned their heavy guns on them.

But if the British had superior naval power, they were outwitted by the determination of the people in Eretz to rescue the refugees. Under cover of darkness, flotillas of fishing boats raced out to the vessels and frantically transferred to land the exhausted children, the women, and the aged. Weary passengers swam and waded to what they hoped would be safety. Often it was: they were greeted hurriedly by Jewish villagers mobilized by the Haganah and taken quickly to a kibbutz where they were given clothes that would help them blend in before the soldiers or the police came to search for them in the light of day. But just as often they would be met on the beaches of the Promised Land with British bayonets and sent off to detention camps in Palestine, Cyprus, or in one case, the island of Mauritius.

Often the landing had to be aborted. Packed with thousands of refugees, the ships would be escorted into Haifa and held there. Nobody would be allowed to disembark, the British trusting to hunger and sanitation problems rather than reason to force the immigrants to return to Europe. In November 1940 the vessel *Patria* was blown up by the Haganah, rather than allow the British to force it back to Europe: 267 people were drowned in Haifa harbor.

Such incidents provoked futile outrage from the Jewish community. Everybody, including the girls at the school, spent days discussing each tragedy and how to prevent the next one. At first Chana was inclined to believe British propaganda, which claimed that every shipload of refugees had been infiltrated by Nazi agents and spies, to form the advance party that would soon hand over Palestine to Rommel. The Germans had already gained a firm foothold in neighboring Syria and Lebanon, which now owed allegiance to the collaborationist Vichy regime. The danger the British had seen in Nazi agitation among the Arabs before the war now became a real threat. At stake were Egypt, the Suez Canal, and British interests that included a considerable portion of the world. Before America entered the war in December 1941, England was fighting practically alone for her very survival. Her cities were bombed, her lifelines constantly attacked by German U-boats. Palestine became not simply a base for defending the empire, but a symbolic necessity to show the enemy that Britannia still ruled the waves.

But as more ships sank and more lives were lost no room was left in Chana's heart or mind for British propaganda. What she saw in the fate of these refugees was the impotence of Eretz Israel, a Jewish homeland but without sovereignty. If it were overrun by the Germans, there would be nowhere left in the world even for illegal immigrants. The Jews knew this and the British knew it—and they exploited it to the full. In the last analysis the British knew they could count on the Jews, not the Arabs, to defend Palestine against the Germans. Half a million Jews would fight the Germans unarmed, with or without British help, rather than accept the fate of their European brothers and sisters.

The Haganah was making secret preparations for just such an eventuality. As the war drew closer during the spring of 1941, plans were drawn up to turn a large area of Palestine into a defensible fortress. This vast modern Masada included the whole of Mount Carmel and the mountains stretching to western Galilee; a part of the coastal plain was to be used for landing planes, the Bay of Haifa as a naval base. The World Zionist Executive—which administered Jewish affairs under the Mandate—authorized the Haganah in May to form a separate underground strike force, which came to be known as the Palmach. Unlike the Haganah, which helped the British by recruiting regular soldiers to serve alongside the Allied armies in the Jewish Brigades, the Palmach was to serve exclusively Jewish interests. When these coincided with Allied interests, as with the ultimate defense of Palestine, the nine companies of the Palmach would cooperate with the British. But they would also turn against the British, running the blockade and performing acts of sabotage, by using the guerrilla training provided in part by the British.

In April Greece fell to the Germans. By June war was raging in Syria and Egypt. Haifa and Tel Aviv were being bombed, and the artillery bombardment was clearly audible in Nahalal, where classes and work were carried on as usual. Pessimism was alien to Chana's nature. She believed that the Allies would win in the end, but she had to consider for the first time the possibility that Eretz might fall. In light of these stark realities she was appalled by the internal squabbling that routinely went on under the name of Jewish politics. How could the fledgling Jewish community in Palestine survive without strong leadership?

Since her arrival in Eretz, Chana had been trying to form a picture of Jewish politics. It was a picture blurred by fragmentation and dissension among many different parties, ideologies, and agencies—all fighting one another rather than preparing to face the external foe. Nobody seemed able to end the squabbles and the nineteen-year-old student of agriculture asked herself: "I feel this responsibility: should I be saying something?" At first she dismissed the thought with merciless logic: even if she had the courage to speak out, she had no opportunity. She lacked the theoretical basis and the practical knowledge of history and politics. Who was she and what had she done that people should listen to her? "Yet I can't come to terms with the idea," she wrote in her diary, "that everything should be destroyed and lost without exerting the slightest effort to influence the outcome."

The pervasive air of pessimism around her inevitably led Chana to meditate on the ultimate questions. "It's noble to die like martyrs and leave the earth to the unclean," she quoted one of her favorite writers. "But if a heroic death is supposed to sanctify God's name, what about life? Could there be anything more holy than life?" Chana did not want to die. But she faced the possibility in this prophetic verse:

> So young to die . . . no, no, not I.
> I love the warm and sunny skies,
> Light, songs, shining eyes.
> I want no war, no battle cry—
> No, no . . . Not I.
>
> But if it must be that I live today
> With blood and death on every hand,
> Praised be He for the grace, I'll say
> To live, if I should die this day . . .
> Upon your soil, my home, my land.

[Translated by Dorothy H. Rochmis.]

The closer the objective reality of mass destruction came, the more Chana rejected the idea of her own death. She believed deeply that life on earth must be meaningful; until she had achieved that meaning, or some part of it, she felt she could not die: "That's how all of us feel, especially the young, in facing death and those who will yet face it during this horrible war. That's how our young country feels, full of resolve and love toward the future."

In early July Chana followed the news anxiously as the German armies advanced deeply into the Soviet Union. The bombings increased over Palestine, causing minor damage and few casualties. On the eighth of July she received a telegram fom her mother, which came via Turkey. Kató wrote only of her worry about her daughter's safety, while to Chana her mother's situation seemed much more dangerous than her own. She felt she lived in shameful luxury. "My conscience is tormented," she wrote in her diary, "that I have it too easy here. I feel the need to do something, something difficult, which would require a great effort, so that I can justify my existence."

Her final exams at Nahalal were at hand and Chana was impatient to complete them and move on. Despite all her worries, she did well, scoring nearly perfect marks; only one other person at the school had matched her. Her success no longer pleased her, especially since she could not offer it as a gift to her mother. The exams, which were spread over two months, were the final hurdles that kept her from the work she had come to perform. What lay beyond was real life, and the hard tasks that she longed for.

This caesura in her life appropriately coincided with the completion of another of the notebooks that she used for her diaries. This was the third book filled since beginning the first one at the age of thirteen; this last notebook contained three years of momentous changes in her life. Her first entry had been in June 1938, when she was packing for her summer vacation at Lake Balaton. The thought of saying goodbye to Gyuri was the only cloud over her carefree happiness. Zionism still lay several months in the future. The notebook began in Hungarian and halfway through changed into Hebrew; it was started in an old world consumed by old hatreds, and was ending in an ancient new land. She began it as the school-girl Anikó, and ended it as a young woman named Chana. It was begun in peace, and now the world was consumed by war.

Despite the seeming transformation of almost everything in her life, there was also continuity. Even as she was striving toward her new goals, she still felt many ties to the old world. She longed, at times desperately, for her mother and brother, but she also felt a loneliness that she knew could only be filled by someone special. In her outlook she was still a pacifist and a poet. But, as the sounds of killing grew louder, she began to abhor deafness—in herself and others—to the reality of destruction. She had just turned twenty in July and had spent less than two years in Palestine: she did not see yet precisely how or where to apply her percep-tions, but her own strength, her ability to master difficult or distasteful tasks, her own influence over others and her need to help them were all pointing to spheres of activity beyond the chickencoop.

She was looking at this transition at the end of her notebook, the end of school, and the end of twenty years of preparation for life. Now life itself, as she would shape it, could begin. "The time has come," she wrote, "to give back to society what has been lavished on me."

TWELVE

KIBBUTZ

Long before passing her finals, Chana had begun planning her next logical step. From her earliest involvement in Zionism she felt that she wanted to work on a kibbutz, and this desire grew as time went on. Choosing to study at the Agricultural School was part of the Zionist ideology of getting back to the land, of redeeming oneself and "conquering" labor through sweat and toil. The specialist training and skills acquired at Nahalal made every graduate of the school a highly desirable prospect, and recruiters came scouting for the best students. Each kibbutz had a complex set of criteria for selecting candidates; the hardships of the pioneering and communal life required people who would be compatible in philosophy as well as personality. For the same reason, recruits had to consider carefully which would be the right community for themselves. The girls of Nahalal, in addition to their agricultural skills, were much sought after because most pioneer settlements faced an acute shortage of females.

Chana's holiday excursions had been part of this search for the ideal community. As she was finishing school, the search became more focused on both practical and political considerations. She began the process jointly with her best friend and roommate, Miriam, but it ended in their separation.

Kibbutzim may all look similar in organization and philosophy, even if location might dictate differences in occupation: some grow citrus, others bananas; some catch fish, others manufacture textile. In fact, the differences between one kibbutz and the next go deeper than is ever apparent from the outside. Some of the sharpest differences are ideological, based on distinct political movements to which most of the cooperative and communal settlements belong. Only by studying these movements, and then visiting several of each type—finding out the origin, ethnic composition and major occupation of each settlement, and then attending meetings with individuals or groups of kibbutzniks—would Chana and her schoolmates come to understand the essential nature of a specific community and its differences from others.

It is easy to discern what appealed to Chana in the concept of the kibbutz. She belonged to a relatively well-to-do, middle-class youth who could take material comforts for granted. Neither obsessed by possessions nor dependent on them, she wanted things mainly for practical reasons. Unlike many of the European immigrants who clung to their lifestyle and clothes as extensions of their personalities, Chana was eager to shed these along with her old life. She was generous and found it natural to share—whether her homework or the latest package sent by Mrs. Szenes.

Communal property was—and is—the most basic tenet of the kibbutz movement, and although ideology played an important role, the reasons for such communism were practical. Most of the settlements were started under extremely difficult conditions, either in tents or in makeshift shacks that had to be shared. The pioneers often came from the same school or youth organization; their bonds were further cemented by the constant dangers from hostile Arabs. No individual could survive as well under such circumstances. It made no sense for people who were sharing a tent to be cooking separately: this gave rise to the communal kitchen, and the laundry that followed. The same common sense applied to the common treasury. If the group needed to buy a tool or materials that would make all their lives easier, they would naturally pool their money. Similarly, it only made sense for the children to be looked after together by members of the group who specialized in child care and education.

Another vital principle was that kibbutz members would receive no wages for their labor. It was common in the early days for members to earn money on the outside (even now many kibbutzniks fill important posts in government, the military, or other aspects of public service); all such earnings must flow into the common treasury. From the same purse the kibbutz provides equally for all the needs of its members, including all dependents, whether children or parents. Perhaps nowhere else on earth has the Marxist ideal—"from each according to his ability and to each according to his need"—been better realized than in the kibbutz. The emphasis is on equality; the kibbutzim are entirely self-governed by the members, each of whom has one vote.

Although in some superficial ways one may compare the kibbutzim to religious communities (communal dining, idealistic rules voluntarily undertaken, unpaid labor, and so forth), there is this great difference: the kibbutz is above all a political organization, in which the members collectively have the power to make their own laws and rules, rather than obeying dictates from a hierarchical system above and beyond. A kibbutz has no equivalent to a Mother Superior or Father Confessor, although dominant

or charismatic personalities usually do get elected and so get their way by
the usual democratic process: persuasion, tact, and compromise.

Chana and Miriam spent August 1941 in seminars sponsored by Noar
Oved, the Working Youth organization that prepared pioneers mentally
for kibbutz life. There they learned a great deal about the history and
ideology of various kibbutz movements. They also tramped around the
countryside from one settlement to the next, asking questions and working
for a few days with people who might become their future family. Although
they were attracted to Kibbutz Gesher, where they had attended a week-
long seminar, in the end they decided against joining. Chana liked Gesher
but also saw several drawbacks:

> The kibbutz is perhaps too young, although that's not a strong reason
> for not joining. But the planned site for the new kibbutz is six hundred
> feet below sea level, and the heat is unbearable. I'm having doubts
> because the doctor ordered me to spend part of each summer up in
> the mountains to help my heart . . . I don't have the strength to give
> up half my life. That may sound extreme, but it's true. Given the
> climate and the work, there would be no life during the summer
> months. I feel I'd be giving up too much. Of course, this isn't a good
> reason either. Hundreds of people go to live in the Negev, the Bet
> Shaan Valley, or even by the Dead Sea. I'd go too, if I already had
> ties to a group there. But it is very difficult for me to choose such a
> place, when I can contemplate alternatives with a complete freedom
> of choice.

Despite the low altitude, Chana was attracted to the atmosphere around
the Sea of Galilee, and she spent three days in Hatzer Kinneret with a
group of Hungarian-speaking pioneers from Transylvania who were planning to establish Kibbutz Maagan on its shores. She had met some of these
young men when they were still part of the established settlement in Afikim,
which she visited in her first year. Now they had accumulated enough
experience to start out on their own. Much as Chana liked them, she would
have faced the same problems of altitude and heat as in Gesher. Besides,
she did not want to start her new life surrounded by people who spoke
her native tongue. So she reluctantly said goodbye and left them to their
dreams of Maagan, little suspecting under what conditions she would meet
them in the future.

At the end of August Chana and Miriam returned to Nahalal. They had
work to do, things to pack, and farewells to make. The village was celebrating its official twentieth birthday. The school had mounted an exhibition of photographs depicting the growth of two decades. Chana could

not help noticing how amateurish the exhibit was; she thought the village itself, and the faces around her, provided better testimony to what had been achieved.

Chana spoke of this in the valedictory talk she was asked to give on graduation day, September 1. Her speech was brief and simple, describing the transformation of the girls from protected and carefree youths into responsible, serious agricultural workers, ready to develop the land of Israel. Where they had arrived in Nahalal speaking a dozen different languages, now they all spoke with one voice. Chana's address ended with an expression of gratitude to the school and to all the parents who had borne the loss of their daughters, so that they might study and grow. In the following words, she was clearly thinking of her own mother: "And we send our grateful thoughts to parents in the Diaspora. They gave up what was most precious to them so that we could take our place in the world, holding our heads high. We cannot thank them with words. If our work and our life bring blessings around us, while giving satisfaction to ourselves—that will be our gratitude."

It was September sixth, the last Shabbat of the last week, the last morning of the last day in Nahalal. Miriam and Chana were stripping their room bare, making room for its next occupants. At last they sat down to talk, realizing they would now go their separate ways. Although they had not selected their future kibbutzim, it was clear that their different objectives would lead them to different settlements. Miriam in the end went to Kibbutz Hatzor, a large agricultural community about an hour southeast of Tel Aviv. It was less radical in its philosophy than the kibbutz that had attracted Chana more and more during the past month. Lately the two girls had spent endless hours arguing about their differences; sometimes raising their voices until the girls in neighboring rooms banged on the wall and begged them to go to sleep. Chana was feeling the pain of impending separation as she summed up their friendship to her diary:

> She is deeper, more deliberate and given to extremes. She could get worked up about nothing, while I am much more superficial, easygoing, and tend to see what is good and positive in life. Miriam often remarked that she found my judgments and decisions facile. But I showed her the lighter side of life. She is more impulsive, quick to explode; I am more cool, likely to weigh things. Her insights are more theoretical, mine practical. I could go on, but this is the point: I could turn with all my problems to her, I could confide in her completely. I knew that she understood me and I always valued her advice highly. She turned to me likewise. This helped both of us to overcome problems, large and small. But that wasn't all. We watched the world through the same eyes. We enjoyed the same jokes, laughing at our-

selves and passing judgments on everybody else. We understood each other from a single word or allusion. We teased boys the same way, yet we both would have welcomed that special one, if we could have found him. But, since we could not, we laughed even more at those who tried to approach us.

Theirs had been an intense friendship for two years. They were both independent and tough-minded young women now. Their parting was an assertion of those qualities.

After another month of traveling and searching for the ideal community, Chana narrowed her choices to two. Although she was still greatly attracted by a kibbutz at Ginnosar, on the northwestern edge of the Sea of Galilee, she also began to consider joining a group of people who were planning to found a kibbutz near the Roman ruins of Caesarea. Chana visited the site, on the Mediterranean seashore, roughly halfway between Haifa and Tel Aviv. She found nothing there except the dream and the will, and steady planning by people who seemed to know what they were doing. She liked the combination. Characteristically, she was reluctant to join an established kibbutz where the hardest work had already been done. Here she would be part of a group of pioneers whom she admired; together they could create a new world out of sand. The future kibbutz had a name already. They called it *Sedot Yam,* or "Fields of the Sea."

THIRTEEN

THE COMMON GOOD

Chana spent the last three months of 1941 commuting between Kibbutz Ginnosar and the group that was planning to settle at Sedot Yam. It was usual for a prospective member to spend a brief trial period with a kibbutz. This test was advantageous to both parties. No matter how ideal a match looked on paper, only by getting to know the people and how they worked together would Chana find out if she was compatible with them. And while individual kibbutzniks expressed interest in having her join them, ultimately the whole kibbutz had to approve every new member. So Chana spent a week or two at each place, doing regular chores, attending meetings, and discussing the experiences of members. It was a slower and more agonizing process than Chana would have liked.

By the end of October Chana had visited the Sedot Yam group several times. They had not yet made the transition to the site they had selected near Caesarea, having maintained a temporary base for five years at Kiryat Chayim. The *chaverim,* or members, worked at regular jobs in and around Haifa to earn money and acquire the skills to establish and support themselves on the land. Because they would be living by the seashore, they looked to the sea for their work: fishing, building and repairing boats, handling cargo. Several members were serving in the merchant marine and spent many months on voyages across the Pacific. Less obvious, but equally important, were the things they had to learn about living and staying together as a group. During those five years, many came and many left. The ones who stayed were obviously the best suited for the communal ideal and the particular dreams for Sedot Yam.

Chana came to know the group during a crucial period, when the long-awaited transition from Kiryat Chayim to Caesarea had just begun. Out of a total membership of about 120, 30 pioneers had recently moved into tents on the future site of their kibbutz. She was with them on the beach on October seventeenth when they celebrated the Festival of Water, the drilling of the first fresh-water well. It was her first visit to Caesarea, and she fell under the spell of this place, where sand and surf, the old and the new clashed. But it was not just the beautiful landscape that made her want to stay.

"I saw the beginning of a new project, and I wanted to join in. I know that in many ways they need me, just as they offer me a great deal. I still have my doubts, but I am attracted by their dedication to a vision, to the work itself. It is the only force that binds the members together."

There was a certain irony in Chana's choice of a kibbutz where she was least likely to use her agricultural training. The sand dunes of Caesarea were not likely to be transformed into fields and orchards. For one thing, there was not enough fresh water to irrigate; when they dug in the sand, salt water seeped through. Under the sand they found not soil but vast quantities of marble stones, columns, statues, coins, and other antiquities from the time when it was a busy seaport for the Roman province of Judaea. Eventually the kibbutz excavated the site properly, and unearthed an entire amphitheater, which now stands next to the settlement. But in the early years these hidden treasures were considered a nuisance, which delayed permanent construction.

Nor did the plans include starting a poultry farm. At Kiryat Chayim, Chana had helped out with the small hen coops that contributed to the kibbutz's everyday needs; she did not enjoy this work as much as she had imagined she would while studying at Nahalal. She craved a larger scope, and the infinite sea symbolized that scale better than a chicken yard.

At the end of December, Chana gave up on Ginnosar and began a formal period of probation with the Sedot Yam group, at the end of which both parties could make their final decision. She had enough reservations of her own to leave most of her clothes and personal belongings in storage with the Krauses in Haifa.

During the first few months, like other unmarried members of the kibbutz, she moved frequently between Kiryat Chayim and Caesarea. Her assignments were the usual mundane jobs in the kitchen and the laundry. Because the kibbutz needed money, she was occasionally asked to take a paying job on the outside. She wrote about one such experience, when she was sent to do a day's washing at a private house: "At first I felt only scared because of the difficulty of the task and the responsibility involved. Then I felt strange about doing this kind of rough work: serving in a private house. I thought of my mother, my home, and my pride hurt." Her careful self-analysis revealed that it was not just her upbringing that made her shrink from publicly performing Rózsi's work; rather it was the way she had been looking at it. She now began to see her labor as part of her voluntary contribution to her community. In the end she even enjoyed the eight and a half hours of heavy-duty washing and sang all the way back to the kibbutz: "I felt a sense of accomplishment in knowing that I can do this too."

Still, Chana hoped she would not be doing such tasks for long. If she minded anything it was that domestic chores kept her more at Kiryat, where the majority of the membership and all the married couples lived. But she was prepared to do quietly whatever they asked of her, and continued to observe. Almost immediately the cultural committee in the kibbutz began trying to recruit her. She was hesitant at first, but realized that they needed her as more than just an observer. Most of the sabras had a much more narrow education than Chana and welcomed the contributions that European immigrants could make. Hence, Chana's highly developed cultural sensibility was of great value to the group. Unfortunately for her, there were few people she could talk to. She met another girl called Miriam, the highly educated daughter of a Frankfurt professor. But Miriam Neeman was already married and soon to have a baby, which prevented the forming of a close friendship.

Partly as a result of her loneliness, Chana used most of her free time for reading. In January 1942 she devoured Gorky's novel *The Mother,* then the *Communist Manifesto,* and then turned her attention to trying to understand Kant. As the war made correspondence with her mother and Gyuri more difficult, she put more of her feelings into her diaries and poems. But there was no one at the kibbutz with whom she could share these deepest feelings, so she was particularly delighted when her old friend Miriam visited. Besides the hours of intimate conversation they enjoyed, Chana could show Miriam a poem she had written in Ginnosar, contrasting the joy of winter plowing with the death sowed in the frozen fields of Russia, where many young Hungarians of Chana's age were dying for Hitler's cause:

> *In the black fields on a dark night*
> *Candles kindled, scattering light*
> *In the furrow's festive joy.*
>
> *In the dark night on white fields*
> *Bonfires flared, flames spread . . .*
> *Worlds were destroyed.*
>
> *In the black fields,*
> *The future's sparkling song,*
> *The tractor sang.*

In the white fields
There groaned
A dying man.

[Translated by Ruth Finer Mintz.]

If she still felt isolated among her new community, the hours of solitary writing provided other rewards. Finally Chana felt sufficiently fluent in Hebrew to undertake a major literary project. In early 1942 she began working on a play, which later became *The Violin*. It is her most ambitious work in an arena where her father had scored his greatest literary successes. But while Béla wrote witty boulevard comedies, far removed from the realities of everyday life, Chana dealt with some of the practical and painful problems of her life. *The Violin* has considerable biographical interest, and sheds as much light on Chana's life and thinking at Sedot Yam as anything found in her sparse diary entries during this period.

In the opening scene the heroine, Judit Stern, is leaving her middle-class home in an unspecified but unmistakable Central European city. Her mother is helping her pack, and Mrs. Stern forces her daughter to bring her violin to Palestine, even though Judit knows that she will not have time to practice there. The loving but tense banter is interrupted by girlfriends and uncles who vociferously oppose Judit's decision without really understanding where she is going or why. The only exception is a boy called Zvi who is emigrating with her.

The next scene shifts to a kibbutz in Palestine. Judit seems to have adjusted well to her new life, although she is anxious about her family and cries when she gets mail from home. Zvi is in charge of a Zionist cultural event, and asks Judit to play something on her violin. She refuses, claiming to be out of practice since she has come to the kibbutz. When Zvi presses her, she cries out:

When I came here, I thought I'd be able to play after work. After work I'd become Judit Stern again, who has these clever fingers, and a feel for playing the violin. Well, I tried and I was mistaken. At first I did not want to admit it to myself. After I spent a day working outside in the orchards, or in the laundry, I could not concentrate on the violin. And my hands . . . *(she looks at them)* . . . could one play with such hands? *(During the speech she moves toward the piano in the corner, where her violin is resting on top. She leans against the piano and strokes her violin.)* At first I didn't think much about it, I was so overwhelmed by my new impressions. Only after a few months did I start to feel that something was lacking, that I was missing something very, very much.

Zvi feels that Judit must try to play for her own sake. She must overcome the difficulties and the fatigue: "Should we give up reading and studying, just because we often fall asleep at our books?" Judit agrees to try. The next scene depicts the concert a month later. Despite her nervousness, Judit scores a tremendous success. In fact, a violin teacher from Tel Aviv, who hears her performance, comes backstage to offer her a scholarship. He feels that she has only a year or two before her talent will atrophy. Studying with him would mean taking a leave from the kibbutz, where she is needed. Zvi is shocked by the idea, but Judit wants to bring the question to a vote in the general assembly. After explaining her dilemma, she asks the kibbutz to decide. Speeches are made by kibbutz members both in favor of her going and against. Zvi listens in silence; when he is asked for his opinion, he declines to give one. There are eight votes in favor of her leaving, and eleven against.

The play ends with an unexpected twist: Judit defies the ruling of the kibbutz and decides to leave, although she realizes that she will probably never be allowed to return. She is packing when Zvi brings news that finally the kibbutz has received a grant of land that will make it possible to settle in the Galil. The realization of that long-held dream changes Judit's mind:

JUDIT: I thought it'd be easier. I'd make a decision and go. I'd learn to master the violin and concentrate on nothing else. But I feel I can't leave now. You're going to build a settlement. I can't bear the thought of all of you going there without me. Nobody can help me—mother or friend—with a word of advice.

ZVI *(takes her hand):* You expect somebody else to say the word? You've said already that you won't leave, that you can't go. Because the music of your life is more precious to you and that's the music you make here among us. You must stay, because we need you, Judit, because I . . . *(He falls silent.)*

JUDIT *(surprised):* You . . .

ZVI: You must have known . . . *(Silence.)*

JUDIT *(gets up and goes to one of the beds where the violin is):* And this violin—what will become of it?

ZVI: You'll play it from time to time, to celebrate our aliyah, the first harvest, the fifth anniversary of the new kibbutz . . .

JUDIT: No, I don't think so, I should put this away, and keep it . . .

ZVI: For whom?

JUDIT: The next generation. For our children.

ZVI *(standing close to her):* For our children, Judit? *(They look at each other with a loving smile, the violin between them.)*

And the curtain falls on this idyllic ending. But until this last moment, when the dream imagined in the first scene is suddenly revived, every scene of the play is tense with frustration, disappointment, and conflict, both within Judit and in the kibbutz around her. Given that the violin is a thinly veiled metaphor for Chana's desire to write—her whole sense of individual creativity—the play accurately reflects the conditions and sacrifices in her life at Sedot Yam.

Throughout her first year, Chana fought for a permanent transfer to Caesarea, where she felt the real challenges lay. But when the leadership finally approved it in November 1942, she received it with mixed feelings. The transfer was connected with an earlier decision in May to place Chana in charge of managing food supplies. Chana had protested in vain that she had neither the training nor the talent for the job.

There was more to her reluctance than modesty. Chana was caught in a bind: the attraction of starting a community from scratch remained undiminished; she even liked the work much of the time, because it was so difficult. But she was having trouble defining her own goals and separating them from those of the group. She was ashamed to admit to herself that sometimes she thought the work was too mundane. In her readings of Herzl and other Zionists it was easy to forget that the reality of founding a country was made up mostly of endlessly boring, exhausting, and menial tasks: clearing stones, building privies, finding vegetables in the market and doing the laundry in sea water. The old doubts about wasting her talents resurfaced, a dilemma clearly expressed in *The Violin*. Perhaps she could be more useful to the kibbutz if she learned new and different skills. As in her play, the chaverim thought otherwise, but Chana agreed to abide by their wisdom.

At least she could use the superb training from Nahalal to draw up menus that were nutritious and balanced. The real problem was where to get supplies and how to pay for them. In Nahalal they grew everything, had their own chickens and eggs, more fruit and vegetables than they could ever eat. At Sedot Yam the hard work and miserable conditions made the young men and women constantly hungry. Supplies often ran short, and of course it was to Chana that all complaints were directed. Her choices were limited. The new kibbutz depended on the sea for food; what little cash Chana had at her disposal she used to buy things from the Arab vendors in the village at Caesarea.

With such daily battles against physical want, she often felt the work was draining rather than adding to her store of knowledge. In her diary Chana worried that she might exhaust her spiritual reserves. Typically, she reached for the closest image, the flickering kerosene lamp she was writing by: would it be sufficient to light her way? And then her mind soared to

the stars: "There are heavenly bodies that can give out light without receiving illumination from another body. Do I have that capacity?" And
she turned to a favorite quotation from a Jewish writer, Haim Hazaz,
which summed up her own aspirations: "All the darkness cannot extinguish
a single candle, but one candle can light up all the darkness."

Outwardly Chana remained enthusiastic. She was deeply involved in the
affairs of the kibbutz and with the people around her. The communal life
appealed to a part of her nature, and she shrugged off the physical dis-
comforts of tent life and the lack of essential facilities. Once she wrote in
her diary that it was dark and her fingers were too stiff with cold to hold
the pen: yet she managed to write that sentence. Her mood would swing
from exaltation about the beauty of the physical world to despair about
her own place in the world—then swing back to joy, as she walked along
the ancient shore and sang raucously, competing with the waves. The
surroundings evoked a new, mature poetry, more suited to Hebrew. This
simple, Haiku-like sigh has been the inspiration for many Israeli *chanson-
niers:*

> God—may there be no end
> to sea, to sand,
> water's splash,
> lightning's flash,
> and the prayer of man . . .

[Translated by Ziva Shapiro.]

Still, as the first year at Sedot Yam wore on, she began to ask herself
whether she received enough recompense from her life. She realized how
little of her former *joie de vivre* remained. She had almost forgotten what
it was like to be really carefree. The taste for happiness was ruined by too
much duty, tension, and anguish for the world. At other times she identified
with Scarlett O'Hara, from *Gone with the Wind*—one of her favorite books
in this period—because she felt that she too was always postponing difficult
decisions; time did not exist in the present, only in the future or the past:
"I'll think 'some other time' about the meaning of life, about social values,
about the responsibility of human beings, about what is going to happen.
Always, 'some other time,' " she wrote once in frustration.

Yet in fact she was thinking about serious issues all the time. No matter
how exhausted or dispirited she was at the end of the day, her diary during
these months contains page after page of tortured reflections, written by
the flickering kerosene lamp while others in the tent were asleep, her own
eyes kept open by the fierce turmoil within. She felt ashamed at being
dissatisfied with her work: "I can't rid myself of the thought that I'm wasting

years that should be spent learning, developing further. If I could become a real expert at something, I would help the kibbutz and find greater satisfaction for myself at the same time . . . But, that's a lie—another voice says. I am learning all the time—gaining experience of life."

In her diary, Chana urged herself to offer up all her personal ambitions to the communal ideal, to hold nothing back. Not only must the common good come first, but its goodness could not be challenged. Only her individuality seemed imperfect, inadequate. Working in the Haifa dockyards, one of her colleagues asked Chana bluntly whether she was a "good" person. She laughed the question off at the time, but returned to it anxiously in her diary: "Perhaps I'm not good. I'm cruel to those who are close to me, who love me, who are good to me. I only *appear* to be good. I'm cold-hearted to those who are dear to me, perhaps even to myself."

The ideal itself was beyond question; she had invested too much effort and pain to question it now. But she had lost much of the fervor of her early years in Eretz. She saw herself growing apart from, rather than merging into, the collective will. At one point she compared herself to a droplet of oil bobbing about in the sea. Sometimes she floated on the surface, sometimes she was submerged; she was always separate.

She tried to relieve her loneliness by visiting Miriam at her kibbutz. Sharing with her former roommate some of her fears and disappointments helped, but her return to Sedot Yam brought the painful reminder that Chana had not found anyone like Miriam in her own community.

Missing the intimacy of a close friendship made Chana long for her family more acutely. But communication among them had grown more difficult; the practical problems posed by censors, geography, and war were only augmented by the emotional separation of their vastly different circumstances. Chana found it harder and harder to write cheerfully about her daily activities, and she did not want to burden her mother with her doubts and disappointments. If only Gyuri could finally get to Eretz. But after the occupation of France his letters became sporadic, then ceased altogether.

FOURTEEN

OVER THE PYRENEES

Gyuri was in the midst of cramming for his second-year exams at the Textile School in Lyons when Paris fell on June 14, 1940. The exams themselves were interrupted by several air raids. On June eighteenth, as Gyuri fought his way through the crowds to the school, Lyons was in total chaos; thousands of people were trying to leave town in any vehicle they could find. When at last he arrived, he found the big modern building completely deserted. Finally he came upon the janitor, who told him that everybody had fled.

For a moment Gyuri felt lost. Although he had discussed this eventuality with several friends and his mother when she visited a few weeks before, the various options suddenly seemed impractical. How could he get back home to Hungary, which in any case was fighting on the side of the Germans? Switzerland was a safe haven, but her borders were closing except to the wealthiest foreigners. Even those, if they were Jewish or undesirable in some other way, were pressured to move on. The Swiss were anxious to preserve their neutrality at all costs. Already the tiny mountain federation was surrounded by the Nazis in Germany and Austria to the north and the east, their Fascist Italian allies in the south; now the conquest of France had closed the ring.

Two possibilities remained for Gyuri: England and Spain. The former, though desirable, was the next country likely to fall. Hundreds of thousands of Belgians, Dutch, French, and other Europeans were desperately trying to get across the English Channel, which had saved the island kingdom from so many foreign invaders. But it seemed impossible to get to one of the northern ports, which had fallen to the enemy. All train and bus schedules were thrown into chaos by the advancing German armies, and the millions of people fleeing from them.

Dazed by these realizations, Gyuri tried to locate school friends and acquaintances who had cars; they had all left in the past two days, while he was immersed in exams. Fortunately, he managed to get his money out of the bank and buy one of the last remaining bicycles in Lyons. After purchasing weatherproof clothes and canned food, he packed fifty pounds of essentials into a backpack and set out that same evening on the crowded road toward the only border that appeared breachable: that of Spain. Gyuri had heard that the long mountainous border offered many opportunities for illegal crossings.

Following the three-year civil war that formed a bloody prelude to the world war, Generalissimo Francisco Franco needed to stay out of the European conflict in order to consolidate his power and rebuild the shattered country. There was no question that his sympathies were with the Axis powers, but at least there were no horror stories about refugees who were caught and turned back by border guards. Another benefit from Gyuri's point of view was Spain's geography: her eastern coast was lapped by the same Mediterranean Sea as Palestine—a few days' sailing away. It would be easier, in theory at least, to get there from Spain than from landlocked Switzerland.

Gyuri had spent several days cycling south when he learned that he could safely return to Lyons, which would remain under French administration as part of a so-called "France Libre." The Germans agreed to occupy only half of France for the moment, to husband their thinly spread forces and allegedly to leave some dignity to their vanquished enemy. Hitler installed a puppet government in Vichy, in the unoccupied zone. Although Jews came at once under severe restrictions, no deportations took place from this free zone, and foreigners like Gyuri were allowed to resume almost normal lives. He spent the next year completing his training in textiles and graduated at the top of his class. There were no jobs available, especially for foreigners, but Gyuri was fortunate enough to be hired as an apprentice. This gave him valuable experience while he waited for his Palestine certificate.

Gyuri watched with growing apprehension as events unfolded in the occupied zone. Jews were stripped of their French nationality and property. The compulsory wearing of a yellow star further isolated them from the mainstream of society. Later they were put into concentration camps. One notorious camp at Drancy was 80 percent filled with foreign Jews, including a large number of Hungarian citizens. Following the Bastille Day celebrations in 1942 the deportation of Jews from Paris began, and by August many thousands had been taken to what *The Times* of London called an unknown destination, but which would soon be known to all as Auschwitz. The Vichy government was now eager to collaborate with the Germans in deporting Jews even from the free zone, and French officials carried out their German masters' orders with ferocious zeal. Some Jews disappeared from Lyons, others fled; increasingly in the summer of 1942 Gyuri felt his life directly threatened.

In November the Allies landed in North Africa and the Germans, fearing an attack at their soft underbelly in southern France, set aside the fiction of the free zone and occupied the rest of the country. After his 1940 dress rehearsal, Gyuri was better prepared to flee. Thousands of people, including hundreds of Jews, had already crossed the Pyrenees. That they did not come back was considered grounds for optimism. In addition to civilian refugees, British Intelligence had organized regular escape routes into Spain both for Allied soldiers and for French deserters who wanted to join the Free French army in North Africa.

The day after the fall of Vichy the Jewish Agency appealed to the Allies and neighboring neutral countries to admit Jewish refugees fleeing from the free zone. And as reports of "the final solution" began to reach the West, London and Washington also put pressure on Franco not to turn back Jewish refugees; they strengthened their case by offering to pay for their keep in Spain and guaranteed that the refugees would soon leave for Palestine. In the end fewer than a thousand Jews were saved through this action, but one of them was Gyuri Szenes.

Gyuri spent several weeks planning his escape and obtaining—through the black market—the false papers without which it would have been impossible to move around. He sold the Leica camera that Anikó had brought him on her visit to Lyons, to pay for his *carte d'identité,* which was made out for Georges Charbonnel. The name was a French variant of Szenes, meaning "Coalman," which would make it easier for him to remember. His forged papers gave his birthplace as Lille, a town in the north of France that had been bombed to bits by the Allies. It would be hard to check his personal data should the authorities become suspicious of his story.

Gyuri and a school friend named René decided to leave on the night of December fifteenth, buying in advance two train tickets to Perpignan, near the Spanish border. That evening Gyuri ate dinner as usual at his modest *pension,* telling his landlady he was going on a climbing trip in the Pyrenees. When he had told the same transparent story to his coworkers and playing partners at the Ping-Pong club they all quietly wished him luck. After dinner he walked to the apartment of René's parents and stood at the doorway, holding his small suitcase. René's mother opened the door. Gyuri knew at once that something had gone wrong when she refused to let him in.

"He can't go with you," she whispered, "it's too dangerous. His father and I wouldn't have a moment's rest if we let him go." In the background

Gyuri could hear an intense argument going on in the living room between René and his father.

"I'm sorry," she said. *"Bonne chance, eh?"*

This was hardly an auspicious beginning, but Gyuri had no choice but to proceed to the train station alone. He had no family in France; he could not hide from the Germans, who checked hotels and rented rooms. At the station, despite the late hour, he found an enormous crowd. The wartime trains were jammed with soldiers coming home or going to the front. The train south was filled with German soldiers. Gyuri found a corner in the train's crowded corridor where he could sit down on his suitcase. He tried to be as inconspicuous as possible.

All night the train rolled southward; at dawn it pulled in at Narbonne. Teams of German and French guards working together boarded the train to check passports and papers. After four years Gyuri's accent was flawless; any suspicions could have been explained away by regional dialect—he was, after all, from Lille. By midmorning the train arrived in Perpignan. The little town was swollen with refugees from the north and with Germans who anticipated an Allied attack from the south. Gyuri noticed increasing numbers of antiaircraft units during the last hour of his trip: he was glad to see the Germans on the defensive.

His first mission in Perpignan was to find a hotel room and recover from the sleepless journey. The adrenaline of the escape had given way to a weariness that could lead to mistakes. He needed his wits about him, for the most dangerous part of his journey still lay ahead. At last, he found a small nondescript hotel. On the usual police card, which asked the purpose of his visit, Gyuri wrote that he was en route to visit relatives. With quiet satisfaction he noted to himself that this was no lie.

The forged papers were only a part of the package that Gyuri had bought with his Leica. He was also given the name of a man who made his living by smuggling people across the border. Until recently, this had been a lucrative and fairly safe occupation. If one were caught, the punishment might be a year or two in prison—the same as for smuggling cigarettes or other contraband. With the German occupation, the price of saving lives suddenly became the loss of life, with the result that the smugglers of human cargo dropped out of sight. After two days of following meager leads Gyuri finally made contact with his man in a café. He learned that a group would be leaving Perpignan the next evening. The smuggler told him every detail of the escape, every scenario in case things went wrong. From the way he spoke, it was evident that a lot could go wrong.

On the evening of December eighteenth, Gyuri took the bus from Perpignan to Longeuil. After a short while, the bus stopped. Announcing that there was mechanical trouble, the driver told everybody to get out of the bus. He had been well paid, of course, for staging the breakdown just before the German control point. According to plan, they were less than a mile from the border, but the illegal route was not a direct one. Outside in the wintry dark, Gyuri grabbed his luggage and walked unobtrusively behind the bus. He could barely make out the turnoff leading over the mountains a few yards away. Seeing several people drifting in that direction, he followed them, just as the smuggler had instructed him. It was about seven o'clock when they started to climb.

The mountain road became a path, and then it seemed to disappear. In the clear moonlight they saw it meander uncertainly among thorns and bushes. Despite the cold, they were sweating with exertion. Gyuri was in better shape then the dozen or so others, but even he was growing tired. They climbed for six hours without pause, carrying their scanty but awkward luggage. It was essential to reach the other side before dawn.

There were no markers, no fence, and no guards in the mountain wilderness to indicate the border between France and Spain. The snow-capped crags sparkled in the blue light of the moon, but the little band had no time to admire the vista.

If anything, the descent proved more difficult than the climb. Gyuri found himself slipping and sliding several yards, dragging his suitcase. Some older people stopped to regain their breath, but the guide went relentlessly on, occasionally whispering "Vite, vite!" to those lagging behind. Gyuri was amused to hear one woman complaining about her stockings, which were being snagged.

It took more than six hours to make the descent but by early dawn they reached the outskirts of a small village some ten miles inside Spain. They were desperate for a resting place and found a run-down barn in the middle of a field. One of the women insisted on walking on to the village. She went into a tavern and was followed on her way back. The tired party of refugees woke up midmorning to excited shouts outside the barn. When they peeped out they saw that they were completely surrounded by gendarmes and border guards. The fugitives were all placed under arrest with the utmost courtesy, their captors reassuring them repeatedly that they would soon be on their way to Barcelona when everything would be straightened out.

It soon became obvious that their chances of escaping notice in Spain had been much slimmer than the smuggling operatives had led them to believe. The entire border region was crawling with guards, keeping tight control not only on foreigners but also on the movement of Spaniards, all of whom needed permits to visit even the next village.

The captives were taken into the village and interrogated individually at police headquarters. Again the tone was polite, even friendly. Gyuri, along with the others, had discarded his expensive identity papers up in the mountains. They had been instructed to deny being French, to avoid possible repatriation. Some in the group decided to be English; but others, including Gyuri, feared that their English was not good enough. It was safer to pose as French-Canadians. The Spanish police showed no surprise at the story of how they had been robbed of all their papers. Gyuri improvised a name he thought might pass for a Quebecois: he became Julien Andreans.

Following the friendly investigation, without the slightest warning, they were all subjected to a thorough body search. Gyuri had converted all his francs into Spanish pesetas before he left Perpignan. He still carried almost seven hundred pesetas, which was then equivalent to about fifteen thousand francs. He had the presence of mind to stuff two hundred pesetas between the soles of his shoe where they had split; the rest joined a growing pile of banknotes that the Spaniards had confiscated from his much wealthier traveling companions. The guards vouchsafed that the money and other valuables would be scrupulously returned in due time—a brazen lie, as it turned out. The misfortune of being parted from his money was temporarily relieved by the supper and clean beds that their captors provided. Though exhausted and under arrest, Gyuri felt exhilarated. The threat of deportation and death seemed to be gone; at least the Spaniards showed no sign of planning to exterminate him.

The next day, being Sunday, passed uneventfully. The following morning, the twenty-first of December, they were piled into a truck and driven a short distance under escort to a local jail. The day was spent in a seemingly endless round of formalities. Gyuri and his companions were continuously interrogated by a tribunal of judges. There were more body searches, and they received no food all day. That night Gyuri was squeezed with fourteen men into a cell roughly six feet by ten. They tried to sleep sitting up or standing. They had not washed and their empty stomachs growled.

The next day the prisoners were taken from their cage for further rounds of questioning, fingerprints and mug shots. The authorities now behaved as if they had captured internationally famous criminals. After another sleepless night in an even more crowded cell, Gyuri was transferred with two hundred other refugees to a medieval dungeon in nearby Figueras. The place had been in use since the Spanish Inquisition. A grim-faced guard opened the enormous gate; he shut it behind them with his huge key and an air of ominous finality.

Lined up in the yard, they were given yet another and more thorough strip search. Gyuri was astonished how many knives and razors had survived the previous search; one of the new prisoners still managed to cut his throat that night. The prison officials took great delight in the endless formalities of admission procedures, before herding the prisoners into dank and frigid cells. By now they barely noticed that they were fifteen in a space designed to accommodate five. The regular inmates consisted mostly of political prisoners from the losing side of the civil war. The definite length of their sentences, varying from five years to life, seemed almost enviable compared to the uncertainty faced by the fugitives from France.

The authorities kept the new prisoners in the dark about their fate. Gyuri gradually realized that this was a technique to secure their cooperation. The guards continued to treat them with courtesy and kept talking of their transfer to Barcelona as an imminent reality. But their actions contradicted such promises. After long-awaited showers, their heads were shaved: they were now barely distinguishable from the regular prisoners. Finally they were served a bowl of watery soup, in which a few cabbage leaves floated like shipwrecked sailors on a vast ocean. In the absence of spoons, they quickly learned how to drink the tasteless concoction from the bowl. After the "meal" there was a head count in each cell, which was performed three times a day. Their elderly guards could only count up to three—*uno, dos, tres*—and then would start again four times, keeping count with their fingers. At eight o'clock the light went out, and the tired prisoners tried to find oblivion hunched up on the cold floor.

At ten the following morning they were allowed into the courtyard, which looked like a cross between a beehive and an Oriental bazaar. Three very long lines formed instantly: one to the canteen, where those with money could buy food, another one for the washrooms, and the third for the toilets. It took all morning to get through two of these lines, and since one could not afford to give up the toilets, those who had money for the canteen had to choose between food and cleanliness.

Gyuri still had a few pesetas tucked away. He was amazed by the canteen, which offered several brands of exotic cigarettes, tropical fruits, and other delicacies that had long been rationed or unavailable in France. Gyuri bought some food at an exorbitant price, and felt compelled to share it with his friends who had no money left. He observed longtime residents, mainly Arabs, roaming the yard for discarded peels and cigarette butts, which they scooped up as soon as they were dropped. They would then either consume these treasures or trade them. It was Gyuri's introduction to the economics of a prison black market.

On Christmas Day, the authorities announced that British subjects would receive a blanket and fifty pesetas, courtesy of the British consulate. As a Canadian, Julien Andreans qualified. He bought some figs and nuts in honor of the king of England.

Despite the unsettled future, Gyuri quickly settled into the prison routine. Among his cellmates, six claimed to be fellow Canadians. But they could not speak a word of English.

"Are you French-speaking Canadians?" Gyuri asked them in French.

"Oui, bien sûr," they replied in pure Parisian accents. Two genuine Belgians prattled away in Flemish; all Gyuri could make out was their frequent appeals to the deity. They were passionate smokers, gradually converting all their earthly goods into cigarettes. A Romanian Jew had wandered through so many countries that he spoke a private Esperanto. A Polish infantryman claimed to be a French pilot. He slept almost all the time, between twenty and twenty-two hours a day, but woke up unfailingly when the meals were served. Gyuri sometimes watched him sleep standing up, like a horse.

It was harder to get used to boredom and the apathy it bred. No books, pencils, or paper were allowed. The authorities even forbade playing cards, although the prisoners managed secretly to improvise a pack, and this helped somewhat to pass the time. A prison newspaper appeared once a week, containing hardly any news; the quality of the paper rendered it useless for sanitary purposes. The prisoners spent much of their time exchanging rumors, generated by new arrivals or the black marketeers who sometimes bought information from the guards.

Toward the end of December, rumors increased about the promised departure for Barcelona, but the coming of 1943 brought nothing to celebrate. On more than one occasion the guards ordered them to get their things ready; then the order was canceled. It was hard to know whether this was deliberate torture on the part of the prison authorities, or if they themselves were victims of a larger bureaucratic hoax.

Finally on January tenth, following compulsory Sunday Mass, there was a roll call. About one hundred and fifty prisoners, including Gyuri, were told to present themselves with all their belongings in the main hall of the prison. Their thrill was somewhat dampened when the guards handcuffed them in pairs. A large contingent of mounted police, in extremely colorful uniforms, then drove the ragged band of prisoners on foot through the medieval gates and into the streets of Figueras. The native population accompanied them with their stares all the way to the railroad station, which had been surrounded by a ring of security police. Four carriages were reserved and, much to their surprise, each prisoner got a seat. As the unfamiliar landscape passed by the train window, they wondered if they would get to the promised land, currently defined as Barcelona. Instead, after a brief ninety-minute trip, they arrived at the town of Gerona, which boasted a jail much bigger and less crowded than the one at Figueras.

Following the now-familiar procedures for admission and body search, the group was shown its new suite—a large room where all one hundred and fifty would be staying together. Fighting broke out immediately as the most enterprising prisoners tried to secure the few spaces near the windows. Once they had settled in, guards brought in a caldron of soup. Much to the inmates' surprise the liquid had the consistency of real soup. The guards were also markedly more considerate. Next morning began with café au lait. A canteen visited their room, with all kinds of provisions for those who could pay. The authorities informed the British subjects that they would henceforth receive a regular allowance of fifty pesetas a month. In the days that followed, Gyuri was becoming resigned to his lot, and even began to enjoy himself. He ignored the rumors that they would only be staying here for a week at most.

There were problems, of course: fetid air, pervasive filth, and an astonishing variety of lice, ticks, fleas, and roaches. Gyuri staked out a few square feet of territory in the corridor where a cold draught at least kept the air fresh. Despite the inconveniences, he could appreciate the advantages of his present situation. Food was relatively plentiful and he began to regain the pounds he had shed at Figueras. The group included a diversity of interesting people, some of whom gave lectures in their subjects, taught languages, and recited poetry. Gyuri joined several committees that organized prison chores and planned cultural events. One of these was a concert improvised with mouth harmonicas, with piano and cello provided by the authorities. The artists were rewarded with a double portion of soup. Gyuri wondered if they might not have been more inspired had they been given the soup in advance.

On the twenty-third of January the authorities announced that refugees with sufficient financial means would be freed and given permission to stay in Spain. This threw everybody into feverish activity, trying to figure out a way of getting enough money from relatives or friends. So many letters were written that stamps suddenly became the hottest item on the black market. A number of people who had long claimed to be penniless now remembered large notes sewn into their coat lining. Gyuri had no relatives or friends to contact in Spain, so he remained calm. As it turned out, very few gained their freedom this way.

But one day three French medical students were released. Gyuri knew that one of them belonged to a Zionist organization in Lyons; he now tried to send a message with this young man. So far he had not written to anyone, not wanting to risk getting anybody into trouble, and also because he thought his family might be more frightened by receiving a censored letter from a Spanish jail than if they did not hear from him. He had no idea whether this attempt would reach anybody and if it did, he never found out.

About five weeks after his arrest, when he felt generally content and settled in, Gyuri began to have nightmares. He dreamed in one that he was climbing mountains and crossing borders. Suddenly, behind the mountains, he found himself back in Budapest. As he walked through his native city, people looked at him with amazement. They did not understand what he was saying, because he could only speak Spanish. In another dream he was a tourist visiting a foreign country, and he found himself surrounded by armed soldiers. He could not break out of the ring, except by waking up. After such nightmares, it was a relief to find himself in the safety of the prison.

FIFTEEN

DECISION

Early in January 1943, while Gyuri was waiting to be released from the jail at Figueras, Chana experienced what she called a shattering week. After months of worry, guilt, and helplessness, all her frustrations and doubts were suddenly merged into a single crystallized resolution: "I must go back to Hungary. I must be there during these days and help organize the emigration of Jewish youth. I must bring my mother out from there."

The fog she felt around her lifted; suddenly it seemed clear what she must do. At the same time she realized that most other people would consider her idea absurd or her motives suspicious. Some might think she was going back because she could not stick to her Zionist principles, or claim that she was putting her mother—in no more danger now than she had been three years before—ahead of the needs of the kibbutz, and of Eretz Israel.

Chana first debated the idea within herself, trying to assess the obstacles from every angle. Once she saw that her decision stood up to her own scrutiny, she discussed it with a few trusted colleagues, some of whom were already training to join the Jewish Brigade. They were all men, and although sympathetic to her reasons, they thought it unlikely that the British would accept a young woman into such dangerous service. Besides, there was no evidence that any rescue mission was planned for Central Europe. Who was concerned about Hungarian Jews when the fate of Allied countries still hung in the balance? Chana listened politely to their objections and marshaled arguments of her own. She applied for a short leave from the kibbutz and, traveling to Tel Aviv and Jerusalem, tried to find officials in the various Jewish agencies who might support her plan.

Although her restlessness was focused on the futility she felt in her kibbutz life, Chana's decision was in reality a reaction to larger events. Its roots went back to a year earlier, when correspondence with her mother—which had been regular as clockwork for two years after Chana left—

became erratic. Some letters were delayed several months; often they did not arrive at all. When things got desperate Mrs. Szenes turned to the Red Cross, which had a wire service for tracing lost relatives. Only twenty-five words were allowed, Hungarian was not permitted, and these telegrams received more thorough scrutiny than letters. In the middle of January 1942, Mrs. Szenes sent a Red Cross inquiry to care of the Kraus family, having no firm address for her daughter after Nahalal: "Darling! Nothing since your news in September. Everything in order here. Gyuri is writing regularly; his plans with Jeanette became impracticable. Thousand kisses to you; greetings to the Krauses." The coded reference to Jeanette clearly referred to one of Gyuri's attempts to leave France.

The kibbutzniks remember that when Chana first joined Sedot Yam, she talked constantly about her mother and brother; her face lit up with love and admiration for them. As 1942 wore on, they noticed the tension rise in her when the mail arrived. She often sat by herself, holding a letter or the occasional telegram, crying quietly.

She tried to keep her worries from others, and even from herself. Entries in the diary are terse and factual: "No news from home or from my brother." "I got a letter from home yesterday. Oh, it's so hard." "I keep silent about my mother and brother. It's so hard even to speak." She watched the war like a fire raging out of control, getting ever closer to where her loved ones were trapped.

In August 1942 she received a letter from her mother that she was well, only her hair was turning a little gray. "What made her hair turn gray can be read between the lines," Chana wrote in her diary: "How long will things go on like this?" Mrs. Szenes was physically still safe, but with the banning of Béla's books, she had no livelihood; only by subletting the larger part of her house could she make ends meet. In November, the Nazis marched into Lyons; after that Chana had no idea about Gyuri's whereabouts. In the same diary entry describing her inspiration to return to Hungary she mentions her deepest fear: "Whenever I think of my mother and brother, I'm incapable of thinking of anything else. At times a terrible fear grips me: will we ever see each other again?"

The first and greatest impact of her decision was to change the way she felt about the war. She had been writing about the coming war for seven years and she had lived with its effects for four. For a third of her life she had felt weak, small, and futile. The decision to stop being a spectator was both frightening and exhilarating, a wrenching inner change from her pacifist ideals to an active battle for the lesser evil. The sudden determination to do something went through her like lightning, leaving her charged with such energy as she had not felt for years. Compared to that force the realistic tasks of persuading the kibbutz or the British to let her take on the German Reich seemed easy.

In late February 1943, a young man whom Chana had met at the Hatzer Kinneret paid a visit to Sedot Yam. He belonged to the Hungarian-speaking group that came from Transylvania in the late 1930s and was planning to found Kibbutz Maagan at the south end of Galilee. Like many Zionist immigrants, Gyula Rosenberg had shed his Hungarian Christian name and was now called Yonah Rosen. In a conversation that lasted far into the night, Yonah told Chana that he was helping to organize a mission to rescue the Jews of Central Europe. The Haganah had already approved the plan as a project for the secretive Palmach. Yonah's immediate task was to recruit people who spoke Hungarian and knew the countries where it was spoken: Slovakia, Yugoslavia, Romania, and Hungary itself. Yonah was sharing this highly confidential information because he knew how anxious Chana was about her mother and other friends trapped in Hungary. He also hoped she could recommend volunteers for the mission.

Chana was thunderstruck. Here was her own idea, one she had been carrying for six weeks in the strongest safe of her heart, and others were already doing something about it. She felt immeasurably strengthened, and saw it as a special sign that her own plan would succeed. Her feeling of isolation vanished. She did not know, and Yonah could not answer, if she would qualify for the mission. Yonah's voice revealed his doubt whether the shadowy men who had sent him would allow a twenty-one-year-old girl with no military training or experience to join them on the basis of her language skills.

Her sex was not a problem: both the Haganah and the Palmach were open to female volunteers. And Chana had already dealt with the Palmach, which kept the Jewish navy—consisting of a few disguised fishing boats— at Sedot Yam, and operated a marine training camp on the beach, specializing in rescuing illegal immigrants; she was responsible for feeding these recruits, who sometimes numbered a hundred. Yonah promised to recommend her as a native speaker with strong personal motivation to volunteer. But he also made it clear that every part of the plan required final approval by the British military, without whose assistance it would be impossible to mount such an operation in occupied Europe. At this stage there was no knowing whether the mission would even take place, let alone succeed.

Chana knew that she would do everything in her power to join the mission. For the moment, it sufficed that she did not have to fight alone for her idea; that Eretz Israel would not sit by helplessly watching the destruction of European Jewry.

That night she lay awake, trying to imagine her return home. How would she cross the border? By military transport or on a train with forged papers? Yonah mentioned parachute training—what would it be like to jump out of an airplane? How would she inform her mother? Or would she simply ring the bell one day at the little gate on Bimbó-út? What about the rescue of her Zionist friends? And what was happening in Budapest right now, tonight? Were people in hiding? She realized how little she knew about the practicality of the tasks facing her.

In the weeks that followed she continued her preparations. Word from Yonah indicated that the project was progressing very slowly. The Haganah's original plans called for a more ambitious rescue effort, dropping entire companies, each consisting of a hundred or so regular soldiers, into several Central European countries. These plans were scaled back by British Intelligence, which supported the idea as a rescue mission—not for Jews, but for Allied airmen shot down over Central Europe. By this time, the armament factories were producing a surplus of warplanes, but there was an acute shortage of trained pilots; it was essential to bring back as many survivors as possible. Clandestine contacts with partisans and local resistance groups, especially in Yugoslavia, were nurtured for the purpose of maintaining such escape routes.

For the most part different agencies of the British military were fighting one another in Cairo, bringing the project to a bureaucratic stalemate. The Near East High Command and Churchill's war cabinet were engaged in a larger debate about giving sophisticated arms to the Haganah, which fought the British in that other war to establish a Jewish homeland. As Allied prospects improved steadily during 1943, the British no longer felt they needed the Jews in a Doomsday scenario to save their empire. So their thoughts turned back to the Arabs and how best to appease them.

Even if she was accepted by the Palmach, Chana still needed permission to leave the kibbutz. Many of the senior members were already serving in the Jewish Brigades with the regular Allied armies. Others were hoping to be called up soon. They were older, they were men, and they already had the backing of the kibbutz. Chana had barely joined the line. What would she do if the general assembly refused to let her go? Chana was thinking about Judit Stern's dilemma in her play. She had not written an ending, because she did not know how she would react in her own situation. When she wrote the scene of Judit's defiance of the collective decision, Chana may have been rehearsing her own stand.

Meanwhile she lived in two worlds. By the end of May, a new dining room had been built at Sedot Yam, the third permanent stone building to go up. There was talk of moving the married women and children to Caesarea, but the site was still far too primitive, and the pioneers still lived in tents. They were surrounded by intractable sand dunes, which produced ancient marble instead of cabbages. The kibbutz was still struggling to secure enough land from the Jewish National Fund to make the long-term settlement viable. Meanwhile the kibbutzniks invested their hopes in the sea. At the end of May Chana watched with satisfaction as a dozen Sedot Yam fishermen brought back the first catch.

In the middle of June, the kibbutz approved Chana's volunteering for military service. For months she had been thinking about little else, and during this time she lobbied hard to convince a majority of the chaverim of the seriousness of her commitment. In the end her passionate determination and sheer force of personality carried the vote.

Béla and Kató Szenes in the early 1920s soon after the birth of their two children.

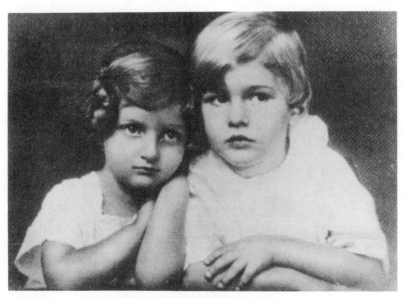

The Szenes children in 1924: Anikó aged three, and Gyuri aged four.

Kató and Gyuri in the garden of their house on Rózsadomb.

Anikó, aged sixteen, ready for her first ball.

Chana, with her favorite cow in Nahalal.

Building the kibbutz at Sedot Yam.

Chana and Gyuri at their last reunion in Tel Aviv, the night before Chana began her mission.

Memorial for the fallen parachutists in the Cemetery for Heroes on Mount Zion.

Kató Szenes with Prime Minister Golda Meir at the Roman theater in Caesarea celebrating the 25th annviersary of Sedot Yam in 1965.

Chana Szenes lying in state in front of Haifa City Hall in 1950.

My dear George!

I have again a chance to write you some words and so I doo, though there is not much I can write. The most important is my very-very best wishes to your birthday. You see, I hoped for this time to celebrate it already together, but I was mistaken, well, the next one — let us hope.

I would like you George to write once some words to Mopli in our colony, I did not write to them very long time, but I think much on them and are quite „O.K"? I have some reason not to write them for the moment.

What news about mother? Pleas write me about everything, your letters reach me sooner or later and I am so glad always to read them.

My dear, best best greetings and thousand kisses to you Hanna

1944, VI 6.

Chana's last letter from Yugoslavia to her brother.

SIXTEEN

WHEEL OF FORTUNE

The yard at the Prision Provincial of Gerona had four tall watchtowers, one in each corner, with bayoneted guards posted in front at all times. Gyuri watched the changing of the guards each noon. Half an hour later the Barcelona express sped temptingly close by. And this in turn was a signal for the main event of the day—the stew. After the soup was consumed, all too quickly, the prisoners would savor its memory by historical comparisons of its thickness with soups past.

It had been a balmy winter, without a drop of rain for six weeks. During the day Gyuri took his shirt off to bask in the yard, which had once been used as a soccer field. There were still a couple of goalposts at either end, but he also saw grim reminders that a deadlier game had been played here. The brick and plaster of the ancient walls showed innumerable holes where people hostile to Generalissimo Francisco Franco had been shot. The civil war, which lasted three years, until the spring of 1939, had caused at least 170,000 military casualties. It was a conflict characterized by immense savagery and treachery on both sides: Stalin sent his secret police to shoot Communist fighters in the back. The killing did not stop with Franco's victory, but the whole country was turned into an enormous prison camp for the defeated Republicans and their allies. During the Second World War, while Spain was neutral and supposedly at peace, at least another 100,000 people were executed in jails throughout the country. As Gyuri became fluent in Spanish and met veteran prisoners from the civil war, he learned firsthand about the destruction of a nation's spirit.

Because of the political prisoners, there were no books or newspapers in the jail. The authorities, who permitted trade in every other kind of contraband, took a very dim view of anybody caught reading. Gyuri thought he could be totally content at Gerona if only it had a library. To pass the time, he became interested in cooking. The culinary art suffered from exceptional limitations in the prison, which gave his hobby the additional advantage of being time-consuming. He supplemented his meager rations of bread with careful purchases from the canteen, scrounging leftovers and trading cans. He would spend hours preparing a salad with onions and tomatoes—using a can to chop them—a couple of small fish sprinkled with crumbs or leftover potatoes, and even a few drops of lemon, to make the most delicious concoction.

He spent much of his days watching the endless buzz of traffic in the courtyard, as people bartered their valuables for food and cigarettes. An exclusive gang controlled the risky business of trading in foreign currencies. People were amassing dollars and pounds sterling to help them reach a safe haven if they could buy their release. But the authorities were unusually severe on the currency black market. Gyuri witnessed two people caught and put into solitary punishment cells. Three weeks later they re-emerged so thin that he barely recognized them.

Those who had managed to preserve a few heirlooms in Figueras now let them go almost without regret. Diamond rings and gold cigarette cases became all but worthless under the merciless appraisal of the black mar-keteers, who could easily afford to wait for another day or week, until the hungry owners dropped the price, as they always did.

At the end of January a new administrator took charge of the prison. Change was at once palpable. The soup was diluted and fights broke out over the smaller portions. People scraped imaginary remnants from the soup caldron and licked their bowls so clean that they looked like new. A fresh cache of precious objects flooded the market, but found few buyers. The price of gold watches fell precipitously. "I don't need this, but I tell you what—I might be able to do you a favor," the usurer muttered in the time-honored words of his trade, and the ex-owner would already be rush-ing with his few pesetas to the canteen to buy a pound of figs.

Coincidentally there were difficulties with the transfer of money paid by the British consulate, which meant that the regular recipients could not supplement their diminished diet from the canteen. Soon Gyuri found himself too enervated to move. With the hunger, the mood inside the jail also turned dark. Rumor now had it that they would not be set free until the end of the war. "What if this is another Hundred Years' War?" the pessimists joked. But these rumors were contradicted by other news. With fresh German defeats in Africa and Russia, the tide seemed to be turning in favor of the Allies for the first time, a fact that was not lost on neutral Spain. Suddenly the prisoners were permitted to write letters abroad.

This opportunity posed a dilemma once again for Gyuri. For three months he had been out of touch with his mother and Anikó. He knew of no Zionist organization in Spain, and it was useless to write to Lyons, which was under German control. In the end he wrote some cautious postcards to Budapest and to Palestine, using his false name and pretending to be conveying news about his friend Gyuri.

After ten days of near starvation, he became so weak that a virus laid siege to his system. He ran a high fever for several days, wrapped in his heavy overcoat on the cold floor. He later thought that he recovered only because of the desire to be avenged on cellmates who kept tripping over him many times a day. There was no medication and the prison hospital was reserved for more "serious" cases. In his delirious moments Gyuri would see the warm clean bed of his childhood where his doting mother confined him at the slightest symptom of a cold. And when this ideal picture dissolved into reality, he wept like a child.

But his athletic young body somehow cured itself, and Gyuri woke each day to a sun that was a little warmer and more springlike than the last. The administration launched a new campaign against lice, and even distributed sheets for the first time. As usual, the aggressive inmates claimed more than their share and he was too weak to get one. Fights erupted at the slightest provocation. Gyuri longed for a book or magazine that might take his mind off the constant tension. He was worried that he might do something crazy. But the situation continued to improve. Gyuri managed to buy a smuggled book, which he devoured three times within as many days. It was a Spanish adventure story about a German pirate ship during the First World War. He felt an almost forgotten sense of vicarious thrill when the boat was finally dispatched to the bottom of the sea.

Other improvements followed. Several of his cellmates, who admitted to being French, were freed. Gyuri was just reconsidering the wisdom of his claim of being Canadian when the British consul raised his allowance to 550 pesetas a month. This enormous fortune enabled him to supplement the meals with anything the canteen had to offer. He even saved enough by the end of February to buy a complete set of underwear, socks, and expensive shirts from Arab vendors.

As his energy returned, Gyuri eagerly embraced any skill, any bit of knowledge that came his way. He had noticed that those who found reasons to complain about everything gradually fell into apathy and depression, while those who tried to make the best of their bad situation remained alert. To maintain his sense of reality, Gyuri played elaborate mental games to make himself believe that his condition was not only tolerable but in fact voluntary. He imagined that he had been prescribed a period of prolonged rest after the strain of studying so hard. He could not read because newspapers or even fiction might be too exciting for his strained nerves. He slept on the bare floor because it was prescribed for his posture. Indeed, after a few weeks his back was straight as an ironing board. And here at least he was spared the complicated system of figuring out ration cards, which had bedeviled him in France. He did not have to shop, his meals were brought to his house. And instead of working in the textile factory, bending over machines, the British consul was paying him a salary three times what he had ever earned before. In this sanatorium of his imagination, he could omit his studies without any pangs of conscience, and his sole duty was to enjoy the sun during the warmest hours of the day.

The authorities provided unstintingly for his spiritual needs. Mass was said three times a day. Not being a Catholic, Gyuri continually regretted the lack of opportunity to commit sins he could afterward confess. From the window he could see well-built peasant girls working in the fields, bending their full hips and letting their skirts slip up their legs. He had a hard time concocting imaginary justifications for why his particular regimen forbade sexual activity. Remembering the works of Émile Coué, whose system of autosuggestion was quite the rage, he repeated each morning a few hundred times the line "How great it is to be here!" Sometimes this helped. More often, he would have gladly sold all of Dr. Coué's slogans for five minutes of freedom walking in the fields.

About the middle of March the prison was rife with rumors that the British and Canadians would soon be transferred to Caldas, a town in the Pyrenees. They had heard little about the place except that they might have greater freedom there. Gyuri was suspicious of all rumors by then: it was equally possible that they would be taken somewhere worse. But the transfer for a hundred and fifty of them came on March twenty-fourth, when Gyuri had been in jail for more than three months. His hair had grown again, he had gained weight, and he felt that with a little sprucing up he could look presentable again to the outside world. Looking at the old walls of the courtyard during the final roll call he suddenly felt sentimental. He wanted to recite a poetic farewell to each prisoner, each guard, each stone that he had stared at for so many hours.

Caldas de Malavella turned out to be a pretty little resort town. Because of its proximity to France, some people called it the Catalan Vichy: its famous natural springs brought both the sick and the sybarites from far and wide. The ex-prisoners were billeted in the most elegant hotels, all paid for by His Britannic Majesty. As it was still the off season, and the war had kept the foreign tourists away, the whole town welcomed this unforeseen bonanza. The luxury of the first-class hotel—with its splendid halls and salons, separate rooms for reading, smoking, games, and dining, its inviting swimming pools surrounded by deck chairs, spacious suites equipped with gorgeous bathrooms—struck the new visitors as a bizarre fantasy. Gyuri wanted to savor everything in case he was awakened from his dream: he had a shower, then took a bath, visited the game rooms and played in turn Ping-Pong, pool, piano, and cards. He attacked the reading material piled on the coffee tables, devouring half a dozen illustrated magazines. He ordered an array of expensive dishes from a long menu, amazed at the sight of waiters in tailcoats attending to his every wish. His sole regret was that his stomach could digest only moderate amounts of the rich food. After the meal he went to the smoking room, where brandy and coffee were served, while more servants offered an unending supply of the finest cigars and cigarettes. Finally, worn out from all these sensations, he sank into a clean and warm bed. The next morning he awoke exhausted. He had grown so accustomed to sleeping on a hard floor that his back hurt from the bedsprings.

During the next few days the new arrivals explored the little town. Wondrous tiles and mosaics greeted them everywhere in the beautiful Moorish-style villas, with their lush, exotic gardens. The elegant shops brimmed with every possible luxury. Most intoxicating of all was the free-dom to walk aimlessly anywhere they wanted, to explore the town and its surroundings. The only restrictions imposed by the authorities, who still kept a close watch over them, were a roll call each evening at 8:30, followed by an informal curfew that restricted them to the hotel grounds. Since their day began at seven in the morning, this did not present any hardship. Gyuri took vast pleasure in walking out past the town, wandering amidst the productive fields and orchards already in bloom. His eyes followed the exuberant color to the point where they met with the more sober greens of the forests on the mountain slopes. He thought he could never have enough of these views.

He used his newly acquired Spanish to talk with the townspeople, who showed a great deal of warmth to the newcomers. The conversation was restricted to the simple routine of their lives and the immediate region; Gyuri could rouse no response when he tried to bring the subject around to international affairs or politics.

Commingling with the local population also brought an inevitable prob-lem. As other convoys of recent prisoners arrived, the little town found itself host to five hundred young men who had been starved for female company. They had time on their hands, money in their pockets, and one thing on their minds. The young men knew of the severe moral code in this most Catholic of countries, but they were wholly ignorant of the ex-traordinarily intricate courtship rituals that had evolved from a chivalric code of honor of the Middle Ages. The girls were well chaperoned, and the young foreigners were welcome to visit at their windows, where they sat in the cool of the evening with their embroidery and sewing. Their conversations were monitored by careful parents, brothers, and aunts, hiding behind shutters, while invisible eyes followed their every move. Gyuri came from a society in Budapest where the distinction between nice girls and those who meant business was clearly drawn. He understood well that these window romances would at best improve his Spanish. But in case naive coquetry might mislead any of the foreigners, the benevolent authorities provided them with occasional passes to the larger town of Gerona where their needs might be fulfilled in time-honored fashion.

During the next few weeks they all settled into the good life, adjusting to the ways of town and vice versa. The little cinema, which before their arrival had played Spanish movies once a week, was now doing a roaring trade with four films in French and English. The taverns, tobacconists, bakeries, newsstands, and other confectioners were similarly delighted with this foreign invasion. Gyuri had developed a pleasant routine of rising early and going for a walk in the morning dew. After a hearty breakfast he would put on his shorts and engage in a strenuous tennis tournament. Before lunch, he would read either the newspapers that he purchased in town or a Spanish novel. After lunch, when the natives were settling into their siesta, he sat out on the terrace, soaking in the sun, which grew warmer every day. This was a good time also for chess with one of his regular partners, and in the late afternoon he would walk a couple of miles to a nearby lake to join the bathers in a strenuous swim. He had always enjoyed sport, but he had a special reason to exert himself: much to his embarrassment, he had put on more than twenty pounds since Figueras. By 6:30 in the evening, he was back on the terrace, curled up with an English book. At about eight, he heard the orchestra warming up; and after the nightly roll call, supper was served at nine. There was time still for a stroll in the garden or, if Gyuri could persuade one of his playing partners to face losing, a few rounds of table tennis and pool.

Pleasant as this schedule was, especially compared to the horrors he had just endured, Gyuri saw the risk of becoming seduced into accepting this fairy tale as reality. Although he was preoccupied with the sensuous experience of getting his body back into shape, he was growing aware that his mind was getting flabby. He noticed how, along with his companions—with no control over their lives and no decisions to make—he was becoming dangerously passive. He decided to break his routine one day by getting a pass into Gerona. Rather than buying sex, he was driven by a need to experience real life as it was lived simply and naturally by people with everyday concerns. It happened to be a market day, and the entire town was bustling around the colorful boutiques and stands. He had a hundred pesetas saved up, which he spent quickly; he hungered to do whatever those other ordinary people were doing, to be normal, like them. After a few hours he caught a bus back into Caldas, returned to the hotel, and went into the reading room. But he did not want to read any of the cheap novels there. For a long time he stared into an emptiness that was his life, and gradually he began to feel a sense of purpose returning.

That evening Gyuri mapped out a schedule of projects to keep his mind in shape. He set himself courses to improve his skills in languages. He would memorize and recite poetry; study history and philosophy. He made efforts to establish contact with the world that had once held his future. He wrote to Chana, hoping that she would send him news about his immigration. He also wrote to Hungary, but under his assumed name and without daring to put a return address on the envelope.

Even paradise becomes boring, and the other men were growing restless, too. Now that they had physically recovered from their hardships, they remembered their original plans and began to think about resuming their lives. Conversations centered more and more on the possibility of leaving Spain. Escape was not considered seriously after a few people tried it and were quickly recaptured; they were returned to the Prision Provincial in Gerona.

By late May Gyuri's efforts to plan his own future were beginning to pay off. He had established contact with a tiny Zionist group in Barcelona, which in itself was powerless to help him. But they did arrange for Gyuri to meet with Wilfrid Israel, an emissary of the Jewish Agency from London who was searching thoughout Spain and Portugal for Jews who might qualify for certificates of emigration. Israel was encouraging, noting that Gyuri's age and close family connection in Eretz gave him a good chance. Then in early June, Gyuri read a newspaper account of the shooting down of a civilian plane between Lisbon and London. Wilfrid Israel, who would plead Gyuri's case in London, was on board. (So was the great actor Leslie Howard, also of Hungarian Jewish parentage, who played the perfect Anglo-Saxon gentleman in the movies. Apparently, the Germans believed Winston Churchill was traveling on the plane.)

In the middle of June, the "Canadians" were informed that henceforth they would be considered French. At first this was interpreted as good news, because more than three hundred French had left Caldas during the previous two weeks. However, the transports had now stopped and so did the free English cigarettes. As Frenchmen, their allowance was halved. And now the rumors said they would not be freed as promised, but sent instead to Miranda, an infamous detention camp. On July thirteenth the French contingent was anticipating the next day's Bastille Day celebrations when the sound of a military reveille awoke them. Looking out from his suite, Gyuri saw that the entire hotel was surrounded by troops and armored vehicles. After dressing, he and his fellow guests were greeted by the commanding officer, who looked despondent as he gave them the painful news that they had a few minutes to pack.

The sudden change in their fortunes could not have been more brutal. After months of luxury in balmy Caldas, their nightmares had faded. Once more they were herded at gunpoint to the railway station, and then into cattle cars. There they sat locked up, waiting for most of the day while the July heat turned each wagon into a furnace. News of their transfer had spread rapidly through the small town; many townsfolk came out to bid them farewell, and brought little gifts, but the guards allowed no civilian contact with their prisoners. Gyuri could hear from inside the wagon one of his girlfriends begging a soldier to pass on a package of homemade biscuits. Although he had longed for change, Gyuri's young heart rebelled against this cruel spin in his wheel of fortune.

SEVENTEEN

PREPARING

In the summer of 1943, the rescue mission was still bogged down in Cairo, although some recruits were being trained. Yonah wrote occasionally to Chana, but he did not tell her that her chances seemed slimmer than ever. British Intelligence was at first vehemently opposed to sending young women on such a mission. Besides the traditional reasons, much of their reluctance was based on intelligence reports about what the Gestapo did to spies. It did not make pretty reading. The Haganah liaison officer with the British Near East Command, Captain Moshe Dayan, suggested that Yonah should present only the male names for training in Cairo, at least to begin with. Once the project was more established and obtained greater support within the British command, one could propose Chana and other women volunteers.

British Intelligence was mainly interested in two skills among the recruits: parachute jumping and operating a transmitter with the Morse code. Therefore they preferred volunteers from the Jewish Brigades, who had already gone through basic military training, British style. But some of the volunteers had demands as well. A few of Yonah's recruits dropped out from the project after complaining about the lack of training. Their complaints were directed to Eliahu Golomb, one of the Haganah chiefs, who was in the middle of delicate negotiations with the British. It had taken a long time to convince the British to combine their objectives with that of the Haganah—which was to rescue Jews, not just British airmen—and Golomb had no desire to create further friction at this point, regardless of any Jewish volunteers who did not like these priorities.

"I'm willing to go and tell them of your complaints," Golomb told them, "but first I want to know who among you is willing to go on this mission without preconditions. If you insist on conditions, whether it's training or anything else, I'm going to suggest to you right now that you go home." When several did, Chana benefited in two ways. First, the departure of these men made room for her. Second, the Palmach stepped up its own training of the recruits, which was much more thorough than the British program, especially in clandestine and sabotage work. Best of all, she did not have to wait for British permission, since the Palmach had its own training programs, which she could start right away.

Her first seminars were not military but ideological. They were provided by the Noar Oved, the same Working Youth organization that had attracted Chana to her kibbutz. The classes were designed to orient and even indoctrinate volunteers about Jewish ideals and values, including the causes of anti-Semitism and the Holocaust in Europe, which provided the rationale for Zionism. The Jewish Agency and the Haganah considered it of the highest propaganda value that anybody representing Eretz Israel to the Jewish Diaspora should carry a Jewish message of hope in this darkest hour.

After the hardships of Caesarea, Chana enjoyed the luxury of the Ruttenberg mansion in Haifa, where she attended the month-long seminars. Here she also celebrated the fourth anniversary of her arrival in the same city: "Everything was new then, everything was beautiful. Everything belonged to the future. One figure only drew me back into the past—my mother standing at the train. Four years! I did not believe then that the chasm separating us could become this deep. Had I known . . . but perhaps I did know, only I did not want to admit it."

Reviewing her years in Eretz, Chana felt much satisfaction. But as was her way, whenever she did her spiritual accounting, the diary dwelled more in the debits column. Preparations for her mission, nerve-racking because of rising tensions alternating with long periods of waiting, gave her an unsettled, temporary feeling that she was still only preparing for the next step rather than setting down roots. The close comradeship at the kibbutz and now among soldiers had not resolved her growing sense of loneliness.

"I'm very clear now that my loneliness is not caused by external factors. I must be peculiar in some way or lack the communal spirit, and this keeps me apart from other people. It's especially hard when it comes to boys. It appears that I love, or at least *could* love somebody. But . . . there are too many objective 'buts' in the way and I lack the courage to overcome them."

There was a fellow kibbutznik who might have been that special person she had often thought about: "I had a chance to speak to him, but I still left. I really did want to talk to him, very much. I had been waiting for it all week. We did talk for a few minutes and then it was up to me whether we would continue. I didn't have a good reason for leaving but I left anyway. I couldn't do otherwise. I can't explain everything, but I do understand. Too bad."

As so many times before, she dismisses the "boy-question":

Well, my heart is not exactly about to break into little pieces. And yet I'm scared by something else. I am twenty-two years old and I have no joy in life. I can't remember the last time I was really happy, looking forward, or joyous, if only for a few minutes. I feel a certain indifference. Sometimes I catch myself asking: "What is this? Is my whole life going to pass like this?" And again, this isn't caused by anything outside; it's inside me. I have no real complaints about my life; I'm quite content. I cannot remember a time when I felt more satisfied. On the contrary. And the mission has an extraordinary attraction for me. Yet I've forgotten how to laugh, really laugh with all my heart, as Gyuri and I when we wrestled on the sofa and rolled down on to the floor.

The Palmach field-training program left little time for such introspection. Chana returned for a series of courses during the second half of 1943. It was a very thorough program, which became the foundation for perhaps the most admired fighting corps in modern times. Yigal Allon, who took charge of the Palmach in 1945, gave these objectives for the training of each member:

The emphasis is on developing [his] power to react quickly, to think clearly and logically, to make the best use of [his] weapons, to know how to exploit to the full natural conditions (terrain, darkness, etc.), and to operate both as an individual and as a member of the group. All this required, of course, maximum physical fitness and mental readiness, and was supplemented by direct instruction in the value of certain moral qualities—in particular, conscious discipline, responsibility, comradeship, and the sense of cause and purpose.

Chana possessed the required moral and mental qualities in abundance. She was physically fit because of the unceasing activity at the kibbutz. What she lacked was military training, of which her sole experience came from doing occasional guard duty at Sedot Yam. (Although the Arabs of Caesarea were on the whole peaceful neighbors, no Jewish settlement could afford to let its guard down.) The Palmach program included thirty-seven days and twenty nights of basic training, with fifteen days of marching; additional training for such independent action as ambush and infiltration, searching people, guarding an area; and guerrilla techniques of harassment and deception. The program was extremely arduous and particularly effective in weeding out those not suitable for the rescue missions. In between these training sessions, which she was forbidden to discuss, Chana returned to Caesarea to do her regular work and wait for the mission to begin.

In Cairo the battle continued within British Intelligence about Palmach participation in the mission. The A Force—which was more sympathetic to the Jewish cause—was now gaining ascendancy over the dilatory Intelligence Service, largely due to the enthusiastic efforts of Squadron Leader Lawson, an English officer from a totally assimilated family whom the war helped to awaken to his Jewish roots. He had a strong supporter in Colonel Tony Simons, who was pushing the project through the chains of the Near East Command. But they encountered the old questions about the value of the intelligence to be gained and whether it was worth the risk of collaborating with the Palmach in light of the deep divergence between British and Jewish aims regarding the future of Palestine. Simons and Lawson both supported the Haganah's moral imperative to do something, no matter how little, to save some of Hitler's victims from the gas chambers and crematoria that were consuming tens of thousands of Jews each day. And from a military point of view they argued that the rescue of a single shot-down pilot, who could fly a bomber again, would justify the mission. One final attempt at obstruction by the Intelligence Service was to seek the opinion of the British high commissioner for Palestine. In the venerable hand-washing tradition of Judaean governors, the diplomat replied: "By all means. I'll be glad to have them off my hands." The decision had been made at last.

In September, the Romanian group left, but the Hungarians were told to wait. It was frustrating, but the Jews of Hungary were not in the same life-threatening situation as those in neighboring countries. Chana, who heard less and less frequently from her mother, Évi, and other friends, was neither patient nor reassured, however. Even though Allied victory seemed more than a mirage for the first time in four years, people feared that it might come too slowly and late to save European Jewry. Chana had to be prepared but accept that the call might not come for several more months—even years.

She tried to make the best of this period. During the long months when she heard nothing from Gyuri and letters from her mother were intermittent, Chana learned much about waiting. Preparing for the mission had helped to diminish her sense of futility and impotence. In the meanwhile, she had several projects to attend to. When she finally received word from Gyuri in Caldas, she wrote back reassuring him that she was doing everything to get him to Eretz Israel. At the same time, she tirelessly exploited every opportunity to bring her mother out of Hungary. Here she received some unexpected encouragement from high-ranking British officers, who said they would try to get an emigration certificate for Mrs. Szenes as soon as possible. They told her she might even arrive in Palestine before Chana's own departure. But while she grasped every straw of hope, Chana was worried whether her mother could be persuaded to leave Budapest, whether she even realized her own danger. In late 1943, Chana wrote her a hasty note: "There's a wonderful opportunity right this moment to come and join me. I have made all the necessary moves on this end to make your journey possible within weeks, possibly days. I know, darling, how very sudden this is, but you must not hesitate. Every day is precious and the road may be closed or new difficulties could arise." By the time Mrs. Szenes received the letter, that particular opportunity had indeed evaporated, but Chana kept trying new avenues while waiting for her call.

At the kibbutz endless chores occupied most of her waking hours. In her spare moments Chana went swimming, walked on the beach, sat on her favorite rock and gazed out at the inhuman splendor of the Mediterranean. When she needed to feel reassurance about the value of human activity, she could look back from the beach and within her purview compare the new settlement with the Roman ruins, the Crusaders' castle, and the ancient Arab village. Much had been achieved during the past two years: not just the physical buildings that anybody could see, but those invisible bonds of common purpose and understanding that make for a community. She felt the pride of having started something and sensed the loss of having to go away, if only for a brief time. She began to realize it would not be easy to leave this infant kibbutz or to give up the free air of Eretz. She wanted to gulp and hold it in her lungs, so that she would not have to breathe the poisonous atmosphere of hatred in Europe. "I want to breathe this air on them," she wrote, "so that they could feel what freedom is."

EIGHTEEN

PING-PONG

The slow journey to the notorious prison camp of Miranda de Ebro took almost two days, during which Gyuri could not sleep nor lie down. Although the train stood at several stations for hours, the prisoners were never allowed to disembark and use the sanitary facilities. The wagons were filled with the stench of vomit and excrement but the guards did not heed the cries for relief. After the transport arrived the second night, they had half an hour's march to the camp, where they were greeted by a two-hour line-up while the authorities filled out the usual admission forms. Although the prisoners were assigned bunks in the barracks, most of them simply dropped in the middle of the courtyard and fell asleep.

The scene that greeted Gyuri's eyes the next morning was more depressing than anything he had experienced so far. Nearly five thousand people were crammed into a space roughly six hundred by twelve hundred feet. The bunkbeds were piled four levels high. The new arrivals were mostly left with the uppermost bunks, which meant considerable risk at each climb, not to mention the heat that rose to the top and hung there. Many people actually preferred to sleep on the ground outside. Searchlights criss-crossed the whole camp, dramatically silhouetting the guards along the walls with their rifles at bayonet. Beyond the walls was a tall fence, which was electrified.

Worse even than the crowding, the pervasive filth, the merciless heat, and the constant danger of dehydration were the human predators. Miranda was a well-established jail with a great number of semipermanent residents who had been there since the early years of the civil war. Most were political prisoners but there was a substantial class of common criminals who constituted an underground network of chieftains, enforcers, usurers, and other providers of services who had grown wealthy at the expense of a constant supply of greenhorns. Gyuri found all the familiar goods and services on the flourishing black market, with a few new twists as well. It was possible to hire a construction crew and have private quarters—with electricity, if desired—built from tin cans and crates. Miranda also boasted gambling dens, private laundry, and open trade in homosexual favors. There was a private dentist who spent days extracting one of Gyuri's infected wisdom teeth with a pair of pliers.

Miranda was a far more brutal place than Figueras or Gerona. A few enterprising individuals lived well at the expense of the masses who lacked the financial or mental resources to engage in business. Gyuri saw the powerful exploiting the weak, in a microcosm of the outside world. But inside the camp there were no brakes on the unceasing intimidation and thievery. Fighting with knives was an everyday occurrence, and murders were not uncommon. Gyuri tried in vain to find his own little corner, where he could tune out this inferno.

Arriving prisoners brought a constant supply of news from the outside. By the end of July 1943 the Allies had liberated most of Sicily and were preparing to land on the Italian mainland. Mussolini had been forced to resign and some French inmates organized a mock subscription drive to pay for his one-way ticket to Miranda. Il Duce never arrived, but many others did every day from various prisons, causing an acute shortage of bunks. Some of the inmates had been to many exotic places and spun wonderful tales about Indochina, Madagascar, and Tahiti. Sitting in the cool of the evening they entertained their listeners with stories more tall than true.

"I could buy a wife in Saigon for two francs," said one of the French veterans.

"And leave her for one," reparteed another. The prisoners made plans to visit such places after the war; in the meantime they were simply happy to forget for a few hours the hunger and misery of Miranda.

After two weeks Gyuri discovered a Hungarian colony in the camp. It had fifteen members, some of whom had also come via France. They had spent years already at Miranda, for having helped the Republican side during the civil war. Because of their seniority they belonged to the privileged caste in the jail and Gyuri was astonished to see how their domestic set-up resembled what he remembered of life in Budapest, lacking only women to make the illusion complete. Despite ideological, social, and even religious differences, they welcomed Gyuri into their makeshift homes as a long-lost brother or son, and from that day he hardly ever saw his former comrades.

The Hungarians had special connections with the intricate underground network, so it was easily arranged that Gyuri would relieve one of their number for a three-week cooking stint in the camp hospital. This was a plum job, because only ninety meals had to be prepared. The ingredients were of a choicer quality than those in the mass kitchen, which provided meals by the thousands. Naturally, a cook must frequently taste what he prepares, and nobody noticed if a couple of extra rations disappeared. Despite what he had learned about improvising salads at Gerona, Gyuri found cooking hard work. The heat around the ovens was all but unbearable. By the evening he looked like a chimney sweep, and he had to wash his clothes each night.

Gyuri never finished the three-week assignment. On August twenty-fifth, there were the usual rumors of liberation; this time they centered on inmates who had been arrested during 1942. Familiar with every variation on the theme, Gyuri went about his kitchen duties as usual, until a friend came running to tell him about his name being on a list that had been posted on the camp noticeboard: a group of twenty-five were to leave for Madrid that afternoon. On his way to pack his few belongings, Gyuri dropped by the camp office where an even greater surprise awaited him— a letter from Chana, the first one to reach him in fourteen months. He did not have the time to savor his sister's news, needing every minute to say goodbye to his friends and prepare himself for the next adventure. Everybody had an errand for him: to mail a letter, to contact somebody for money, to call an embassy—to remind the world of their existence.

Within two hours the small group of prisoners was assembled, clutching their bags as they waited at the gate outside the electric fence for the final formalities of release. It was clear from their official safe conduct that this was not a transfer to another prison or camp; they were actually going to be set at liberty. After nine long months Gyuri would be free again.

Finally it was time to go. Tentative at first, with each step the ex-prisoners felt more confident as their feet regained the spring and gait of free men. On the way to the railroad station, the local people greeted them with more than common courtesy, as if they had known what they had suffered and wished to disassociate themselves from any blame. At the station, they were shown into the restaurant, where the French Red Cross had set up special tables laid with fruits and other delicacies. An hour later they were on the train to Madrid. It was crammed full, but none of the refugees cared. They were free to get off the train and therefore content to remain on it.

They arrived in Madrid the next morning and immediately went to the Red Cross to begin the long process of establishing their identity. There was no point in maintaining the pretense of being French or Canadian any longer, so he became Gyuri Szenes again, a Hungarian citizen. His last ties to France were now severed, with few regrets on his part.

At his own request Gyuri was referred to the Palestine Emigration Office in Madrid, where he learned that it might take several more weeks, perhaps months, to get the right papers for certification, as his file had been lost with Wilfrid Israel's plane. Gyuri could do nothing but wait. He was ready to savor the pleasures of the Spanish capital, except that he had practically run out of money, and there was no prospect of any income. Tens of thousands of unemployed young men were looking for work in a country that was among the most backward in Europe, and that had not recovered either from the Depression or from its civil war. Gyuri needed a work permit for any regular job and his recent experiences with Spanish jails reminded him not to break the laws of the land.

He was lucky to find a cheap back room, where the landlady spoiled him as an adopted son. All day he roamed. Occasionally he stopped at a café for a few hours of reading and watching the crowd. But increasingly, Gyuri became preoccupied by problems of survival. Daily his dilemma grew worse. Even if his letters reached his family, it was problematic to send money out of Hungary or Palestine. He thought Chana would have none to send him, since kibbutzniks owned nothing, and it was more than likely that his mother's means were severely restricted.

One day Gyuri was drifting aimlessly down a Madrid street when he noticed a large arcade that offered opportunities for playing pool and table tennis. More than ten weeks had passed since he had wielded a cue or racket in the balmy days of Caldas, and he was seized by an intense desire to play. He watched a Ping-Pong match in progress and then screwed up his courage and challenged the winner to a match. The other spectators in the hall exchanged meaningful glances; Gyuri had no idea that he had just challenged the champion player of the Madrid Club. Winning the match was to change his life in Madrid.

Immediately he was invited to join the Castille Club; he now had a place to go during the day, to play and talk. The other members were young men from rich and politically powerful families; sport was an aristocratic pastime in Spain. His playing partners began to take him places, always finding a tactful reason for paying his bill. His meager clothes and refugee status did not need further explanation. One of the boys, by the name of Pago Francisco, introduced him to his parents, who were prominent in Spanish society. The mother was happy to find somebody with whom she could practice her French; after some tactful questioning, she learned that Gyuri had advertised to give French lessons but so far without results. Within a few days Pago brought Gyuri a note from his mother, asking whether he would be willing to take on a student, the son of a friend of hers, for 150 pesetas a month.

Gallego Coman was nineteen, very rich, and interested only in the pursuit of pleasure. Instruction had little effect on him, until Gyuri found the motivation to get his hedonistic student out of bed. Gallego was planning a trip to Paris, where he planned to impress the cocottes and demimondaines with his fluent French. He adored French chansons, and as soon as he got Gyuri to teach him the words in the latest pop song, he would rush to call one of his girlfriends in the middle of the lesson and sing it to her over the telephone.

Gallego was generous and took his young teacher to elegant places, shrugging off Gyuri's share of the expense with a reference to his immense personal fortune. He often offered to introduce Gyuri to one of his many girlfriends in town, adding, "Don't worry, I've arranged everything so that she is madly in love with you already." Then they drove together to a house, where two apartments faced each other at the top of a flight of stairs. Gallego pushed the bell on each door. Almost simultaneously two beautiful young women came to the door. "You choose," he said, "you're my guest." Gyuri looked at each girl: one was blonde, the other dark. He chose the dark one. He was not looking for true love, but he knew which color was likely to be genuine.

As his social contacts increased there was no shortage of pupils, including the children of a genuine duchess. He still found plenty of time to play at the club, and his reputation as a formidable Ping-Pong player quickly spread throughout the fashionable circles of Madrid. One afternon a large black limousine, sporting diplomatic plates and the ensign of an unfamiliar country, pulled up to the shabby tenement where Gyuri lodged. A driver with immaculate white gloves emerged and came to Gyuri's apartment to invite him for a Ping-Pong match with His Excellency the Ambassador of the Republic of China. Gyuri had heard at the club that the Chinese ambassador was a passionate competitor who would invite the top three or four players in Madrid regularly to his residence. Now it was Gyuri's turn. As the limousine sped through the exclusive diplomatic district toward the mandarin's palace, he thought gratefully about his early training at the Duna Sport Klub in Budapest, which had produced so many world-class table tennis players. And he also reflected on the differences between the genial openness of Spanish society, which he penetrated so easily after a few weeks, and his years in France where most private homes and social circles had remained closed to him.

The ambassador himself stood in front of his residence to greet Gyuri with a smile. His friendliness was partly to compensate for the fact that he knew no European languages. However, sport is an internatonal language and His Excellency and the young man from Budapest had no problems understanding each other. The ambassador had an agile, ageless body; he moved around the table like a cat. Several times he cried out in admiration of a particularly finessed return or serve—*"formidable!"*—the only word he seemed to know in French. They played several hours without a pause, until about 2:00 A.M., when they agreed to resume their match at a later date. His Excellency's wife translated his opinion that Gyuri was the best player he had met in Madrid, and Gyuri agreed that they were well matched. Then it was time for a small banquet of unfamiliar delicacies, after which sleepy butlers served the finest selection of cigars and cigarettes. Gyuri felt he had earned it all.

From then on he became a regular visitor at the ambassador's residence. The peak of his career came when he won the Madrid championship for the Castille Club. This was an exhibition game attended by hundreds of people, and during the banquet, he was presented with a cup that had been donated by the Chinese ambassador. It was filled with champagne, which custom demanded that the winner drink. Gyuri had won a number of cups in Lyons and Budapest; this was the only one that he managed to keep during his long flight to Palestine.

The middle of December marked the first anniversary of Gyuri's departure from France. He reflected on the extraordinary vicissitudes of the past year, which in retrospect struck him as more appropriate to a picaresque novel than real life. He had lived through more during the twelve-month than in the previous twenty-three years, yet it felt now as if only a few days had passed since he embarked on his escape across the Pyrenees.

New Year's Eve found him among a crowd of wild celebrants massing around the Puerta del Sol, waiting to ring in 1944. They were watching the large clock on City Hall. By ancient custom a person had to eat a dozen grapes during the twelve strokes of midnight, to prevent a catalogue of catastrophes during the ensuing twelve months. The tradition meant a bonanza to grape vendors, who would be starting off the year with a good omen. As a refugee Gyuri was more impressed by the abundance of grapes in the middle of winter than by the superstition itself. As the clock began its chime, an eerie silence descended on the assembled crowd, followed by the sound of thousands eating and swallowing grapes. Then pandemonium broke out. All evening there had been the expectant build-up of emotions that now sought release, aided by the usual byproducts of the grape. Gyuri was swept forward by the human tide and the horde of attractive, happy people dancing and singing. When he staggered back to his lodgings in the early dawn, sporting a funny hat and a false beard, his landlady almost fainted. Apparently, the assumed beard had rendered Gyuri's face into an astonishing likeness of her dear long-departed husband.

The grape-eating ceremony seemed to pay off much sooner than he had expected. On the very first day of the New Year Gyuri received word at the Palestine Office that his certification papers had arrived, and that they were trying to include him with a small party of emigrants scheduled to sail from Cadiz within a month.

Gyuri was seized by travel fever, although this time his joy was tempered by regret. Madrid had been good to him, and in a few short months he had established himself and felt at home. He had many friends, a fledgling occupation as a successful teacher of languages, a flourishing reputation among sportsmen. He had his first taste of self-supporting adulthood in the Spanish capital. Yet he knew that a man needs to do more than just play Ping-Pong and seek pleasure, that he ought to be seriously thinking about setting down permanent roots. How could he consider his life normal, when he had been completely cut off from his family?

On January fifteenth, a specially reserved train to Cadiz was scheduled to leave at midnight. By nine o'clock the platform was a Babel of voices as the Jewish emigrants gathered, speaking a dozen different languages. Hundreds of Spanish friends brought presents, flowers, and food to the travelers. Not a few somber beauties were tearfully wrapped in the arms of boyfriends, each pair silently swaying on their feet: finally the words had run out, and only the pain of parting remained.

The Palestine Emigration Office had gathered an aliyah of about five hundred people: of these some four hundred had recently arrived from Barcelona. Gyuri even met somebody he knew from his school in Lyons. Almost everyone met long-lost friends from various jails and holding camps, and the questioning began about the fate of others. This absorbing occupation carried on far into the night, after the train had begun its long journey south. After more than thirty hours the sleepless travelers were made to wait another two at the Cadiz station. Finally they were driven to their hotels. It was early morning and Gyuri went straight to bed. When he woke in the afternoon he saw from his window the Atlantic Ocean for the first time. After lunch, he decided to go exploring the picturesquely untidy streets of this southern town. The local newspapers had reported the arrival of five hundred Jews, and curiosity—officially no Jews had lived in Spain since 1492—drove many of the inhabitants into the streets to look for them. Gyuri saw some superstitious natives cross themselves, averting their eyes, while others betrayed disappointment that the visitors did not have horns and hooves, as they had imagined.

A full week went by in Cadiz. Finally, on the twenty-fourth of January, the *Nyassa,* a Portuguese vessel hired by the Zionist organizations, arrived from Lisbon with 170 passengers to pick up another 560 in Cadiz for the first aliyah to leave the Iberian Peninsula. At midnight the ship steamed out of the harbor. The younger members of the group danced the hora on deck and sang pioneer songs in broken Hebrew. Others plunged into heavy debates about the politics of Palestine, a land that they had never seen and that was not yet a country. There were future partners putting together business deals, matching limited funds with limitless dreams.

Many of the passengers felt no Zionist zeal to build a Jewish homeland: they were tired refugees who had lost everything and been hounded through the concentration camps of Europe. They were not looking forward to having to start a new life under conditions they knew would be harder than those they had enjoyed before the war. Already aboard this ship they could see the problems: the lack of a common language and of background between Jews from different countries. Gyuri, who counted himself among the idealists on board, wondered if these different languages, incongruous traditions, and outright antagonisms could ever coalesce and be reconciled in Eretz Israel.

The first day at sea proved pleasant, and despite the season, most people basked on deck during the short sun-filled hours. By next day, a nasty storm drove everybody below deck, and the ship was filled with the groans and moans of the seasick. Gyuri was lucky to escape with a bad headache. Two days later, as they were approaching Crete, still a German stronghold, the captain decided to hold an air-raid practice. Everybody was supposed to find his life belt and then rush to line up for an assigned lifeboat. The results were far from reassuring.

Gyuri thrilled to the exotic islands and distant shores he remembered from Homer and other classics of his school days. The myths were becoming real; he could feel firsthand how the crafty Ithacan and his frail companions were tossed about the wine-dark sea. Poseidon, god of the sea, displayed his awesome anger by rearranging the decks and clearing the dining tables with a single tilt.

The seasickness had one unexpected side effect: an epidemic of wedding fever swept the ship. Eretz Israel had such an imbalance of genders that it was acquiring a reputation as a place where the most unmarriageable girls stood an excellent chance of finding a husband. Gyuri thought that the females on the ship belonged mainly to this category and avoided them. However, some of his companions, weakened by sickness and hunger, began to panic about the prospect of living mateless in the promised land. So each tilt of the boat that swept some maiden into a young man's arm ended in a promise of marriage.

There was but one girl who held Gyuri's thoughts as the steamer headed to the eastern shores of the Mediterranean. His excitement grew as he tried to imagine the long-awaited meeting with his sister. How much had she changed in the past five years? How was she coping with the problems of the kibbutz? Would he be joining her there? He had grown used to making his own decisions, but he had to admit that there was much he did not know and would have to learn all over again in another new country. Yet, unlike the other tired refugees huddling on the ship, he was exhilarated by his prospects. He was ready to give all his strength and energy to a higher ideal than daily survival. He knew that from now on he would not be doing the work alone.

On the last day of January, just before dawn, Gyuri hurried on deck expectantly. The storm had delayed their arrival the night before. Now the engines were turned off and the ship was moving very slowly toward a harbor that lay shrouded in dense fog. But above this curtain arched, with improbable suddenness, the ridge of Mount Carmel, as the first tentative fingers of dawn streaked the sky behind it. In a few minutes, the sun rose and its fractured rays sliced through the mist, falling gently on to the sea as if laying a golden carpet of welcome before the ship. Then, dramatically, the curtain of fog lifted, and Gyuri beheld a breathtaking view of Haifa Bay, its far shores stretching north to the medieval citadel of Akko and The Lebanon, and the pretty harbor with its white stone houses, dotting the steep hills and ravines of Mount Carmel. Nearby, their outlines still ragged in the mist, a flotilla of Jewish fishing boats stood revealed. The fishermen were all shouting one word: "Shalom!" There had been very few legal immigrant ships recently that could simply sail into Haifa harbor. Now the steamer was passing a number of British warships docked at the piers, and all of them were lined with dock workers wildly shouting "shalom!" By now even the weakest passenger had climbed on deck. As they crowded to get their first look at the promised land, a solemn quiet descended upon them. Spontaneously someone began to sing the Hatikvah, and the chorus of voices grew, at first tentative and dissonant, until they became unison, their different backgrounds and plans melting into a thundering hymn of defiance to everything they had endured to come home.

NINETEEN

MEETING IN ERETZ

British officers boarded the *Nyassa* in Haifa harbor and started to process the immigrants' papers. Jewish stevedores—giants with swarthy complexion and bulging muscles—swarmed on the decks, tossing three or four suitcases at a time like feather pillows. They refused to accept tips from *olim*, as the new immigrants were called. Upon disembarking, the passengers were funneled by the British authorities into a quarantined area, keeping them away from the people who came to meet them. Palestinian Jews knew about these precautionary measures, and therefore few people came to meet the boat. Gyuri did not expect anyone to meet him, but he immediately began to make enquiries about Sedot Yam. Within minutes he was introduced to one of the stevedores who turned out to be a member of the kibbutz and offered to tell Chana that evening of his safe arrival.

The immigrants were transferred under escort to Atlit, a transit camp on the coast just south of Haifa. There they were to be interrogated by British officers, who believed that the Germans used both the legal and the illegal transports to infiltrate Palestine with their agents. The process of debriefing could take anywhere from one to two weeks. Some relatives followed them and stood anxiously outside the barbed wire, but no contact was permitted. It was frustrating for Gyuri to find in the land of his dreams a reception much like the one that had greeted him in Spain.

By the evening of his first day in Eretz, Chana had found out and managed to send a welcoming card into Atlit, indicating that she hoped to see him the next day. Since the rules had been made amply clear, Gyuri could not imagine how she would do this. The next day, he was idly sitting in the barracks when a young British officer asked Gyuri to accompany him to the guardhouse, outside the gates. They entered a small room, and before Gyuri could focus his eyes in the semidarkness, a young woman flew into his arms and squeezed him in a tight embrace. She was laughing and crying, and gradually the words began to pour out incoherently in

Hungarian. She continued to hold him, as if to make up for the pent-up emotions of those lost years. It was only when they disengaged and he could take a better look at her that Gyuri realized that his little sister was wearing a British uniform.

"What does this mean?" he asked in their native tongue. But she switched to English, to include the officer who was still in the room, trying to look busy during this passionate reunion: "I am leaving the country in two days, Gyuri. I have to go for training in Egypt. I hope to be back soon."

"But you . . . you've always been a pacifist," was all he could bring himself to say. He was fiercely disappointed that his sister would be gone by the time he got out of the camp. Chana seemed to want to reassure him but her explanations, in a language that was foreign to them both, only made her imminent departure more mysterious.

"I am with the Women's Auxiliary Force. We can't talk now, but believe me, Gyuri, I'm doing everything to get a few private hours for the two of us before I leave." Then she turned a dazzling smile to the officer: "And it's going to work, isn't it, sir?"

"I don't know . . . The rules are very strict here," the young Englishman muttered and then indicated that the interview was at an end. Chana kissed her brother again and left. As the officer took Gyuri back to the camp, he explained how unusual it was for even this brief interview to be granted: a compromise had been worked out to accommodate the very special circumstances of his sister.

Gyuri sat on his bunkbed and a gradual depression took hold of him. This reunion had been so different from anything he could have imagined. All the questions he had, all the answers he wanted to hear, all those years they had to catch up with, and there was no time for any of it. He hadn't even asked about their mother. What if they did not see each other again for a long time? He did not want to doubt Chana's promise of arranging a longer meeting, but he was also experienced in the ways of officialdom; while he remembered that it was very much in his sister's nature to be overly optimistic. His fellow immigrants did nothing to bolster his hopes. Some of them claimed to have the highest connections inside Eretz who were sending letters into the camp promising to cut through the red tape and get them out of Atlit within three days. But within three days Chana would be gone, and he did not really understand why.

The next twenty-four hours were among the slowest that Gyuri had ever endured. It was the afternoon of his second day at Atlit and there was not the slightest hint that he would see Chana. He was sitting despondent under a tree, trying to read, when a civilian carrying a briefcase came up to him. He asked for Gyuri's name, first in Hebrew and then in English.

"You come with me now," he said abruptly. Gyuri followed him to an old taxi that was waiting out of view, already filled with other civilians. They made room for him in the middle of the back seat. One of them gave his hat to Gyuri and politely forced him to put it on his head so that he would look more like everybody else. Then the taxi sped toward the gate. The guard gave them a cursory glance and waved them on.

The people in the car were representatives of the Jewish Agency, the only civilians allowed inside the camp to take the new immigrants' data and help them find jobs upon release. The Agency was extremely reluctant to jeopardize this privilege, which had been won after much bargaining, so Chana must have pulled the highest strings to arrange for this kidnaping. But Gyuri felt the tension in the car, even though he could not follow the Hebrew conversation. He was left to his own bewildered thoughts.

The taxi sped along the coastal road that connects Haifa with Tel Aviv. To the left they were leaving behind the wild southern slopes of Carmel. The widening coastal plain was covered with orchards, trees laden with every kind of citrus and even bananas. Ancient Arab villages dotted the high ground; the more functional and drab houses in neat rows were Jewish settlements. After about half an hour, one of the people in the front seat addressed Gyuri in English.

"A couple of miles off this road is Caesarea. If these sand dunes weren't so high, you might see Sedot Yam, the kibbutz your sister is building."

Gyuri looked toward the sunset and saw nothing but mountains of sand, with a few hardy shrubs. He had read how the whole country used to be sand or swamp, and he marveled, as Chana had before him, how much had been done to transform the land—and how much still needed to be done.

Within the hour they arrived in Tel Aviv at a hotel near the seafront. Chana was waiting anxiously in the lobby. She thanked in Hebrew the man who was responsible for smuggling Gyuri out of Atlit and arranged for her brother's suitcases to be held by the Jewish Agency until he had an address.

Finally they were together, alone, to catch up with the missing years that constituted one quarter of their life, and almost all of their adult existence. They looked into each other's faces, trying to read at one glance everything they had gone through, and especially what was happening inside each other right at that moment.

For Chana it was agony to be sitting at last face to face with her beloved brother, and yet unable to pour out her soul. Her superiors in the Palmach specifically forbade any talk of the mission; she was only allowed to mention the training in Cairo as routine paramilitary service that was common during the war. She did not want Gyuri to know how dangerous her mission was, that there was a possibility she might never return. Chana herself was not ready to face that finality.

A month before, when it looked unlikely that Gyuri would arrive before her own departure, she had written him a long letter, which she now brought with her, wondering whether to give it to her brother:

> I must explain something to you, my Gyurka, I must excuse myself. I must be prepared for that moment when you will stand inside the borders of Eretz waiting for that moment when after six years we finally see each other, when you will ask: "Where is she?"—and they will give you the brief reply: "She isn't. She isn't here."
>
> Will you understand? Will you believe that this was more than a childish love of adventure, more than some youthful romanticism that drove me? Will you sense that I had no choice, I had to do this? There are events that render one's life meaningless, a worthless plaything, or else compel one to action, even if it means sacrificing life.
>
> I'm so afraid, my Gyurka, that passionate feelings will turn into empty slogans. I'm not sure that you will feel behind my words all the doubts and misgivings, the hard struggle that gave birth to the new decision. It's so difficult, because I'm alone. If only there was someone with whom I could discuss this freely and without fear, if I did not have to bear all this burden alone—if I could talk with you. If there is anybody who can understand me, I believe you are one of them. Who knows, though—six years is a long time.

And now Gyuri was sitting in front of her, his face all gentle questioning, and she could not even say what she had written him in December in that unsent letter:

> The day after tomorrow I'm starting on a new project. Perhaps it's foolishness, perhaps it's fantasy, perhaps it's dangerous. Maybe one out of a hundred—maybe one out of a thousand—pays the ultimate price. Sometimes the price is less, sometimes it is more. Don't ask. You will know what I'm talking about.

Gyuri, of course, had no inkling what his sister felt. She told him only that she was forbidden to talk about the training program in Cairo because he was so new to the country and still being treated with suspicion in case he was a German spy. She promised to write more details in a few weeks, or perhaps she would be even back by then. It sounded plausible, and whenever Gyuri asked a question that involved them in the future, Chana quickly deflected it or spoke generally about the wonderful time they would all have after the war.

In truth, Chana did not trust herself to discuss her decision to return to Hungary with the one person she could trust most in Eretz Israel. What if Gyuri thought her plan insane and pleaded with her not to go? He was the only person who might have talked her out of it. She had invested more than a year of her life in the mission; could she give it up on the eve of leaving? Gyuri's opposition and possible arguments would stir up all the doubts she herself had felt, and she did not want to leave carrying his disapproval. It was much easier to avoid the subject; besides, there were so many other things to talk about: plans for Kató's arrival, which might be imminent; advice to Gyuri about life in Eretz and in a kibbutz. In all this, Chana projected a picture of rosy optimism, while trying to balance her comments with a more realistic description of the harsh pioneer life.

Gyuri listened eagerly, both absorbing the information and marveling at this splendid, self-confident, and committed being whom he was proud to call his sister. And even when he could not fail to sense the anxiety underlying her excitement, he was so completely under her spell that he decided to postpone any questions he had until she found the right moment to tell him.

After a few hours of animated discussion, they went together to a send-off party for Chana's group. Her entry was greeted by enthusiastic cheers. Most of the crowd consisted of military men and a few women; apart from the Haganah commanders there were many officials from the Jewish Agency, including Golda Meir and Moshe Sharett, both future prime ministers of Israel.

Chana introduced Gyuri to her Hungarian-speaking comrades: Yoel Palgi, Yonah Rosen, and Peretz Goldstein, who said they felt they knew him intimately, since his sister never stopped talking about him. Chana had already explained to Gyuri that she had arranged for him to spend his first few months in Maagan, where these chaverim were building a kibbutz. Chana felt that this beautiful place by the Sea of Galilee, where life was less difficult than at Sedot Yam, would help Gyuri to acclimatize to Eretz. Later, when he learned Hebrew, he might join her at Sedot Yam or choose whatever life appealed to him.

Gyuri had no plans of his own beyond that day. And he was too tactful to bring up a letter she had written to him about Maagan three years back, giving extensive reasons why she did not want to live in that beautiful place among Hungarians.

Chana made her excuses to leave the party early; she wanted to spend as much time as possible with her brother before leaving for Cairo in the morning. As she and Gyuri were strolling along the Tel Aviv beach in the cool winter night, he heard the familiar whirring of a camera. When he turned around, a young photographer hurried toward them, handing out his card and asking for money to develop his picture. He clearly took them for lovers as they walked in a close embrace. Chana thought it would be nice to have the souvenir, so she paid the man and gave him the address at Maagan, where the picture should be sent. Gyuri had forgotten all about the incident when several weeks later he opened an envelope; in it he found the only photograph of Chana and himself in Eretz Israel.

TWENTY

HOSTILE TERRITORY

Their basic training completed, the Jewish commandos traveled from Palestine to Egypt to practice their parachute jumps and learn espionage from the British. It was the beginning of February 1944 when the thirty volunteers arrived by jeep at the military compound outside Cairo. There they were given comfortable accommodation in real houses, a far cry from the barracks or the tents to which the kibbutzniks had been mostly accustomed. They had been brought together for the last few weeks of intensive training to transform them into a cohesive team so they would act together under pressure. Some met here for the first time; others had known one another since childhood, like Yoel Palgi and Peretz Goldstein, who had emigrated together from the same town in Transylvania and belonged to the same kibbutz as Yonah Rosen.

Yoel had joined the group only in late December. He had regular army experience and was not looking forward to jumping. But Chana put him at ease as soon as they met, lying about how much she had enjoyed her first jump over the Emek. Even before he spoke to her, he noticed her tall, shapely figure in the gray-blue air force uniform, which matched her eyes. But what captivated him completely was her charm and straightforward manner: "All the anxiety I felt that day was suddenly gone, as if it had never existed. I held her hand for a long time. I felt a mystery how this girl could so utterly win my heart from the very first moment."

The courses in espionage training turned through constant repetition the glamorous stuff of spy stories into routine tasks. Chana and her comrades spent weeks learning the Morse alphabet, taking apart and putting together a wireless transmitter, translating ciphers from books, taking clandestine photographs, forging and altering documents. The trainees were given intelligence briefings about the situation in Central Europe and methods of interpreting such information for their own purposes. They were taught to take elementary precautions: how to tell if they were being followed and how to shake off the tail; how to communicate with one another and protect themselves by knowing only what was absolutely necessary for their individual role in the mission. To know more could endanger their comrades or themselves, and the course gave grim details of what could happen to them if things went wrong. They were instructed, if under interrogation by counterintelligence, how to lie, how to conceal or give misleading information; what to do with their equipment, given the time to do anything; what kinds of torture they might expect. Such advice had to remain vague, since no one could predict another's threshold of endurance.

In Cairo the debate continued about the objectives of the mission. The Haganah was inclined to the view that Hitler and his death squads might inflict more destruction in retreat than they did in conquest. If lives were to be saved—Jewish and others—quick and effective action was required to hit the enemy's weak spots. But British Intelligence knew in early 1944 that the Hungarian government was making tentative steps toward disengagement from a lost war. After the devastating destruction of its armies at Voronezh and Stalingrad, a few military and political leaders began to urge that Hungary declare neutrality or follow the Romanian example of switching to the winning side. On January twenty-fourth there was a high-level meeting between Hitler and General Szombathelyi, chief of the Hungarian General Staff, who asked for permission to withdraw his beaten armies from the Soviet Union. This request was repeated on February twelfth by Admiral Horthy, who explained that the troops were needed to defend the Carpathian passes against the Red Army.

With the number of powerful pro-Nazi officials and informers in Budapest, Hitler was only too aware of these moves and he was unlikely to watch idly while losing one of his few remaining allies. He could not ignore the possibility that the jittery Hungarians might deny passage to the retreating Wehrmacht. If he needed more proof, there was Horthy's reluctance to deal with the Jewish problem, which to German eyes was more acute in Hungary than it had ever been in the Reich itself. Hungary's Jews were still permitted to walk about and mix with Aryans, even after emphatic demands from Hitler to the Hungarian government that it take appropriate measures.

All this added urgency to the rescue plans: Hungary was a haven now not only for close to a million Jews, but also for hundreds of Poles, French, Czechs, and other refugees or escaped prisoners of war from defeated countries. In Cairo several plans were put forward to drop commandos into various parts of the country in time to organize effective resistance, which might even forestall occupation by the Germans. But others thought they would be taking an unnecessary risk by entering Hungary this way. The government might have some Anglophile members, but the country as a whole was full of pro-German Fascists. There was no ready-made support group to help the commandos the moment they touched ground, and the Jewish community itself was known to be divided between a Zionist minority and the Jewish mainstream, which supported successive anti-Semitic governments out of patriotism or fear that worse could follow.

On the other hand, almost ideal conditions existed just south of Hungary, in neighboring Yugoslavia, where partisan forces, organized into regular army units, had been fighting the Germans and their Fascist collaborators for a couple of years. They even managed to control large areas of the country, for a long time the only liberated territories in occupied Europe outside of the Soviet Union. The success of the Yugoslav partisans, led by Yosip Tito, was not lost on the Allies. The British in particular had developed wide-ranging contacts with them, making frequent runs of arms, medicine, and food supplies to support them. The Jewish commandos would provide further help by guiding shot-down Allied pilots through partisan territory to the Adriatic coast where they could be picked up by ships or airlifted into liberated parts of Italy.

In selecting Yugoslavia as a staging area for commando operations against Hungary and neighboring countries, the British military minimized the obstacles. Vast areas of difficult and dangerous terrain separated the partisans from the Hungarian border; besides, Yugoslav Jews, who might have helped the mission, had been mostly liquidated with the active cooperation of the local regimes. Sending Jewish commandos into such a situation increased rather than lessened the danger. Yet the British asked the Haganah to find additional volunteers who knew Yugoslavia and the languages there. That is how Reuven Dafni, a native speaker of Serbo-Croatian, joined the group. He was a few years older than the others and had considerable military experience, having already served with the regular British Army.

Like Yoel, Reuven Dafni also noticed Chana at the first meeting of the paratroopers, but he was struck by her sharp questions and firm opinions rather than her appearance. He was surprised to find out afterward that she was not a support staff member, but a comrade on the mission. When they were introduced, Reuven was struck by Chana's enthusiasm, later describing the feeling as being touched by a sacred fire. As he got to know her in different moods, he grew more impressed by her ability to make jokes one moment—her laugh was so contagious that she could even make their Arab driver smile uncomprehendingly—and the next be feverishly planning a tiny detail of their mission.

Now that the mission was moving forward, Chana felt generally optimistic. Her letters to Gyuri, which Yonah carried back to Maagan, were full of enthusiasm and sparse in details: "It is difficult to write at the moment, because everything here is a military secret and I'm worried about the censor. In brief: I'm doing well, there are lots of soldiers here from

Eretz (boys and girls) so I'm not wanting for company. The days are occupied, in the evening we go to the movies, or I stay at home to read. Fortunately I'm staying in town, not the camp, and so I can take advantage of my free time."

In another letter she described a visit to Luxor and the Valley of the Kings, but she was no longer the carefree tourist: "I don't have the patience for such things. It looks like I might be moving from here next week, and I feel the tension of beginning the new project."

Chana spent a great deal of time worrying about Gyuri and how he was finding his new country. Beneath her concern lay the guilt of not being completely honest with him. She saw before her his quizzical face, just before parting, when she impulsively decided to give him the letter she had so painfully composed in case they missed each other. Gyuri gave it only a cursory glance, caught up in their farewell, but Chana knew that he would be rereading it for all the meaning hidden between the lines. She felt she was also letting down her mother once more, by not being there to greet her and even more, by causing her worry. She wrote to Gyuri: "If Mummy arrives in Eretz in my absence, you must try to explain the situation. I know, my dear, that this is a hard task and I don't know how much Mummy will understand my decision. I can't find words to express my pain that I should be causing her anxiety once more, and that we can't be together. All my hope lies in the two of you being reunited soon."

The new phase of the mission, which Chana mentioned mysteriously to Gyuri, began with their leaving Egypt on the thirteenth of March. The commandos were flown on the first leg of their journey to Bari in liberated southern Italy. Five paratroopers were on Chana's plane, including the Italian-born Enzo Sereni, who was excited about returning to his native land. Despite his Zionist commitment, he immediately felt at home on Italian soil. Chana, anticipating her own ambivalent feelings about going home, challenged his forgiving views about the Italian people: had they not supported fascism for two decades? had they not quite recently bombed Tel Aviv? Reuven listened to their argument—how Chana marshaled each point with her uncompromising logic and sent it to do battle with Enzo. She was unwilling to concede a single point, appearing completely sure of herself and of being right. Reuven wondered what it would be like to work with her in the months ahead. When he shared his concern with Enzo, the latter replied, "She may not be the easiest to work with, but then this is no ordinary girl."

During the phases of the mission Chana would come into contact with many new people, some of whom became close comrades, like Reuven and Yoel. Others met her only for a few days or even minutes, and their memories are preserved in verbal snapshots. She affected all of them deeply: the English soldier at the parachute supply depot, who wanted to marry a girl like her; another English officer, in overall charge of the operation, who could barely overcome his astonishment at her self-confidence; and the hard-bitten sergeant-major, a Scotsman, who confided to Reuven, while checking his parachute: "In all these years I've seen hundreds of you chaps, but she is the first girl." An American parachutist who happened to be at the airbase was so moved by seeing her that he went up to her, a complete stranger, and silently shook her hand. Chana gave him her radiant smile, which was so open and appealing that the Yank became flustered and left without a word. Enzo came to say goodbye as they were climbing into the airplane. He shook Chana's hand, too, wishing her luck: "Remember, only those die who want to." They were both to be exceptions to Enzo's maxim within six short months.

The paratroopers took their positions inside the plane. Reuven and Chana faced each other across the front seats immediately next to the hatch. They were crammed, barely able to move in their winter coats, carrying heavy packs and the parachutes on their back. The noise of the engines made conversation impossible. Reuven surveyed the anxious faces of his team members, lost in thought. Then he met Chana's gaze in the semidarkness. Her face was radiant, filled with a childlike smile, the happiness of finally being on the way. She stuck her thumb in the air, as a sign of victory. That image of her would stay with him for the rest of his life.

Despite instruments and the best available reconnaissance maps, flying a military aircraft at night over enemy territory in 1944 was risky at best. The areas controlled by the guerrillas had borders that fluctuated daily with the fortunes of war: they could not be mapped. The slightest change in weather conditions or the angle of the plane when the jump was made could make the difference between landing in safety or fatal trouble.

The wind was stronger than expected on the night of March thirteenth, and perhaps Chana's lighter weight had not been given due consideration. As a result she drifted hundreds of yards off course. As she crashed through the crown of a giant pine, the chute became a giant web trapping her. Her dangling feet sought firm ground, while her arms still clutched the threads that further entangled her. She could not struggle too much for fear of drawing attention to her presence; yet she could not remain exposed and disabled in the air.

It took several minutes for Chana to cut loose and lower herself onto Yugoslav soil. She sat in the dark, rubbing a bruised ankle. For a moment she feared that the fall might have sprained it. She dragged herself to the nearest mound for cover. She could see nothing in the pitch dark, certainly no friendly partisans greeting her with bouquets of flowers as a liberating hero. As she listened to the darkness, she heard no familiar whistles from comrades with whom she was supposed to regroup on the ground. There was only menace in the March wind rustling the treetops. The reality of her loneliness and helplessness was vastly different from what she had imagined so vividly about this moment. All the fears she had managed to suppress now assailed her.

After what seemed like half an eternity she finally heard some cautious footsteps and muffled calls. The sounds were coming closer; maybe remnants of her parachute had been sighted. She hugged the ground and tried to stop breathing, at least until she could make out what language they were speaking. If they were Germans, they might have dogs and she would be lost. If they were friends, they should recognize her British uniform. Chana heard two men stop about ten feet from her. They were standing on the spot where she had fallen and were obviously trying to decide which way she had gone. Like most educated Hungarians, Chana had heard German most of her life; it was not her favorite language but she understood it perfectly and could speak it if she had to. The men were whispering in a tongue that was unfamiliar. From her position she could not see them and it was too dark to make out their uniforms. She took a deep breath and stood up. Instantly the men turned around with guns pointed in her direction.

"Halt!" one of them called out. She stood motionless. With one gun barrel still pointed at her, the other man switched on a flashlight and carefully examined her. Their tone seemed to confirm that she had passed their test. Then, suddenly, the man held the light closer to her hair and became quite excited. He was staring right into Chana's face and muttering something to himself. The other approached and was looking closely at her hair, which fell softly on her jacket collar. They exchanged animated comments, which attracted another patrol searching nearby. There were now four men standing around her, laughing and pointing in a friendly if disconcerting manner. She was sure that they were sharing the discovery that she was female, which seemed to delight and amuse them. And being Balkan men, they did nothing to hide it. Chana learned later that her initial reception was due not so much to her sex as to a wonderment at the inscrutable British for sending such a young girl to help them.

Even though she could not talk to them, Chana felt a huge release of tension. She smiled and said "hello" and they said "hello" back. Then they led her to an improvised encampment, where she was reunited with Reuven and her other comrades. Some of the provisions dropped from their plane had also been spotted; others would have to wait for daylight. The partisans advised that it was best to move on and avoid attracting enemy attention to the spot. Despite their fatigue, they marched several miles through the forest that night. Their first dawn in Yugoslavia brought them to one of the permanent hideouts of the partisans.

The Jewish paratroopers were careful to speak English in front of the partisans. The British held the view that there was one British Army fighting the war against the barbarians, and that it did not matter whether a particular regiment or commando unit was composed of Gurkhas or Jews. Speaking English was safest; in a country where there was active collaboration with the German occupation forces, anti-Semitism among villagers—and possibly even among the partisans—might cause unforeseen and unnecessary complications. The paratroopers themselves felt that an important part of their mission was to represent the Star of David as well as the Union Jack, to let their persecuted brothers and sisters know that armed Jews were coming to their help. In the end, however, the British view won and the commandos spoke Hebrew only among themselves. (Once they were caught talking by one of the partisan women who understood English; Yoel, asked about the language, improvised: "Welsh.")

It might have been equally dangerous for the commandos to reveal that some of them spoke Hungarian. Large areas of Yugoslavia had once belonged to Hungary. The new borders drawn after the First World War left hostile ethnic minorities stranded on both sides. Hitler used the recovery of these territories to induce the Hungarian government to finally join— in April 1941—his war against the world. In January 1942, the Hungarian army occupied the border provinces and allowed the massacre of thousands of Croatians and Jews; this in turn led to Croatian atrocities against Hungarians still living in Yugoslavia.

Reuven Dafni acted as spokesman with the partisans, because he understood their langauge. But even he pretended to know only English when meeting civilians. On occasion it was difficult to keep up the fiction. One day they were visiting a liberated village, and Reuven instantly recognized a woman there: as children they had lived on the same street. How would he hide his identity from a childhood playmate? It turned out she was also Jewish, something her family had concealed; now she gave them firsthand accounts of the horrible sufferings under the occupation. Chana was particularly moved by this incident, an encounter between the Diaspora and the commandos, who brought hope from a new Jewish society to one that lay in ruins.

Six days after their arrival they heard over the wireless that the Germans had occupied Hungary. Not a shot had been fired that Sunday morning and there was no talk of invasion: permission had simply been granted for friendly troops to cross the country. As it turned out, it would take a whole year for the "friends" to be forced out, after they had plundered and destroyed the entire country, decimating its inhabitants.

To the commandos news of the German occupation meant both private anguish for relatives and friends and drastic changes in the mission. Their careful planning over several months had assumed that Hungary could be penetrated, in the absence of German troops and with a government that was warming toward the Allies. Now these plans were destroyed.

Chana cried in her helplessness. Her comrades, who admired her self-control, were shocked to see this articulate, usually cheerful woman shaken with sobbing. They tried to reassure her that the British had promised to get her mother out. Perhaps Mrs. Szenes was already safe in Haifa. But when Chana found the words, her concern was larger than her own immediate family and friends: "What are the Nazis going to do to the one million Jews there?" she cried. "While we're just sitting there, doing nothing. . . ."

TWENTY-ONE

BLESSED IS THE MATCH

From that day, March 19, 1944, Chana knew no rest. With relentless single-mindedness she reminded her comrades of their original mission—the one that motivated the Palmach, Yonah, herself, and all of them. From then on she never smiled; the mission had become a duty she would do mechanically, her eyes continually searching the northern horizon where the border with Hungary lay. Her mind searched desperately for a way to go back to Hungary and do something, anything, in the face of the catastrophe that she sensed was taking shape there.

But the commandos' orders were to stay with the partisans in Yugoslavia. They discussed several alternatives, even reviving the plan for a night drop near Lake Balaton, if they could be airlifted out of the mountains. The idea was radioed in code to their superiors, who, after ignoring the request for days, categorically rejected it as foolhardy.

March turned into April, and Chana was getting more obsessed with the idea of getting into Hungary. Yoel Palgi, who was dropped into Yugoslavia later and rejoined the group after several weeks' separation, found her completely changed from their Cairo days. Chana claimed bitterly that the partisans only took advantage of the paratroopers, and would never help their rescue mission. They faced a common enemy, but the partisans had a much narrower nationalistic agenda. When challenged by her comrades to support her accusations, she snapped at them, as if her opinion alone should be enough to convince them. She was making them uncomfortable. Mindful of the importance of obedience to their superiors, especially in wartime, they staunchly resisted her arguments. At the same time they were afraid that she might persuade them to disobey. She was sowing the seeds of suspicion, giving voice to their own secret fears.

Reuven Dafni watched with growing frustration the girl with the sacred fire turning into ice. He saw his own fear—the one he had expressed to Enzo Sereni in Bari—coming true. Reuven knew that a war could not be won if everybody followed his own instincts. He was in a quandary. He sympathized with Chana's point of view but deplored the disruptive effect she was having on her comrades.

Moreover, as unofficial commander of the group, Reuven worried not only about morale but also about Chana's health. She was visibly wearing herself out with this obsession; her lovely young face looked more haggard each day. She had trouble sleeping, and often woke from horrible nightmares. He tried over and over to reason with her. Sometimes she would concede that their work with the partisans served some useful purpose. Their minor sabotage operations, blowing up trains and ambushing small patrols, were at least causing problems for the Germans. But most of the time they were on the move, evading attacks from the air and land, marching for days on end through the forested mountains and staying only a few hours in a friendly town, to get provisions. What for? Chana wanted to know.

Reuven and Yonah countered that they were rescuing shot-down American pilots who could go back and bomb the Germans. Wasn't that more useful than a small band of them committing suicide in Hungary? Chana, however, saw the situation in reverse: they were committing moral suicide by doing nothing. Behind her logic was a greater conviction that the mere act of going to Hungary would have a tremendous symbolic value. It was not what they themselves could achieve that mattered, but the inspiration and strength their presence might give to Jews there to fight and defend themselves.

In her desperation, she used every opportunity and all her reasoning skills to convert her companions to her view. And she was succeeding. Yoel, who had been resistant to her previous arguments, now began to listen:

Chana suddenly got up and asked me to go for a walk. As we did, she began to pour her heart out. She was really saying all the same things we had heard before. But this evening she put it in a completely different way. This wasn't the cold person who didn't want to listen to anybody else's opinions. This was a young woman talking, with a feminine passion that was deeper than ours. She talked about her inner struggles, and how she felt she couldn't wait any longer. She realized that she did not always have logic on her side, but this was not the time for logic. She said: "It's better to die to ease our conscience than to go back home without having tried. We're all free and have the right to act in whatever way is right and true for ourselves. This is a matter of conscience, outside of military discipline." I seized her hand and said: "Let's go!"

It was obvious that Chana would have gone alone, but everybody felt uneasy about letting her do that. The partisans claimed that all their contacts in the border regions had evaporated following the German occupation and the only traffic with Hungary was through smugglers. The commandos decided to head toward the border and began several weeks of arduous marches, during which they continued to carry out sabotage operations with different partisan units along the way. The Palestinian commandos usually carried sealed letters of recommendation to new partisan units issued by the group they just left. On one occasion they failed to locate a particular unit and Reuven, before destroying the letter, opened it and translated its contents:

> We're sending to you British officers, one of whom knows our language thoroughly; the others are beginning to understand it. Be careful what you say in their presence; talk only about the enemy, nothing about ourselves. They are heading toward the Hungarian border. Do not help them with our units there. Let them work with the smugglers.

Understandably, the partisans were mainly interested in any help they could get from the British, and not in any reciprocal aid to them. As Communists, they felt much closer to the Soviet Union than to the Western Allies. They were fighting a desperate war of national liberation against a foreign occupation force and its local puppets. As long as this strange and somewhat naive group of idealists who had arrived by parachute could persuade the British to keep dropping supplies to them, they were welcome. When the visitors shifted their interest to Hungary, which was after all fighting on the German side, the partisans grew uncooperative.

The Palestinian group now shared Chana's cold fury at being used. Again they discussed the possibility of asking the British to drop them directly into Hungary. In the end they decided to mount their own mission and cross the border with two small units in separate places to double their chances of success. Chana was to go first with Yoel and Peretz Goldstein. Reuven would follow later with Yonah Rosen and a man named Abba Berdichev. The rest would stay in Yugoslavia as a logistical base and backup: contact would be through wireless in code.

Another sixty miles of hostile territory lay between them and the Hungarian border. It took twenty-six days of endless marches and backtracking—the rest of May and the first week of June—to get within striking distance. With each day, Chana's heart bled away drop by drop. As new problems arose, the plans had to be changed. Yoel and Peretz had veered off toward the east; they were going to create an alternate route for Jewish escapees, via their native Transylvania. The Romanians were now eager to switch their allegiance to the Allies, which would make the rescue mission easier.

Before they parted, Chana and Yoel discussed different strategies for contacting each other in Budapest. The safest place would be the most obvious, they agreed, so they decided to meet in front of the central synagogue on the corner of Dohány-utca. They would come there after Shabbat service every week until they met. In case such services were no longer permitted, they arranged a Sunday rendezvous in front of the Roman Catholic basilica on Szent István-tér. Yoel was also going to contact Dr. Rezső Kasztner at the Jewish Rescue Organization in Budapest. He was a lawyer and long-time family friend from their native town of Kolozsvár in Transylvania.

Their partisan guides led Chana, Reuven, and Yonah into the border region. Once there, true to their instructions, they refused to offer further help. The Palestinians established their own contact with the smugglers, who had just brought out a small band of eight refugees, including a strange character who called himself Albert. He was an older man who spoke in Hungarian, while claiming to be a British agent and bringing a proposal from former Prime Minister Miklós Kállay about setting up in London a Hungarian government in exile. He was trying to get to Istanbul; there was an obscure connection between his mission and the fact that the former head of the Hungarian government had been hiding out at the Turkish embassy in Budapest since the day of the German occupation.

The group included two escaped French prisoners of war and two Jewish boys from Budapest with connections in the Zionist underground. One, who spoke fluent Hebrew, was called Kallós. He belonged to the Shomer Hatzair movement, and had already made his aliyah. He worked two years in Eretz Israel, and then returned to Budapest to help others emigrate. The only person he managed to rescue was his friend Fleischmann, a stocky young man with blue eyes. On their journey south they met one of the fleeing Frenchmen, Antonin Tissandier, whom they called Tony. He had escaped seven times from prisoner-of-war camps and had spent the past two years hiding out in Budapest. Now he planned to join the Free French forces fighting in various areas of Europe and North Africa. The one woman in the group was a Jewish girl of Chana's age who was escaping with forged papers.

The tale they told of Jewish suffering exceeded anything Chana and the commandos could have imagined and confirmed their worst fears. Everybody knew, of course, about atrocities committed by the Germans and their local collaborators. But it was the systematic ghettoization of every single Jew in every town and village, before deportation to Poland, that filled them with despair. The details these refugees gave of the roundups of hundreds of thousands of people, their kidnaping from their homesteads and communities where they had lived for generations—all this was simply beyond comprehension. And as they talked about it, two or three transports were still leaving Hungary each day, every transport carrying twelve thousand people packed into cattle cars. In another week, another eighty-four thousand people might be gone. There were already no Jews known to be free anywhere in rural Hungary, and those in Budapest were forced to wear a yellow star and suffered new restrictions daily. Everybody was waiting for the doom that would surely come.

Chana could listen to such accounts no more. A low moan from the depth of her frustration turned into a howl of rage. She told Reuven she could not wait another day, even if she were court-martialed on the spot. She begged passionately that they all go immediately and save as many people as they could.

Reuven responded with caution. They were out of radio contact with their British command post, and he thought it important to check out Istanbul Albert's identity. After all, high-level pressures might stop the killings more effectively than any action they could take. The group decided to send Yonah east to the Papuk Mountains, where Yoel and Peretz were assumed to be in touch with the British. At the same time, these three commandos could explore alternative routes for entering Hungary.

But Chana would not wait for Yonah to get word back to them. Instead, she talked three men in the group into taking her back into Hungary. Kallós and Fleischmann hoped that, with the commandos' aid, they might rescue their families. Tissandier saw fresh hope for eight hundred French prisoners of war held in and around Budapest. The Jewish girl offered her forged papers to Chana.

Reuven decided to wait for Yonah and the instructions he might bring. He felt deeply unhappy about Chana's improvised arrangements and was especially concerned about the lack of contact with peasants on the other side of the border. The commandos had no clear idea of how the local population felt toward the Germans, the British, or the Jews. Reuven had heard of no large-scale resistance movement since the occupation in March, and the gently rolling, open countryside in southern Hungary made guerrilla warfare nearly impossible. To Reuven's eyes Chana would be going into hostile territory with no support system or contacts; she could not rely on help until she arrived in Budapest.

On the other hand he failed to make Chana reconsider. She saw each word of advice as a delaying tactic, as yet one more attempt to talk her out of her mission. Finally, Reuven accompanied her small band of volunteers on the last leg of the march to a village where the partisans had reluctantly agreed to help them cross. They discussed the code words that would identify messages from Chana: Hakibbutz Hameuchad, Sedot Yam, and Caesarea. They were to use code names assigned in Cairo; Reuven was "Geri" and Chana was "Hagar," the name for Hungary in medieval Jewish texts.

During this same conversation, Chana asked Reuven if he had any cyanide tablets. She had no fear of death in the abstract, but she began to worry about how she might react under torture. Cyanide would give her some control, an alternative. Reuven considered her request and then refused. Under the circumstances he felt that such defeatist thinking might further jeopardize the slender chances of the mission. Chana remembered a scene in Cairo with Yoel and Enzo Sereni during their training. After being urged by their instructor to see a movie with some grisly torture scenes, Enzo had suggested that they take cyanide with them, feeling that no one could hold out against the Gestapo's torture. Yoel would have none of it. He stomped out of the room, refusing to listen to such defeatist talk. In those days, Chana had agreed with Yoel. She could not imagine taking her own life.

Reuven felt a turmoil of emotions, seeing this young girl, full of life, venture forth into vast danger that she clearly underestimated. It did not matter that she had asked to take that responsibility on herself. He could not help her, but he was not going to aid her suicide. What if she panicked and misjudged the situation? What if she swallowed the poison and there were other ways out? He felt angry with himself for doing so little to prevent her from going.

Chana asked Reuven to stay in the village. She did not want him to take any unnecessary risks. The local partisan unit that was going to guide her back to the Hungarian border arrived at seven in the evening, instructing Chana's group to be ready within fifteen minutes. Now that she was nearing her goal, Chana's customary cheerfulness returned. In this last quarter of an hour she radiated the same calm Reuven remembered from their first meeting. In her old bantering tone she joked with Reuven about the near future, when the war would finally be over and all of them safely back in Eretz Israel: "I've got this terrific idea. Why don't we stay together for a while and rent one of those big tour buses from the Egged company? We could visit all our kibbutzim and tell tall tales about our heroic exploits. We will party up and down the whole country from Dan to Beer Sheva and have a grand old time, don't you think?"

She laughed, her enthusiasm brooking no contradiction. Reuven walked to the end of the village with Chana and her rag-tag companions, this tiny band that was about to take on the Third Reich. He insisted that they walk in the opposite direction from her destination; it was best if the villagers did not know which way they went, in case they were questioned.

As she shook hands with Reuven, Chana, embarrassed as she usually was when her emotions took over, took out a carefully folded piece of paper and gave it to him.

"Here. Just in case . . ."

"What is it?"

"It's a poem."

"A poem? Now . . . ?"

"I want you to have it." And she was gone, catching up with the others. Just at the end of the road she swung around and waved a final "shalom" to him before she turned the corner, her steps bouncy, almost dancing, and disappeared into the dusk.

Reuven stood by the road, his fist clenched with emotion. He was still angry with her. His doubts about her military competence assailed him: was this a commando who had coolly estimated the risks, or a hopeless romantic, scribbling verses in these last minutes instead of studying maps? Reuven felt so disgusted that he barely noticed crumpling the piece of paper that was still in his hand. Poetry . . . ! And he threw the ball of paper into a roadside bush.

He slept badly that night. His mind was tortured with images of Chana and apprehensions about her fate. He rose early the next morning and went for a walk. Without noticing, he stood near the spot where he had shaken Chana's hands for the last time. As he recollected the scene, he was seized by shame. Even if not all soldiers wrote poetry on a mission, this was a keepsake, something precious that a comrade had entrusted to him—and not just anybody, but this enchanting and quite extraordinary girl. And he had thrown it away! Frantically he began to search the bushes, which all looked alike now. And then he saw something like a cottonwood flower caught on a branch. Very gently Reuven untangled it, smoothed out the crumpled page, which had been torn from a notebook, and read the four lines:

> Blessed is the match consumed in kindling flame.
> Blessed is the flame that burns in the secret fastness
> of the heart.
> Blessed is the heart with strength to stop its beating
> for honor's sake.
> Blessed is the match consumed in kindling flame.

[Translated by Marie Syrkin.]

TWENTY-TWO

CATASTROPHE

When Chana set out toward the border, she was for all practical purposes alone. Her only companions on the mission—once planned for thirty highly trained commandos—were three refugees whom she had just met. She could not be sure whether they would really risk going all the way back to Budapest, and she could not discount the possibility that one or more among them might be working for the Germans. Kallós and Fleischmann had limited experience of clandestine work within the Jewish underground. Tissandier had French military training and was obviously resourceful, but no spy. If caught, his accent would give him away immediately. But the main problem, as Reuven rightly foresaw, was the lack of local contacts. It took Chana several hours to persuade the partisans to help her cross the border. With great reluctance they finally agreed to guide the little band to the river Drava, where a local fisherman took them across. Not far beyond lay the border and the village where the smugglers might help them to get to Budapest. The partisans would wait a few days at an agreed place, in case Chana and her companions managed to send back some forged papers for their use. But that was all they were willing to do.

On the night of the seventh of June the four of them set out for the Yugoslav-Hungarian border, carrying on their shoulders the sum total of the Allied rescue effort at that moment to save the Jews of Hungary. Using a compass and a map that Kallós had brought with him, they tried to find the border village of Murska where the smugglers lived. It was not a very good map and they disagreed about their own location. Because the territory was so often disputed between two countries, each side used its own names for every village, river, and landmark. Some of these were similar in Hungarian and Croatian; more often new names were deliberately chosen. As a result, almost from the start they were lost.

After several hours they realized that they had been going in circles. Finally they reached a fair-sized river, which surprised Kallós; he could not recall anything except small streams in this area. This looked like a branch of the Drava, in which case the village they sought—and the road to Budapest—still lay on the other side. They walked upstream for more than two hours in the dark, hoping to find the ford he remembered so clearly. There had been heavy rain in recent days and the river was near flooding. They saw no boats, and no bridges were indicated on the map. They would have to swim across the river without getting their essential equipment wet. Chana was preoccupied with keeping the transmitter dry. Tissandier had tried to persuade her to leave it behind, arguing that it would be hard to explain if anyone stopped them for questioning. She insisted it was a vital part of the mission: the only immediate contact with her comrades, the British Army, and anybody else who could provide help.

She carefully removed the wireless from its leather carrying case and took it apart as she had been taught in Egypt. Then they quickly undressed and bundled the radio parts and their weapons into the clothes. It was obvious that they would have to cross several times, using one arm to hold the baggage above their heads and the other to swim against the strong current. Holding each other's hands in the dark, they felt their way into the frigid water. It cut into Chana's flesh like a surgical knife; the pain created instant numbness. She remembered the pleasure of wading into the gentle decline of Lake Balaton on a hot summer day, with her cousins Évi and Pali squealing with delight and shouting mutual encouragement. Then she pictured Gyuri treading water out in the distance, daring her to swim out to him. The splendid backdrop of vine-covered hills faded into the bright contrast of desert and water. It was the Kinneret and the Golan, where she imagined Gyuri working now in the kibbutz. She felt happy that there was such a place and that her brother was safe there.

Four times they swam back and forth. When they got everything across they were so exhausted that they needed half an hour's rest. They huddled in the cold moonlight and listened to the sound of their teeth chattering.

It was time to move on. After they crossed four small streams, Kallós was sure that one more stream would bring them to the border. Tissandier wanted to turn back before it got light and they would be forced to hide for the entire day or risk discovery by border patrols. Chana would not hear of it. As she reassembled the wireless, looking for the missing headphones, she was beginning inwardly to agree with the Frenchman that they should have left the equipment behind, but she was not yet ready to admit that she might have been wrong about the whole mission.

The first streak of dawn painted the eastern sky. It was too late now to turn back. Cold and wet, they gritted their teeth and kept marching. When the sun rose, they decided to hide for a while in the bush. All was quiet and peaceful, a glorious morning in early June. Then they glimpsed a small village less than two miles ahead. Kallós was sure that this was the place where they had met the smugglers. It meant that they had already crossed the border into Hungary without realizing it.

They decided that Kallós and Fleischmann should go down to the village, as they were native Hungarians and somewhat familiar with the area. Chana and Tissandier would wait for them in the clump of bushes. For a moment Kallós hesitated about leaving them. If they were caught, Tissandier could get along in Hungarian with his funny accent, but what if they questioned this Englishwoman? Chana had spoken only in English to Kallós, and with Tony she used French. She never talked to Fleischmann, who had no other languages. As far as they knew, she did not understand a word of their native tongue.

"If it comes to that, I guess I'll have to manage in Hungarian," Chana interrupted their deliberations with her perfect and accentless Hungarian. The three men were astonished by this seeming miracle and began to wonder about all the dirty stories they had told in her presence.

Chana and Tony hid their equipment and extra baggage in a nearby cornfield. Chana was still shivering but there was no dry clothing left. She noticed too late that behind them and not very far away a road wandered up the hillside, exposing them to observation from above. They should have chosen a safer hiding place, but now that this was their rendezvous with the other two, they could not move very far. All they could do was to lie motionless, flat on their stomachs. Several hours passed, and Chana's body stiffened as her uneasiness grew.

Suddenly Tissandier raised his head, and ducked back down. He saw a detail of soldiers heading toward them and recognized their uniforms: they were Germans.

Fearing the worst, Chana and the Frenchman started to crawl in the opposite direction, where they believed the border lay. They felt they must be still quite close to it and a wooded area was only a few hundred yards away. If the soldiers passed, they could wait for their companions more safely there and go back to retrieve the wireless later. At that point they saw another troop also leaving the road for the fields, cutting off their escape. It became clear that there were still more soldiers in the woods, methodically sweeping the undergrowth. Chana and Tony were surrounded in a tightening ring of about two hundred German soldiers.

With lightning speed they buried their weapons and cast off anything that could give away their identity. Then they moved from that spot as far as they could. By now they could clearly hear the commands in German. There was hallooing all around them, as if the hounds had picked up the scent of their quarry. Fueled by adrenaline and having escaped seven times from German camps, Tony grabbed Chana and forced her down to the ground.

"*Vite, vite,* we must be lovers, we must kiss!" and he threw her down on the ground. When the soldiers found them a few seconds later, Tony's head was in her lap and she was playing with his hair. Chana at least did not have to pretend her embarrassment.

There was nothing intrinsically wrong with the idea of two lovers frolicking in the woods on a June morning. It would have made a charming picture in peacetime. The very same picture, however, took on quite a different meaning from the perspective of a wary German sergeant fighting a losing war and searching for dangerous partisans near the frontier. Tony and Chana were still sitting on the ground as two section leaders argued about taking them in.

"Are these the people we're looking for?"

"Why don't we take them?" suggested the other commander. "If we're wrong, they can always come back here and resume where they left off."

Even though the Germans were not sure whom they had caught, Chana and Tissandier knew the game was over. Any doubts they might have had ended when they were taken into the village and learned what had become of their companions.

Kallós and Fleischmann were right about the village, but the smugglers had already left for work. Their wives, not wishing to attract attention, told the visitors to come back in the evening. As Kallós and Fleischmann were heading back to rejoin Chana and Tony, they saw two rural policemen heading toward them. The fugitives could have turned and fled, but as this might have activated a search of the entire neighborhood, they decided to continue walking casually. The gendarmes stopped them to check their papers. Although everything seemed to be in order, the older sergeant decided to invite them to the station for brief questioning. This was an old trick of the Hungarian gendarmes: if suspects came along willingly, the police would let them go. Otherwise they would proceed with a more thorough checkup.

Kallós and Fleischmann were armed with automatic pistols; as yet they had not been searched. The road was deserted, except for a few peasants working in the distant fields. It would have been relatively easy for them to shoot the two policemen—who were walking a few feet behind—before the latter had a chance to aim their rifles. Fleischmann signaled secretly to Kallós with his finger, as if he had it around an imaginary trigger, and then he put his hand into his pocket to reach for his weapon. He saw Kallós do the same, but at the same time Fleischmann heard one of the policemen whisper to the other that they should let the two go after another hundred yards.

Fleischmann relaxed and even took his hand out of his pocket. Before he could glance sideways to see whether his friend had heard the whisper, a deafening report startled him. In an instant he was grabbed from behind in an iron grip and both hands and feet were manacled. As he was swung around, he saw an appalling scene: Kallós had panicked, and instead of aiming at the police, he had shot himself in the head. Blood was trickling from the temples as his body writhed in its final agonies. His revolver lay in the dust next to him.

After a few minutes several peasants who had heard the shot reached the scene. One of them, a young Croatian who spoke Hungarian poorly, told the police, "Over there, beyond the road, I saw another two partisans hiding in the bushes."

The other peasants kept silent in disapproval. They assumed that the unfortunate guerrillas had come to fight against the Hungarians. Even the Fascist sympathizers among them were nationalists first. The two lawmen searched Fleischmann and confiscated the two pistols in his pockets. All his other possessions lay scattered on the ground. The news of a larger partisan operation galvanized them. The older sergeant dispatched his man for reinforcements. He wanted to search the area where the guerrillas were hiding, so that when the German troops came he could have the glory of conducting them to the spot. He could already imagine the promotion that would surely come his way for destroying this vast international conspiracy.

Some of the peasants were pressed into service to guard Kallós's body and the manacled Fleischmann until the police returned with soldiers, border guards, and detectives. The newly assembled troops began to fan out and surround the brush to which the peasant boy had pointed. Meanwhile the detectives rifled Kallós's pockets, where they found, much to Fleischmann's horror, the headset to Chana's wireless.

In less than half an hour Chana and Tony had been found and brought to the scene. Although she could not know how Kallós had died, and she refused to recognize Fleischmann, Chana could see that her mission had ended in a brutally swift disaster. Everything she had dreamed about in the past year and a half, everything she had trained for, had come to an end within the first day and within a few hundred yards of the border.

The three survivors of the mission were taken to police headquarters in Szombathely, the nearest town. They were carefully separated, so Chana did not know what her tormentors had learned from her two companions. They beat her while grilling her about the wireless; she denied any knowledge of it. Then they produced the headset, which they said they had found on Fleischmann. She fell into their trap. She could not let Fleischmann take the blame for her own mistake in bringing in the equipment, so she admitted that the radio was hers and offered to lead them back to the woods where it was hidden. If she had known that the headset had been actually found on Kallós, she could have pretended ignorance and blamed it on the dead man.

After her confession she was taken outside by the guards, where two disfigured creatures were waiting. Chana could hardly recognize her two comrades, whom she had last seen two days before. They looked barely human. Fleischmann's face was completely black and he could barely move. Tissandier's head was one mass of wounds; most of the hair had been torn out by the handfuls. He was entirely toothless. Chana wondered what she herself must look like, although she suspected she had been treated relatively gently. She was tormented, however, because she could not explain to them about the headset and feared that her comrades would think that she had cracked under torture and had given them away.

When Chana's band and their armed escort arrived back at the scene of their capture, Chana saw that several acres of young crops had been completely ruined by the stampeding soldiers. She did not have to wonder long whether their belongings had been discovered. An army jeep that was heading toward them stopped, and a Hungarian officer of the border patrol pointed triumphantly at the familiar carrying case with the radio inside. They had found it without her confession.

The radio was useless without the cipher and Chana knew that she would be tortured to divulge the code, which was based on certain words contained in an innocent-looking volume of French lyric poetry. She still had the book and she had to get rid of it fast without being noticed. The officer drove them to the railway station where they would be taken to Budapest under guard; international espionage required higher echelons than mere border patrol or local police. As Chana got out of the jeep, she left the book of verse on the seat.

They occupied a separate compartment on the train, the prisoners sitting between the guards. It was impossible to talk. The blinds were drawn against curious passengers in the corridor. As Chana looked at the varied countryside of her native land, she felt completely numb. The physical pain was dwarfed by the overwhelming sensation of failure and shame. She would never again be able to face the chaverim, even if she survived this ordeal. The candle of her hope had been extinguished during the past two days; all she wished now was that the rest of her could die. She asked to be taken to the toilet. After some crude joking between the guards, one of them shoved her roughly into the corridor. People were squatting on suitcases or standing everywhere, and it was a struggle to get to the end of the car. Chana felt curious eyes peering at her. If they had any sympathy to offer, she could not feel it. The toilet was occupied and as she waited Chana looked down at the speeding track below. If only she could open the door and jump, all this agony would be over. She tried to undo the bolt, but the guard was quick in stopping her. Defeated again, she was dragged back to the stuffy compartment. Her two comrades looked at her with eyes completely barren of hope.

In Budapest they were taken to the military prison on Horthy Miklós-út. Here the old tortures continued, and new ones were tried. Rózsa, a tall brutal civilian who conducted the interrogations with the aid of several thugs, did not believe she had left the cipher book next to the radio. Why was it not found there? Perhaps it was something she and her friends had memorized? Chana's only comfort was that without the cipher the enemy could not use the transmitter to entice Allied planes into a trap. Whatever she knew depended on the book with the French poems. No matter how much or how long they tortured her, she could not confess to something she did not know. The same went for Fleischmann and Tissandier, whose howls of anguish reached her from the cells below.

Unfortunately, the cipher was not the only information Rózsa wanted. Chana still had not confessed to her real identity, and the papers she had borrowed from the Jewish girl at the border did not stand up to close inspection. So who was she? Whom did she know in Budapest? She was beaten for several hours. Her face swelled up, so that her fingertips found its terrain completely unfamiliar. One of her front teeth had been knocked out and several others were loose.

Still Chana refused to give in, offering another invented name instead. She was grateful for the brief respite this won from her tormentors. But in two hours they dragged her from her cell again. They had found out that she had lied again. Now they attacked her with renewed fury. During that brief pause, with her mind barely functioning, she tried to work out a different strategy. It was likely, she thought, that the British had carried out their promise to get her mother out, just in case of such a situation. Kató must have joined Gyuri by now in Eretz Israel. So what harm would come from giving her real name? She remembered the warm smile that her father's name brought to people's faces, recalling all the pleasure "The Coal-man" had given them through his plays and newspaper columns. Maybe these brutes would suddenly turn friendly if they heard that she was the daughter of Béla Szenes. So, from the depth of her tormented nightmare, Chana made another terrible mistake. She told them who she was.

TWENTY-THREE

PRELUDE TO AUSCHWITZ

The German occupation of Hungary in the early hours of March 19, 1944, caught the Jewish community unprepared for the predictable catastrophe. By then Hitler had ruled Germany for eleven years, neighboring Austria and Czechoslovakia for six years, and had been devastating the whole of Europe for five years. Since 1938, the Hungarian government had imposed specific laws restricting economic and professional activities by Jews. The legal measures culminated with the Third Jewish Law, which took effect in August 1941, forbidding intermarriage between Jews and Christians and defining Jews in racial terms borrowed from the vocabulary of the Third Reich. To win exemption, Jews had to prove that they had converted to Christianity before August 1919 and that their family had come to Hungary before 1848. The new law extended discrimination to another hundred thousand people whose families were baptized for political reasons or had become assimilated one or two generations before. At the time of the Third Jewish Law some eighteen thousand Jewish refugees were expelled from Hungary and slaughtered near Kamenets-Podolski by death squads that included Hungarian troops. Still more refugees kept flooding into the country, reporting on the ghettoes and mass murders in every country occupied by the Germans. Hungarian soldiers serving on the Eastern front told of unimaginable atrocities by the German death squads and their collaborators; almost sixty-five thousand Hungarian Jews had already perished in forced labor battalions.

Still, by early 1944 the Jews of Hungary had good reason to hope that they would survive relatively unscathed. They had escaped mass ghettoization and deportation, and the Jewish population constituted such a large part of the country's economy that its removal seemed wholly impracticable. Indeed this was the opinion of Döme Sztójay, who was installed as prime minister after the occupation. Just a few days before, when he was still the Hungarian ambassador to Berlin, he complained to Herr Ribbentrop, foreign minister of the Third Reich, that "if Germany had as many Jews as Hungary, they would not have been able to go so far in solving the Jewish problem as they had."

Another concrete reason for optimism was that the war had decisively turned against Hitler and his allies. Time was running out on the Nazis, and Hungarian Jewish leaders said to each other: "It took the Germans two years to deport the seventy thousand Jews from Slovakia. We have more than ten times that number." Their hopes were fed by uncensored news from neutral and Allied sources. As early as the spring of 1943 the government of Miklós Kállay had decided to relax censorship, trying to build domestic support for withdrawing the beaten Hungarian armies from the Eastern front. When Mussolini was deposed, Budapest immediately recognized the new Italian government despite German displeasure, but the collision with the German allies was set in full motion when Kállay tried unilaterally to withdraw Hungarian troops from the Soviet Union.

By February 1944, there were unusual German troop concentrations on the Austrian border with Hungary. The Germans claimed that the regular routes to the Eastern front were congested; perhaps they might send some divisions through Hungary?

In early March Hitler learned about secret negotiations between the Hungarian Foreign Ministry and some high-ranking Allied commanders. On March fifteenth, his ambassador in Budapest—Dietrich von Jagow— invited Admiral Horthy, head of state, and top members of the Kállay government for an urgent consultation about the withdrawal of the Hungarian army. Kállay decided not to attend. Horthy met with Hitler at Klesheim Castle on the morning of March eighteenth; "Operation Margarethe," the occupation plan for Hungary, had been set in motion a week before. Hitler demanded that Horthy dismiss the Kállay government, order a general mobilization to support the Reich, censor the press, and liquidate both native and foreign Jews in Hungary. When Horthy refused, Hitler banged the table and screamed, "We'll occupy Hungary!"

"We'll resist!" Horthy replied.

In fact, Horthy was now a prisoner of Hitler, having been betrayed by his own pro-German generals. By the time he was released, the Germans had occupied all points of strategic importance in the country, and the chief of staff had given orders not to resist. Horthy finally arrived back in Hungary on the morning of the nineteenth, to find himself governor in name only. The Germans had the country under tight control in a matter of hours and that day the Gestapo began arresting liberal politicians from well-prepared lists.

On the morning of the occupation, the assembly of the Jewish Religious Community was meeting in a hall next to the great synagogue. As part of regular business it approved various budgetary items and paid tribute to

Lajos Kossuth, the great Hungarian patriot and freedom fighter, on the fiftieth anniversary of his death. Emissaries from the SS came that afternoon to the community offices, politely requesting a meeting with representative members of the entire Jewish community. During the next two days, Obersturmbannführer Hermann Krumey and Hauptsturmführer Dieter von Wisliceny, both of the SS, sought to reassure the Jewish leadership that they could avoid harm if they cooperated with the occupying forces. There would be certain restrictions, as one could expect in wartime, but the Germans hoped that the Jews would continue the practice of their religion and enjoy their educational and cultural institutions. The SS officers urged the immediate establishment of a central Council of Jews that would act as liaison between the German authorities and all Hungarian Jews. They suggested Samu Stern, the respected head of the Jewish congregation in Pest, as president. The new council would coordinate the smooth execution of all the new regulations. Some of the Jewish leaders had heard about the *Judenrat* in various occupied countries, but surely this was different. No mention had been made of ghettoes or of camps, and these German officers were very polite in their requests.

The two hundred representatives of the Jewish community left the meeting reassured that life would go on much the same way as before. Their optimism continued for several weeks, despite frequent arrests and brutal treatment, arbitrary harassment, and confiscation. The endless flood of promised restrictions and regulations was designed to divide the community and to foster false hope, and it succeeded brilliantly. For example, when the wearing of the yellow star became mandatory for Jews, the Germans immediatly exempted "important" Jews, such as members of the Jewish Council and their relatives and protégés, from this mark of humiliation. At the same time the Council was made responsible for selling the regulation-size stars—four inches in diameter—to all other Jews. Occasionally the Germans made a great show of releasing suspects at the Council's intervention, and they were always receptive to ransom and bribes. Such techniques fostered the false idea that the Jewish Council was a powerful organization, while deflecting resentment of the decrees to the Council, which was forced to administer them.

By the end of March, Obersturmbannführer Adolf Eichmann, called "the master" by Gestapo chief Heinrich Himmler, had installed himself in the Hotel Majestic in Buda to begin the crowning achievement of his career, the liquidation of Hungary's Jews. Eichmann, who was put in charge of executing the "final solution" soon after it was adopted in January 1942 at Wannsee, had already made careful arrangements with Rudolf Höss, commandant at Auschwitz, to build extra ovens to accommodate the huge influx of Hungarian Jews. He came now to oversee the massive operation that would render Hungary free of Jews in the shortest possible time. He would start with the eastern provinces already threatened by the Red Army and finish with Budapest, where he faced the greatest danger of resistance. Desperately short of manpower, the Germans were determined to prevent a repetition of the Warsaw ghetto uprising.

So Eichmann, too, called in the Jewish leaders for a friendly chat; he dazzled them with his thorough knowledge of Jewish customs, his seeming respect for religious observances, and his impeccable manners. He took charge of negotiating with them, but he quickly realized that his subordinates and rival predators—both German and Hungarian—had already confiscated and looted a lion's share of Jewish wealth. To the Nazi mind, international Jewry had an inexhaustible supply of money and power: Eichmann decided to seek out the Zionists who still had contacts with the West.

The Zionist groups in Hungary had always been small, and since they chiefly advocated emigration to Palestine their numbers continued to dwindle; since 1939 about six thousand had left. From the end of 1942, the Palestine Aid and Rescue Committee (Vaadat Ezra Vö-Hazalah) had maintained an office in Istanbul; it collected money from Jews in the free world to help those trying to flee Europe. The Hazalah's local office in Budapest was run by a small group of Zionists, including Ottó Komoly, Dr. Rezső Kasztner, and Joel (Jenő) Brand. Although Komoly was best known in the Jewish community, the Rescue Committee's dominant personality and financial manager was Dr. Kasztner, an ambitious lawyer and ex-journalist from Kolozsvár in Transylvania, where both Yoel Palgi and Peretz Goldstein had been family friends. Joel Brand was a businessman who fled from Germany to Budapest in 1935. He was Kasztner's man on the committee.

Just as Eichmann was looking for the Zionists, Kasztner was looking for him. Like Eichmann, Kasztner thought in grand terms, but his ambition was a worthy one: he wanted to save all the Jews of Hungary, and believed he was clever enough to win against Eichmann and the Third Reich. The Jewish Council had quickly run out of bribe money, but Kasztner had access to foreign funds, so he kept his own counsel, made his own plans. He wanted to save one million Jews by himself.

Eichmann's ambition was the opposite: he wanted the glory of killing every one of Hungary's million Jews. He too was a clever and secretive man, and he had many more trump cards than Kasztner. But Kasztner gave him what he needed most—time and secrecy to put his plan into effect. During April the Jews in all the provinces of Hungary were forced into detention camps and ghettoes, having been reassured by the Jewish Council and their rabbis that no harm would come to them.

In May, just before the deportations to Auschwitz began, Eichmann made a grandiose offer through the Aid and Rescue Committee. He told Kasztner and Brand that he would be prepared to let all one million Jews in Hungary go free in exchange for certain goods the Germans needed from the West: two hundred tons of tea, eight hundred tons of coffee, two million boxes of soap, ten thousand trucks, and a few unspecified strategic minerals. Brand was to take this offer to the Hazalah office in Istanbul and try to get the rich and powerful Jews of the West to persuade the Allies to make this deal in order to save the last Jewish community of Europe. Eichmann said that if Brand's negotiations showed progress he would be prepared to halt the deportations; until then they would proceed.

Only complete desperation in the face of complete annihilation could give credence to such an offer. And of course the situation in Hungary was just that. But the proposal also had what Eichmann knew would appeal to Kasztner: it even mentioned the magic figure of one million Jews. So Joel Brand, a little man of no particular standing among the Jews of Hungary or the rest of the world, was driven to Vienna in a Gestapo car, where he stayed as a guest of the Gestapo; he took the plane to Istanbul carrying a German passport and was accompanied there by Bandi Grosz, a well-known Gestapo spy. Eichmann took no chances that the Brand mission might actually succeed.

The same day that Brand left Budapest, the first train with Hungarian Jews reached Auschwitz. The sealed cattle cars, each crammed with one hundred Jews, pulled up right next to the gas chambers: of the four thousand in that transport seventeen were sent into the camp, the rest were immediately gassed to death and their corpses were burned. From the next train, twenty women were directed to the barracks; the rest were killed. And so it went on: each and every day twelve thousand Hungarian Jews were slaughtered.

During this time Joel Brand was sitting in a hotel in Istanbul still trying to reach somebody important with Eichmann's offer. The American ambassador in Ankara seemed interested, but the Allies understandably did not take the offer seriously; helping the Germans at this stage of the war with strategic supplies was out of the question, and where would they put one million Jews? On June fifth, Brand was finally instructed to come to Aleppo to meet with representatives of the Jewish Agency. He arrived in Syria the next day, D-Day, and was promptly arrested. After his release four and a half months later, the British did not permit him to return to Budapest.

On June seventh, the same day Chana crossed the Hungarian border, the Germans completed the first phase of deportations from Hungary. In twenty-three days more than 289,000 people had been brought to Auschwitz and turned into ashes. On the same day, Chaim Weizmann, the architect of modern Israel, went to see Anthony Eden at the British Foreign Office about the Brand offer. Eden was skeptical, especially about American support for the plan. All that summer Chaim Weizmann and the Jewish

Agency made repeated appeals to Eden and the British government to bomb the railway lines from Hungary to Auschwitz and the crematoria themselves. Despite Weizmann's urgent plea, no direct action was approved, although on July eleventh Sir Winston Churchill wrote to Eden:

> Understandably the persecution of the Jews in Hungary is the greatest and most horrible crime ever committed in the history of the world. And this was done with the aid of scientific devices and by a so-called civilized people. It is clear beyond doubt that everybody involved in this crime who may fall into our hands, including those who only obeyed orders in committing these butcheries, must be killed.

On the same day in July Dr. Edmund Veesenmayer, Hitler's plenipotentiary representative in Hungary, declared that the Hungarian countryside was entirely free of Jews. A total of 437,402 people had been deported and most of them would never come back.

On the first day of September, an official in the Foreign Office finally replied to Chaim Weizmann about his request for bombing the death camps:

> I am sorry to have to tell you, that in view of the very great technical difficulties involved, not to mention the diversion which would be necessary of material of vital importance at this critical stage of the war, we have no option but to refrain from pursuing the proposal in present circumstances.

TWENTY-FOUR

MEETING IN BUDAPEST

On the morning of June 17, 1944, Kató Szenes awoke at eight, after a brief and restless sleep. On the Gestapo's orders, she had been up half the night patrolling the neighborhood, making sure that all windows were properly blacked out. The Gestapo had already laid claim to her tiny room in the maid's quarters; a new decree forbade Christians to serve in Jewish households and after many tears, Rózsi had gone to work for Kató's close friend, Judith.

Since Béla's plays had been banned, Kató had had to rent out her own and the children's rooms to supplement her income. Her tenants included a couple of strange Englishmen, one of whom turned out to be a spy. For the past year, the larger part of the house had been rented by Margit Dayka, one of the stars of the Hungarian stage and screen. Talented, warm, and generous, Margit was a Bohemian, whose irregular habits often amused and at times alarmed Kató. Occasionally, a bailiff or tradesman would ring at the door and demand to be paid. The irrepressible actress, who was usually broke, would shout to Kató from her bed: "Tell them, darling, I don't have any money; ask if they'd take my mink coat."

Like most Jews in Buda, Kató knew that she must soon move to the other side of the river, where buildings specially designated with a huge yellow star were filling up with thousands of displaced Jews clutching their few portable belongings. The Jewish houses were prelude to some horror that many Jews sensed without knowing precisely what form it would take.

Since the occupation Margit had tried to help and comfort Kató in whatever way she could. Just the night before, Margit had suggested that she would go to the Housing Authority and requisition the rest of the house for herself, so that at least the Gestapo would not move in somebody else during Kató's absence. Margit also promised to guard Kató's most precious possessions: the books that Béla wrote, pictures of the children, and other objects of sentimental value. Though nobody knew exactly where those trains packed with Jews went to, Margit tried to be as reassuring as possible about how quickly Kató could return and find everything as she had left it.

In preparation for the move, and the worse fate that might follow, Kató had already packed a few essentials. A Jewish couple who had taken a friendly interest in her affairs had been warning her during the past few days not to move into a building marked with a yellow star. Instead, they offered her a forged birth certificate, stating that she was a Christian, and invited her to join their escape. They had planned a route through Romania and heard that if they could reach Constantsa, Zionist agencies could help them board a ship to Palestine. Kató listened with skepticism. In the three months since the German occupation the whole city was rife with fantastic dreams and stratagems of the most desperate kind.

Kató had no reason to stay in Budapest. She had been promised a Palestine certificate many times and she knew that the Hazalah was still issuing them, even if they could not secure exit permits for their clients. But at least the authorities allowed those with certificates to remain at home and not wear the yellow star—favorable signs that they might actually let them out of the country.

As Kató began to dress that morning, somebody rang the bell at the garden gate. A stranger was standing there, saw her peering through the window, and called out: "I am looking for Mrs. Béla Szegő."

"She doesn't live here."

"Of course she does." The man took out a piece of paper. "This is Bimbó-út, number 28. Ah, the name. It's not Szegő: I'm looking for Mrs. Béla Szenes."

"What for?"

"I am a detective, from the state police. Please let me come in."

Once in the hallway, the man explained politely: "You must come with me to the staff headquarters of the Hungarian National Defense. You've been summoned as a witness."

"What's the case?" Kató asked.

"I don't know."

"I must finish dressing. Please wait here."

Kató was baffled. She didn't know anybody in the military. Jews had been excluded from service for years. The only possible answer was Gyuri: he was of military age, but he had left the country almost six years before— legally. It was possible that they had found out about his escape from France and then from Spain, but he was now safe with Anikó in Palestine. And why would that concern the Hungarian military? Did they not have other problems with a losing war?

Worried, Kató decided to wake Margit. The actress hurriedly draped a gown around herself and went to talk to the man in the living room, while Kató retired to her room to dress. Margit launched at once into a cross-examination. The man really did not seem to know the reason for the summons. He was so thrilled to be talking to a famous actress that he would clearly have told her anything he knew.

Kató came back fully dressed, her large yellow Star of David prominently displayed on the upper left part of her jacket, as required by law. Her eyes fell on the dining room table where the forged Aryan birth certificate was lying. Unobtrusively she managed to slip it to Margit for safekeeping. The detective assured both women that Kató would be back very soon, probably that same morning. He was apologetic that they would have to take the streetcar to the military barracks on Horthy Miklós-út, but he could not get a car.

Although the detective seemed honest, Kató had few illusions. It was only too common for people to be arrested on trumped-up charges, or even without them. Many of her friends and acquaintances—writers, journalists, theatrical folk, teachers—had disappeared. Some she knew were drafted into the forced labor battalions, others dispatched to concentration camps. Quite a few vanished without a trace. The best their friends could hope for them was that they might have escaped to freedom. The whole country had long ago turned into a vast prison, especially for Jews; so the fact that she was sitting on a streetcar—albeit in a section restricted to Jews, but still in apparent possession of her freedom—while others were already in prison or camps, made little difference. Only her mind was free when she thought with comfort about her two children, in that unimaginably distant and relatively happy land called Palestine.

Meanwhile, the detective was making an attempt at small talk, mostly about Margit. Seeing that he was quite a simple and decent sort, Kató felt bold enough to ask his permission to make a phone call to her, when they got off the streetcar. She wanted to remind Margit about their conversation the night before; it was even more urgent now that she should go to the Housing Authority as they had agreed.

In Budapest most street tobacconists have public phones, but as soon as Kató began to dial, the woman in charge of the stand yelled at her in panic: "What the hell d'you think you're doing? Don't you know you can't use a public phone if you've got a star?"

Embarrassed by the incident, the detective offered to let Kató use his own phone when they reached his office. Her call to Margit was brief and guarded. When she hung up, the detective casually inquired about her children. How were they doing? Where were they? Kató noticed a world map on the wall, and pointed to Palestine. At that moment a tall man wearing civilian clothes entered the room and asked Kató to sit down. He took another seat next to the desk, ready to take down information on the typewriter. He did not introduce himself, but his name was Rózsa—named after the same flower as the hill where she lived.

The formal interrogation began. After finishing the standard preliminaries of name, birth date, and address, Rózsa questioned Kató about Gyuri's whereabouts. Then he began to ask about Anikó. The questions came in rapid succession and she replied as best she could; Rózsa had stopped typing the answers, and kept trying to find the real reason Anikó had left home.

"I can imagine," he said, "why a young man would want to go out and test himself in the big world. But what reason would tempt a young lady?"

"The same reasons," Kató replied firmly. "Jewish youth has no future in this country. There are no prospects for a decent life here. I'm glad she isn't here to share in our sufferings."

The man grinned and continued probing: where had Anikó spent the past five years, what had she been doing, how often did Kató hear from her and through what channels? The line of questioning at first suggested to Kató that perhaps the military censors did not like something Anikó had written in a letter. But she had no time to follow that thought; Rózsa wanted to know all about Anikó's activities before she left: what did she do at home, in school, what friends, what interests, what kind of profession did she have in mind?

"She always wanted to be a teacher," Kató told him.

"God help us!" The vehement sarcasm in Rózsa's voice sent a chill through Kató. Still, her maternal pride would not let this pass.

"I know you would not take my opinion of my daughter's talents as objective," she told Rózsa, "but it would be easy to get confirmation from her former teachers. Why don't you ask Dr. Lajos Áprily, or Dr. Boriska Ravasz, and Dr. Alice Quant for that matter, whether they think that Anikó would make an excellent teacher?"

The names were well known in the tight-knit society of Budapest, but Rózsa did not seem interested in corroborative testimony. He instructed the friendly detective to type up a summary of the interrogation. As he left the room, he warned Kató that she had to sign the statement under oath. As she repeated a summary of her testimony for the detective, she noticed the file name: "Anna Szenes."

When Rózsa returned he read through the statement, and had Kató sign it, after making her swear an oath. Then he asked: "Mrs. Szenes, where do you really think your daughter is at this moment?" There had been similar questions before, so Kató repeated her answer calmly.

"To the best of my knowledge, she is living and working in an agricultural settlement, somewhere near Haifa." Rózsa leaned down and peered into her face.

"Well, since you want to pretend ignorance, let me enlighten you. Your precious little Anikó is in this building, right next door, in fact. In a moment, I'm going to have her brought in here. You must convince her that it's in her best interest to tell us what she knows. If she won't, I promise you'll never see each other again."

Kató stood as she heard these portentous words, grasping the edge of the table near her for support. The floor seemed to slip from beneath her feet. Dizzy, she closed her eyes and felt in those few seconds her life drain from her, taking all meaning, all faith, and all hope with it. She heard a door open behind her and involuntarily turned around.

Four men were dragging in a young woman whom Kató could scarcely recognize. Her hair was disheveled and matted; her whole face was swollen and bruised. Her eyes, what remained visible of them, reflected an infinite well of suffering. And they were Anikó's eyes.

It took only a moment for Anikó to realize that her mother was present in the room. With the desperate strength of a wounded animal she tore herself free from the grip of the four guards and hurled herself across the room into her mother's arms.

"Forgive me, Mother!"

Kató enfolded her sobbing child, feeling Anikó's racing heartbeats against her own, Anikó's tears scalding her own skin.

"Well, talk to her," said Rózsa. "She must tell us what she knows." Then he repeated his earlier threat: "If you don't convince her to talk, you won't ever see each other again."

Kató sensed only the danger; her numbed mind could hardly guess what circumstances had brought Anikó to that room. But regardless of her own pain and bewildered desire to know the truth, she was certain of this: Anikó must have good reasons for not telling these people what they wanted to know, and Kató would not try to influence her otherwise.

Anikó was equally in shock, having withstood unspeakable physical tortures. As her body was ravaged, her mind had roamed the freedom of the sea and the sand at Sedot Yam. But now her capture was inflicting enormous pain on the person she loved most. If anything could crack her will, it would be this unbearable realization. In that state, at the slightest suggestion from Kató, she might have confessed immediately everything these men wanted to hear. But her mother's unquestioning silence gave her the strength to hold out.

After a few seconds the tense silence produced another outburst from Rózsa. "Dammit, why don't you talk to her?" Kató did not recognize her own voice: "I see no point in your threats; my daughter and I heard you."

"Well, you'd better start talking. I tell you what. We'll leave you alone with her."

Rózsa left with the four guards; the detective stayed. The two women sat facing each other. They remained silent, filled with the anguish of unspoken thoughts. Kató feared that Anikó had returned just to rescue her, impatient that legal methods had produced no results. Perhaps news of the occupation and deportations had made her undertake this reckless and desperate mission.

"Anikó, my darling, am I the cause of what is happening here, because you were worried about me?"

"No, no, Mother, you are not the cause," Anikó hastened to reassure her.

"What brought you here? It wasn't long ago that I got your telegram about Gyuri's arrival. Perhaps he is not in Palestine either?" she asked, bracing for more pain.

"Yes, of course he is, Mother. I sent you the telegram after I saw him. You needn't worry about Gyuri, all's well with him."

Facing her, Kató had a chance to look at Anikó more closely. She noticed that one of her upper teeth was missing. Despite the presence of the detective, she risked the question: "You lost that tooth here, of course?"

"No, not here." Kató watched her bruised child; holding Anikó's calloused hands in hers, she had an overwhelming desire to embrace her. But as soon as she tried, the door was ripped open and the four henchmen rushed in from their listening post. Rózsa followed them into the room.

"No whispering allowed!" he bellowed. "This is enough for today!" He ordered the men to take Anikó away. Then he turned to Kató.

"I've got every right to detain you, but I'm taking your age into consideration. So go home. If we need your testimony, we will call you. It all depends on how your daughter cooperates. If she doesn't, we won't be needing you anymore."

Rózsa warned her not to tell anybody where she had been and what had happened.

"Someone already knows," Kató replied.

"Who?" He was surprised.

"Margit Dayka, the actress."

"How did that happen?"

The detective came to her rescue: "Mrs. Szenes is Miss Dayka's housekeeper. She was there when I went to fetch her."

"Is she going to interfere?" Rózsa asked sharply.

"Very likely, since she isn't used to detectives turning up on her door-step," Kató retorted.

"Well, if she asks questions, you'll just have to say that you aren't at liberty to say. Not one word, remember? And now you can go."

Rózsa left. The detective offered Kató a seat while she recovered strength to depart. This kindly gesture gave Kató confidence to ask, "I beg you to tell me: what's going on here?"

"I swear I don't know." As the detective accompanied Kató down the stairs, he tried to reassure her about Rózsa's threats: "He can't do just as he pleases. Everything's going to work out, you'll see."

Fortified by this sign of humanity, Kató managed somehow to make her way home. It was only one o'clock in the afternoon, but it felt like several years had passed. A knot of curious neighbors stood in front of the house, talking to Margit and waiting for Kató's return. They rushed at her: "What happened? Tell us what happened!"

"Some sort of mistake."

Margit was used to physical transformations in the theater, but she had never seen such a sudden and total alteration in a person's face and posture in real life. She shepherded Kató into the house and gently tried to pry the truth from her. Finally Kató said, "There was no mistake. Something terrible has happened, but I'm not allowed to tell anyone." She was too exhausted to go on.

Fortunately, at that moment the front bell rang. The director had come to fetch Margit to view the rough cut of their latest film. She was reluctant to leave, but Kató wanted more than anything to be left alone. She didn't know how much longer she could restrain her feelings and what she might reveal if Margit stayed.

After Margit left, the Jewish man who had invited Kató to escape with them to Romania knocked on the door. He and his wife wanted to leave Budapest as soon as possible: was she ready?

"I've thought about the whole thing and I changed my mind," said Kató, trying to sound calm.

The man argued: "I don't even know anybody in Eretz Israel, and yet I want very much to go. You have both your children there, you have more reason than most to make the effort to escape. You shouldn't forget how much Anikó has been longing to see you there and how hard she has worked to obtain a certificate of emigration for you."

Kató decided at last to tell him the real reason. She knew him to be a trustworthy person, and if he managed to reach the shores of Palestine at least someone could tell Gyuri what had happened. He heard her story in horror. After what seemed an interminable silence, he finally said: "I can see why you would want to stay here now with Anikó. I am sworn to keep your secret, but I don't think you should. You must tell the story to people who could help. Start with Margit, who might have connections high up in the military or government."

As the man began to say his farewells, Kató noticed from the hallway that a car had drawn up at the curb. Soldiers in SS uniforms poured out onto the sidewalk. One of them called out loudly: *"Wir suchen Frau Szenes. Bitte lassen Sie uns herein."*

Kató called back that she was fetching the key. She hurriedly picked up the forged Aryan papers still lying on the table and hid them in Margit's desk. Then she walked casually with her visitor to the gate, where a detective from the Gestapo was now blocking the way.

"And who are you?" he asked the man in bad Hungarian.

"My wife is a good friend of Mrs. Szenes. I came to inquire how she is." It was common practice for the Gestapo, making an arrest, to take with them anybody who happened to be present. The detective obviously considered it, but finally decided to let the man go.

Four Germans accompanied Kató into the house. After giving his name as Seifert, the detective asked Kató to come with them at once to a hearing. Kató desperately wanted somebody to witness her arrest, perhaps gather a clue as to where she was being taken, and then inform Margit. But she was alone. Even the caretaker had gone off to shop; it was Saturday and the stores would be closed the next day.

"I can't go with you now, because I'm responsible for Miss Dayka's apartment and I have to look after her things."

"You can do that when you come back, after you have answered some questions," Seifert said firmly but politely. "Please get ready to leave."

Kató wished now that she had told Margit about the morning's events. By now she could be contacting important people who might help Anikó. What if they both disappeared without anybody knowing?

She went to her room to pick up her purse and a few things that might be useful in jail, trying not to arouse Seifert's suspicion. He followed her everywhere, asking questions. Which rooms were occupied by Miss Dayka and which were hers? Kató replied that only the back room was hers. What about the furniture and the contents of each closet? He wanted to know where each door led. Such information was preliminary to a thorough house search.

Kató used each reply to delay as much as possible. Suddenly Seifert whipped a picture out of his pocket and held it in front of her.

"Do you know this person?"

The picture in Seifert's hand showed Anikó in the same battered state Kató had just witnessed. Kató tried to decide whether or not she should pretend to complete surprise. After all, Rózsa's warning had been all-inclusive, and it was certainly possible that the German and Hungarian authorities were acting independently of each other.

"Who is it?" she asked.

"Haben Sie eine Tochter, Anna Szenes?" He reverted to German, which Kató understood perfectly.

"Yes, I do have a daughter, but I wouldn't recognize her from this. And anyway, how did you come by this picture?" Ignoring her questions, Seifert simply urged her to hurry up.

"You should lock all the doors. Who else has keys to the apartment?"

"Just Miss Dayka and I."

"When will she be home?"

"This evening for sure."

Finally Kató noticed with relief that the caretaker was returning. Giving her Margit's telephone number at the studio, Kató urged her to call at once. The good woman hastily prepared a couple of sandwiches and stuffed them into Kató's purse. Seifert was now visibly impatient, so Kató knew she had to leave. As she was locking the door, the detective asked her why she was bringing her keys.

"Didn't you say I'd be back by this evening?"

"Yes, of course," said the Gestapo man hastily.

It was almost five o'clock when Kató climbed into the car, which was obviously designed to transport prisoners. In a matter of minutes they drove across the Danube and arrived at the *Polizeigefängnis,* a jail the Germans had converted next to the old Halls of Justice in Pest. Seifert and Kató were dropped off, while the SS men drove off for a night on the town.

Seifert led her to a room upstairs. For the second time that day Kató watched her personal data being typed on a form. She saw that the file into which her particulars were entered was stamped *Eilt sehr*—most urgent. Three others were in the room: a grim-visaged SS man with his death's-head insignia, another young soldier, and a middle-aged civilian who did not look German. Finally Seifert took her keys and left. Obviously he intended to make the house search before Margit returned.

The SS man told Kató to hand over all her valuables. He searched through her purse. After confiscating her money, watch, wedding ring, and pen, he asked her whether she had any more money. There was a small pendant around her neck, where she kept the maximum amount that Jews were allowed. As she hesitated, he struck her viciously across the face. Although she reeled backward from the impact of his hand, she felt completely numb. The events of the morning had deadened her feelings; it was as if she were watching this happen to somebody else.

The other two in the room were evidently upset by the SS man's behavior. The civilian even gestured to her to ignore it all. She found out later that

he was a Jew, the former president of a large corporation, who was now
employed by the Gestapo as a clerk, to keep an exact record of all confiscated items and money. Everything would be returned if she were set
free, the SS man reassured her. As if to prove his point he returned some
of the small change that he had taken from her purse. Then he instructed
the young soldier to take her to cell number 528.

TWENTY-FIVE

TORTURE

Anikó had no time to recover from the unexpected meeting with her mother. Rózsa entered the room and immediately opened with a new tactic—gentleness.

"I'm sorry that we've had to be rough with you, miss. After all, I have always held your father in the highest regard. I regret about your esteemed mother, too. It's obvious how dearly you love each other."

He paused. She listened impassively.

"You have committed a great crime against your country. Fortunately, it's still possible to reverse it. If you tell me where the cipher is, it's not too late to correct your error."

Anikó remained silent.

"If you don't," Rózsa's voice became ominous, "I have no choice but to execute your mother. She will be killed first, right in front of you. Then we will kill you. The decision is up to you."

"No! Don't you touch my mother! You have no right!" Anikó could not restrain herself.

Pleased with his success, Rózsa leaned over and repeated slowly: "I will have your mother killed in front of you." For the first time during her interrogations and tortures, Anikó lost control, crying hysterically.

"You can torture me to death, kill me—but don't—don't touch—my mother!"

"Where's the code?"

"Spare my mother!"

"The code!"

"My mother! Don't hurt her!"

"I'll give you three hours to think, miss," Rózsa said icily. "If you talk, you may see her again. If not, you'll be responsible for her death sentence. I'll make sure it is carried out tomorrrow."

Then he ordered her back to her cell.

Anikó sat in a corner, turned to stone. Her hysterics had subsided but slowly the cold reality of her dilemma awakened greater panic than she had ever known. If she betrayed the code, the Germans would use it to lure Allied aircraft into Hungary and shoot them down. She might have been able to accept for herself the infamy of being a traitor. Nor was she afraid of death; if she was not executed, she would take the earliest opportunity of committing suicide. But it was not only her own life and honor at stake. She felt she was a special emissary from the people of Eretz Israel to the Diaspora. She thought of all her chaverim and the disgrace they would feel when they heard about her betrayal. She still had a choice, if only she could hold out.

She felt calmer as her former clarity returned. But what about her mother? Suddenly all the ideals for which she was willing to lay down her own life faded into insignificance. Even if she could contemplate her own end, how could she condemn her mother to death? Her mother had not volunteered for the mission; she did not even understand what was happening. All the love Anikó felt for this extraordinary woman, all the pain of their five years' separation, all the guilt for causing her mother this anguish now overwhelmed her. It no longer mattered what happened to herself. Her mother must come first, and then the mission, the chaverim, and Eretz Israel. She must not let her own foolish heroism destroy the person who was dearer than all the world.

The guards came to fetch her. Numb, Anikó allowed them to lead her up the stairs. She had decided to give Rózsa the title of the French book that contained the code. After all, there was a small chance that they might not find it, or know how to use it. Probably the cipher had been changed long ago. The main thing was that her mother would live, go to Palestine, where Gyuri needed her. Anikó would end her own life soon, but her mother at least would live to explain why her daughter had turned traitor. Perhaps some might understand.

"What did you decide?" Rózsa's voice came to her through a fog.

Anikó thought that her inner argument had been settled; she was ready to talk. But now an unexpected voice spoke up: was it *really* true that nobody would mind if she had become a traitor? She knew suddenly with brilliant clarity that her mother would gladly die rather than see her daughter betray her cause.

Anikó looked straight into Rózsa's expectant face: "I've got nothing to say. I left the cipher book with the radio."

The last thing she saw was Rózsa's head drop, like a cobra about to strike. She tried to find something to hold on to, but the world went dark as she felt her body hit the ground.

TWENTY-SIX

BIRTH OF THE LEGEND

Prison cell 528 surprised Kató. Despite the heavy security door with its creaking hinges, the room was bright and fairly spacious, with seven white iron beds. Except for the bars on the windows, it could easily be taken for a hospital ward. Half a dozen women looked up curiously at the latest arrival, and one rose instantly to greet her. Kató recognized the Baroness Erzsébet Hatvany, whom she knew socially in literary and theatrical circles. Her ex-husband, the well-known writer and intellectual Lajos Hatvany, had left Hungary and lived in exile. Böske, as everybody called the Baroness, was clearly the leader and chief organizer in the group. She introduced the rest of the women, who were all aristocrats or wives of men prominent in public life. There was the Countess Klára Zichy, whom the count had divorced when she was found to have Jewish blood; she had been arrested on suspicion of hiding valuable old paintings from the Germans. Kató was introduced to the wife of Jenő Vida, the only Jewish member of the Upper House of Parliament; she had been turned in by her valet for an alleged anti-German remark. Next came the widow of another member of Parliament, Lehel Héderváry; she was accused of being in contact with the Western Allies. But the women all knew that they were held by the Gestapo as hostages, and they were most curious about why Kató was arrested. She just did not seem important enough to be a hostage. Was she involved in secret political activity? Who could have betrayed her? Kató held on to her secret.

She felt a sudden pang of hunger. She had not eaten all day, and the sandwiches were still in her purse. As she took her first bite, six pairs of eyes looked at her with the concentration of hungry dogs. She handed over the small package to Böske, who divided its contents into seven equal portions. Kató had learned the first law of prison life. The second followed soon. That evening a dispute broke out about chores. It was the Countess Zichy's turn to clean the cell and she flatly refused to touch the toilet.

"I've never done anything like this in my life, and I don't have the slightest idea how to do it," she argued vehemently. A cellmate volunteered instead, but Böske insisted that letting the countess off would set a precedent and affect morale. Discipline was essential. Böske got her way; she then patiently explained to Countess Klára what a brush was and how to apply it.

Kató's thoughts were far away—with Anikó. Was she still alive? And how long would they spare her? She thought it unlikely that Anikó would ever break down: so why would they let her live? She lacked confidence in her own strength to stand up to interrogation.

After a sleepless night, she rose at five with the others. As much as she dreaded the day, it was almost a disappointment to learn from her cellmates that the Gestapo did not work Sundays. The day passed in slow agony. Forbidden any kind of activity, the women were restless and bored. Some played bridge with cards that Böske had skillfully improvised with bits of cardboard.

Böske tried different ways to get Kató to talk about her obvious grief. Finally her insistence and tact succeeded. While the others were busy playing cards Kató whispered a summary of the previous day's events. Böske was appalled and promised to keep the secret to herself. But she must have said something to the others to explain Kató's depression, because toward evening the countess apologized for the fuss she had caused and volunteered a useful piece of information—that the women regularly received parcels from the outside. She showed the most useful item her ex-husband had sent: razor blades, which functioned as scissors, knife, or pencil sharpener. Kató observed the countess putting a razor blade into a small container on her allotted shelf. Later that evening, as the women made up beds, putting mattresses on the floor to create extra room, Kató unobtrusively passed the shelf and lifted the razor from the box. As her place was next to the window, she hid the blade behind one of the shutters.

As her roommates settled down for the night, Kató found the razor and waited. She could see no better way for herself or for Anikó. At last, with inexperienced hands she sought her pulse. She missed it; the blood did not spurt as it was supposed to. She could feel a sticky warmth trickling on her skin. Her next-bed neighbor stirred and Kató quickly hid under the blanket, pretending to be asleep. Later she tried to complete the job, but with the first light of midsummer dawn, several began to wake. Böske looked toward Kató and her suspicions were aroused; instantly she came over to her bed. Seeing the blood, she rebuked Kató.

"You could get all of us into very big trouble," she whispered angrily, binding up the wounds with a couple of handkerchiefs. "This is what you must do. When they take you for interrogation, wear this raincoat, with the long sleeves. That way they might not notice your wrists."

At seven o'clock a soldier came to the cell and read Kató's name from a list. One of the women quickly slipped a bread ration into her hands. Interrogations went on from early morning until night without a meal. Kató was grateful for the gesture, even though the bread turned out to be moldy.

A van took Kató and a group of prisoners to Gestapo headquarters on top of Svábhegy, an exclusive villa district on one of the many hills of Buda. Kató was herded into a large room with many other women, where she sat down and waited. One woman came up to her and struck up a friendly conversation, but Kató was warned not to talk by another woman, who explained that the first woman was a well-known Gestapo informer. The entire day passed and Kató was not called for interrogation. Arriving back in her cell exhausted, she was handed an official-looking postcard to fill out. It was to inform anybody on the outside about her whereabouts and to request a change of clothes, food, and toiletries. This offered something to look forward to, but it also meant that she could not expect to be released very soon. She had not really believed Seifert when he promised that she would be returning home the day of her arrest. In fact, she had no hope and little interest in her future, only in Anikó's. The outside seemed as dangerous for Jews as jail.

Kató was wary of sending the card. After the deportations, she had few relatives left alive and she did not want their names made known to the Gestapo. She also wanted to spare Margit further visits from the authorities. Finally she decided to send the postcard to her hairdresser, asking her to take it to the lady living in Kató's house. The form stated that parcels could be brought to the prison every other Wednesday between ten and twelve in the morning. Since it was Monday evening, Kató had no idea whether it would reach Margit in time for that week's delivery; she might have to wait another two weeks.

Wednesday morning there was a great deal of excitement as packages began arriving just after ten o'clock. The guards and supervisors opened and examined the contents of each parcel, carefully removing any paper or string, and appropriating anything else that struck their fancy. Near the noon deadline, a large delivery arrived for Kató by taxi. The soup was still piping hot, and all the other freshly prepared food exuded tempting aromas. Margit herself could not boil an egg, so she had ordered everything from a nearby restaurant. After two days of famine, Kató thought she was dreaming. She noticed that the clothes in the parcel were not those she used regularly and included several items from Margit's wardrobe. Kató deduced that her own room must have been sealed off, probably after Seifert's house search.

During the next few days Kató settled into prison routine. The chief activity of the prisoners was trading rumors. The daily ten-minute walk in the yard brought inmates from neighboring cells together. Although talking was strictly forbidden, people were remarkably adept at swapping news, which was kept current by a constant stream of new arrivals, who belonged more or less to the same social circles as the prisoners.

The deportations from the countryside had been completed, but the large-scale roundup of Jews in the capital seemed to be delayed and nobody knew why. Selective arrests continued. Kató's pleasant room became a hellish hole with twenty people crammed into it. As new prisoners were admitted, others were removed. On the morning of June twenty-third, both Böske and Mrs. Vida were taken away, nobody knew where. All the inmates kept their meager belongings packed, because once their names were called, there was no time to prepare.

The morning Böske was taken away, Kató heard her name called for interrogation. As Kató was walking down the stairs accompanied by a guard, a young female prisoner scrubbing the floor whispered to her, without looking up, "Anikó is also here. I talked to her last night."

Kató was overwhelmed by this piece of news. Anikó—alive! She felt a shock of joy, a jolt of energy and hope that drove out her apathy of the past week. She faced the interrogation with much less fear and a new sense of purpose. Seifert fired the same questions at her as the Hungarian authorities had asked the week before. He was much more thorough, but also much more polite than Rózsa. After several hours, Kató found the courage to ask a question.

"Would you tell me please what exactly is going on here? What are the charges against my daughter?"

At first Seifert was silent. Then he said carefully, "Under Hungarian law her life is not in danger. The German laws are more strict."

That evening, soon after she got back into the cell, Kató's name was called again, this time by another prisoner, a woman named Hilde. Born in Berlin, Hilde was bilingual and the Gestapo trusted her with clerical and other responsible work. Sometimes she was even given keys to the cells. When Kató followed her into the corridor, Hilde's voice dropped into a conspiratorial whisper. She instructed Kató to go and look out of her cell's window. This was strictly forbidden, but Kató went and saw across the vast courtyard the waving hands and smiling face of Anikó. Having resigned themselves to the worst, mother and daughter felt indescribable happiness just to be able to glimpse each other across a prison yard.

Every morning now Kató positioned herself by the window. Anikó appeared on cue in a horizontal opening that was much smaller than the fair-sized windows of Kató's room. Anikó's cell was in solitary row on the top floor for those considered dangerous criminals. These cells had only narrow slits near the ceiling with a heavy bar across them. She could reach the window only by standing a table on the bed and then a chair on top of the table. The chair was brought into her cell each morning for a short time to support a portable washbasin. Looking out the window was highly precarious, and Anikó had to be prepared to leap down and disassemble the table and chair before the guard or matron returned.

Mother and daughter slowly attempted to communicate. Anikó began by drawing huge imaginary letters in the air. Kató answered. The process was laborious, the risk huge. They had to be careful not to reveal anything important, in case they were watched. The rest of the cell observed breathlessly what seemed like a miracle: a Jewish paratrooper who had come to help them. Anikó asked about the yellow stars that all the women wore. Kató explained and asked why Anikó did not have to wear it.

"I'm not a Hungarian citizen anymore."

"You're lucky," wrote one of Kató's cellmates into the air. But Anikó, in a gesture of solidarity, drew a huge Star of David on the dusty windowpane. It stayed there for several weeks, until the authorities noticed it and ordered that the window be washed.

Not long afterward, Hilde called for Kató once more.

"Get into that bathroom, quick," she whispered. "But you've only got a few minutes."

Anikó was waiting inside the bathroom. For the first time in years, mother and daughter embraced freely.

"I am mostly resigned to my own fate," said Anikó, "but I can't bear the thought that I dragged you into this."

"Don't worry, nobody's hurting me," Kató tried to reassure her. "My only comfort in this catastrophe is being near you. If I were free, I wouldn't get a chance to see you."

Anikó smiled. The visible signs of torture and beatings had faded, and her hair was neat again. Only the missing tooth was a reminder of the reality of their situation. Anikó laughed at Kató's concern: "We should both be so lucky, that all this episode will cost is a tooth. You must believe me: the physical torture is nothing compared to the mental pain." Hilde began knocking urgently on the door, so they had to separate quickly.

When neither was being interrogated, Kató could sometimes glimpse Anikó in the yard below, taking her ten-minute exercise after lunch. The entire courtyard was not visible from her window, so she could only see her at the end of the line, walking by herself, while the other prisoners were paired. Anikó tried looking up at her mother's window. Although great care was taken to keep them separate, occasionally their exercise periods coincided. Everybody in the prison knew by now about Anikó's exploits, and they all silently prayed that mother and daughter would succeed in meeting. Even during the exercise period this seemed a hopeless task, with Kató in front of her line and Anikó at the back. The supervising matron stood in the middle, and armed guards were posted at strategic points of the courtyard. Anikó would leave the line several times, pretending to be tying her shoelaces; at the right moment she would jump back into the line next to her mother. The woman originally next to Kató simply stepped back one row and the whole line realigned behind them. Talking was forbidden and Kató felt extremely anxious about getting Anikó into further trouble. But Anikó ignored the warning.

"We're in the greatest possible danger here anyway, so we might as well take any chance we can."

Kató was still puzzled about what could have induced Anikó to return to Hungary.

"It's a military secret, Mother. And I wouldn't tell you even if I could, because they might try to get it out of you. In any case, we will win this war soon, and then you'll find out everything."

"I can't believe," Kató probed further, "that it was your enthusiasm for the British cause that prompted you to sign up. There must be some Jewish agenda behind all this."

Anikó squeezed her mother's hand and said, "I'm glad you guessed."

"But I wonder," Kató persisted, "if it is worth endangering your life for it?"

"It must be worthwhile to me." And then to soften her evasiveness toward the one person with whom she wanted to have no secrets, Anikó added, "Believe me, Mother, I have not done anything that would harm Hungary's interests. On the contrary. But many things that are criminal today will bring great honor tomorrow. I shall be vindicated soon."

During these snatches of conversation Anikó told her mother how Rózsa had wanted to bring Kató in for another confrontation a couple of days after their first meeting. He had telephoned the house in Anikó's presence. Margit answered and must have told him about Kató's disappearance. In frustration Rózsa slammed down the phone. "Another Jew-lover! She must be hiding her!" He then ordered a house search, closely following the Gestapo's the day before. Although they were allies, and united in their hatred for Jews, the Hungarian and German authorities were often tripping over each other in pursuing their secretive goals.

For several days after that, Kató sat by the window and watched in vain for her daughter to appear. She heard through the prison grapevine that Anikó was being taken for daily interrogations by the Gestapo on the Svábhegy, returning late at night. Several of Kató's cellmates had met Anikó up there, and the story of how she parachuted into Yugoslavia and her life among the partisans circulated throughout the prison.

Each morning Anikó climbed up to her window, if only for a few minutes. Sometimes, if she heard steps outside the cell, she would disappear abruptly. Inevitably, she was caught at last by Marietta, the most sadistic matron of all. Many prisoners feared Marietta so much that they gave up their cherished ten-minute walk in the yard rather than expose themselves to her humiliations. During the exercise period she stood in their midst wielding a long whip, which she used to make them trot around slowly or fast, like circus animals.

Early one morning Anikó was so immersed in the technical difficulties of conducting her conversation that she completely failed to hear footsteps outside. Marietta had been watching through the peephole; now she tore open the door and caught Anikó still perched at the window. Marietta directed a stream of abuse at her, citing the prison regulations.

"You know that this is most absolutely forbidden. Tell me at once who you are trying to contact and what you've been saying."

Undaunted, Anikó held her precarious balance and replied with equal vigor, "If you must know, I've been signaling and waving to my mother, whom I haven't seen for five years. Maybe you've got enough humanity left in you to understand what that means!" There was a pause; then Marietta turned on her heel and left the cell. From that day, whenever this matron had the morning shift she brought in the chair herself to help Anikó to reach the window. And when Marietta overheard a prisoner remark that the "British" officer never got parcels from the outside, she at once assembled a big package with goods stolen from the others, and sent it to Anikó's cell.

By this time, Anikó's circumstances had improved somewhat, and her solitary confinement was eased. Walking in the yard one morning, Anikó met two Polish children who had spent almost their entire lives wandering with their mother from one jail or camp to another. The little boy was eight, the little girl no more than six. At once they made friends with Anikó, and soon the three of them were chasing one another around the yard, while the guards looked the other way. Using all her persuasive charm, Anikó obtained permission to spend a few days in the same cell with them, where she began to make dolls for these forlorn children, using any rags she could find or scrounge from Marietta and other prisoners. She started teaching them to read and write, and told them long stories. Adults, too, listened eagerly to her amusing and instructive tales about Palestine, about Jews who were fighting and learning to run their own country. It seemed like a fantastic fairy tale in that Budapest jail.

It was nearing the seventeenth of July and Kató was trying to think what she could give Anikó for her twenty-third birthday. She had been sharing Margit's parcels with her, but had held back a coveted jar of marmalade. As soon as her cellmates found out the purpose of this package, they all wanted to add presents of their own: a piece of soap, a pair of rubber gloves, a handkerchief. A supervisor agreed to deliver the presents to Anikó. That evening, one of the prisoners whose work enabled her to

move about the prison brought back a tiny, folded piece of paper with
Anikó's warm gratitude. The marmalade made her especially happy, not
just because it tasted so wonderful, but also because it reminded her so
vividly of the orange groves of Eretz. The note also contained one of the
characteristic balance sheets that Anikó used to make on such occasions.
Looking back on her twenty-three years, she said, her youth had been rich
and diverse; life had offered her much. As Kató read her daughter's reck-
oning in this past tense, which seemed to discount any future, each word
was like a dagger stabbing right through her heart.

In fact, Anikó's note was considerably more cheerful than her real state
of mind, which was expressed in a poem she wrote while pacing up and
down her lonely cell:

> One—two—three . . .
>   eight feet long, two strides across,
> the rest is dark . . .
>   life hovers like a question mark.
>
> One—two—three . . .
>   another week or a month maybe
> will find me here;
>   death, I feel, is very near.
>
> Twenty-three
>   next July I might have been . . .
> I gambled on what mattered most:
>   The dice are cast—and I lost.

Time passed with excruciating slowness and Anikó kept busy making
her paper dolls. She managed to send her mother two of them—a boy and
a girl walking in a meadow. Kató thanked her in a smuggled note: "I hope
you'll give me real babies one day; for the time being I'll be happy with
these."

In early August, Anikó surprised herself with a present she made to
commemorate her parents' silver wedding anniversary. First she covered
an empty talcum powder bottle with silver foil. Then she stuck twenty-five
tiny roses through the holes in the lid to create the illusion of a bouquet:
the stems she made of straw from her mattress and the flowers from cotton
wool, one of the few necessities that could be purchased in the prison. The
bouquet rested on a cotton-wool base made to resemble lace. She also
made a bride doll wearing a long veil and holding another bouquet. To
accompany her gift, she wrote a beautiful poem, which Kató had to destroy,
since all pieces of writing could bring unpredictable and dangerous consequences. But she remembered it for the rest of her life: "Memories, like

paper flowers, do not wither; they remain fresh. How often we look at them with longing, and almost forgetting that—they are not alive."

One day Anikó asked her mother, in their usual sign language, whether she wanted to learn Hebrew. Kató agreed, knowing it would please her daughter. From then on they began every morning "conversation" with language lessons, which Anikó ingeniously adapted to be telegraphed across the yard.

Anikó also amazed her mother with her information about outside events, despite her isolation in solitary. Much of her information came from those endlessly futile interrogation sessions with the Gestapo. She spent a great deal of time with new prisoners in the prison van, and waiting with others for her turn. She was full of encouragement and advice for fellow prisoners, about how to handle the interrogators and especially their own fear of the Gestapo. As these prisoners came back to jail they recounted stories like the following, investing Anikó with a legendary aura. A young girl overheard Anikó asking an SS soldier, who was escorting her into interrogation: "What kind of punishment would you give me, if it were up to you?" To which the SS man replied: "I wouldn't punish you at all, because I have never met a woman as brave as you."

Anikó's window became a sort of broadcast center, where other prisoners could get the latest news. A few days after her birthday Anikó climbed up at the window and ran her index finger across her upper lip and then quickly across her neck. That is how her audience learned about the attempt on Hitler's life that took place on July 20, 1944. Signaling entailed constant risk, but Anikó's daring seemed to know no limits. Although she had won the matrons over to her side, there were plenty of dangers left, especially the prison commandant, Scharführer Lemmke.

Lemmke was a typical Nazi, a sadist who took great delight in beating his prisoners for the slightest infractions. He literally poured salt into their wounds, kicking them in the ribs when they fell to the floor. Making his rounds one day, he observed Anikó cutting out paper letters. Lemmke rushed into the cell, fist raised. He clearly expected her to cringe and beg for mercy, but Anikó looked at him calmly, without interrupting her work: "Please, take a seat," she said.

Lemmke stared at her in disbelief.

"This is that British paratrooper," one of the German matrons whispered anxiously. The commandant nodded, looking around at the simple decorations that Anikó had made to create a home for herself. Lemmke's eyes paused on the bed, where a pair of paper dolls lay in a lovers' embrace.

"What's this?" he asked ominously.

"Dolls," replied Anikó matter-of-factly. The matrons waited fearfully for the explosion. A long pause ensued.

"You are forbidden to make male dolls!" Lemmke ordered at last. "If

I see another male doll here, I will punish you—severely!" Then he turned and stalked out, as if he had just scored a great victory.

From then on Scharführer Lemmke visited Anikó's cell regularly. He would ask politely whether he could sit down, and listened intently to Anikó's calm explanations of why Germany had lost the war. She also told him about the retribution that would come to him and his fellow Nazis for all their crimes. After these sessions, the commandant would leave her cell lost in thought.

Meanwhile Anikó was stepping up her doll production, and her gifts were reaching into far corners of the jail. These became more inventive and elaborate; there were characters from opera, such as Madame Butterfly and Carmen, as well as figures representing the *chalutzim,* or pioneers, carrying spades or pickaxes over their shoulders. These she made especially for young Jews, whom she was instructing in sign language about Palestine and Zionism. Bringing new students to the Zionist cause compensated Anikó somewhat for the immense sense of failure she felt about her mission.

TWENTY-SEVEN

GLIMMERS OF LIGHT

Compared to the terrible torture and beatings she had experienced at the hands of the Hungarians in the days following her capture, the Gestapo were treating Anikó gently. No doubt they were only using a different method to get the same result. They were extremely polite, but the interrogations lasted all day and often half the night, without relief. Most questions were attempts to catch her in a contradiction or trick her into revealing something other than what they appeared to be after. Anikó had some tricks of her own: she never told them that she understood German, so that while an interpreter labored with the Hungarian translation she had extra time to construct her answer.

More than once, after a long interrogation session, Seifert or some other detective would offer her coffee and cigarettes and then turn to her: "And now let's hear again about Palestine." And the girl who had stubbornly kept silent or dodged questions for the past ten hours would launch into an animated description of life in Eretz Israel. Her unfeigned enthusiasm, her total lack of fear, and her bubbling energy after hours of interrogation frankly amazed the Gestapo, and her tormentors seemed genuinely fascinated by her personality. Of course, Anikó gave only the most positive highlights of life in Palestine. She talked about the miracles of Jewish achievement and not of the physical hardships or political difficulties with the British. She could not resist baiting the Germans with her glowing descriptions, and sometimes Seifert would interrupt:

"*Na gut.* We will come and inspect this place for ourselves. Because we will get there too, just like everywhere else."

"And I want to show you around when you do come, just like any other tourist. Because that's the only way you will ever get to Eretz Israel," Anikó would reply with quiet conviction. Now that her mother seemed safe, she was never strident, nor terrified, nor patronizing, nor hateful. She simply refused to behave the way a prisoner of the Gestapo is supposed to behave. She defied every Nazi stereotype about Jews, and they did not know what to make of her.

By midsummer in 1944 it was becoming abundantly clear even to the most ardent followers of the Führer that the thousand-year Reich might be drawing to a premature end. The Allies were in Italy and France, the Russians in Romania and pushing across the Carpathian ranges toward Hungary; letters from the Fatherland alluded to devastating bombings, even though the official news was mainly about tactical retreats for the final victory. Budapest itself was being bombed with increasing regularity. The Gestapo found it hard to believe that this Jewish girl from Palestine had better information from inside their own jail than they did. Yet her words had conviction and the ring of truth; some Germans, wondering what would become of them after defeat, began to feel a terrible thirst for the truth.

Meanwhile another one hundred and fifty thousand victims had been taken to Auschwitz, forcing Kommandant Höss to travel to Budapest and complain to Eichmann in person that his facilities could barely cope with the flood of victims. But Eichmann was in a hurry to round up the estimated four hundred thousand Jews who were still trapped in Budapest. Then, in the middle of July, his plans were stopped. Horthy, still head of state, asked for the suspension of deportations and the Germans were no longer strong enough to countermand him. The regent did not halt Eichmann purely for humanitarian reasons; international pressure on the Hungarian government was growing daily. Reminded by Allied bombers that Hitler would likely lose the war, a handful of neutral diplomats undertook last-minute rescue attempts to save the remaining Hungarian Jews. Protests from neutral countries and pleas from the Hungarian clergy, coupled with blunt warnings from Great Britain and the United States that the Hungarian authorities would be held responsible for Nazi crimes, persuaded the government to permit the emigration of almost eight thousand people to neutral countries, including Fascist Spain.

On July ninth Raoul Wallenberg, a Swedish diplomat working for the American War Refugee Board, arrived in Budapest. During the next six months Wallenberg issued thousands of protective passports offering extraterritorial immunity to Jews on fictitious grounds. Throwing diplomatic caution and niceties to the wind, he threatened and bargained with the Nazis, trying to save the Jewish remnant in Budapest.

Anikó, already in jail, did not know about Wallenberg or other rescue attempts. In the weeks following her arrest she expected a message or signal from somebody, from the people whom Yoel and Peretz must surely have reached. She could not understand how nobody outside the prison walls seemed to know about her fate or that no one had succeeded in smuggling a few words of instruction or encouragement to her. She was bothered enough to mention her worry to her mother. During a brief whispering session in the exercise yard she spoke quickly about trying to get word to the outside. Kató pondered for several days. Finally, on one of the fortnightly occasions when parcels were received, she smuggled a message back to Margit with the empty dishes, asking for two parcels to be sent in future. Margit found the note and immediately informed one of Kató's sisters, Irma, who until then had refused to believe that Anikó was back.

In the middle of August Anikó got her first parcel from the outside. She proudly signaled her mother its contents, which seemed to have been left intact by the prison thieves. To her the most important item was a blue blouse, of the same color and cut as those worn by the Zionist Youth Movement to which Anikó had once belonged. She took this as an unambiguous sign that the right people on the outside now knew about her situation and that this was their way of contacting her. She often wore the blouse during her walks. She never realized that the color and style of the blouse were just coincidence.

Contact from her comrades came at last, but not from the outside. One day, she heard about Fleischmann, whom she had not seen since they were brought to Budapest. He was now a prisoner whose chores took him into various parts of the jail, and somehow he managed to send her a message. From him Anikó learned that Yoel and Peretz had also been brought to the jail. They crossed into Hungary more than a month after Anikó was captured and reached Budapest, where Yoel had tried to meet her in front of the synagogue and the basilica as they had arranged. When Anikó never appeared, Yoel went to see Dr. Kasztner at the Aid and Rescue Committee. Kasztner was very alarmed to see him, so Yoel assumed that he had not seen Anikó either. Kasztner was in the middle of negotiating with the SS a delicate deal for the rescue of a special trainload of almost seventeen hundred Jews, including many of his relatives. He feared that German discovery of his connection with Palestinian commandos would mark the end of his rescue efforts.

As it turned out, the Hungarian police already knew about Yoel and Peretz and had deliberately allowed them to come to Budapest so that the authorities could find out who their contacts were. After this purpose had been served, they were arrested and tortured.

Anikó found out Yoel's cell number and they were able to exchange a few words by the usual sign language. That was how Yoel found out that Kató was also in the prison. A little later, when Yoel and Anikó were being transferred together to another jail, they had time to catch up more fully with each other; later Yoel would write a book about the mission, which reported Anikó's story during this period when she could not keep a diary.

Throughout August the atmosphere in the jail grew more relaxed and morale among the prisoners improved. Anikó's interrogations grew fewer and finally ceased. With more Allied victories, the Germans had bigger problems on their minds. The overcrowding in Kató's cell eased. Some of the prisoners were actually released, usually for a huge ransom. Many more were transferred to a detention camp in Kistarcsa, where conditions were rumored to be far better than in the Gestapo's jail. Some people said that Hungarian police had surrounded the camp to prevent the Germans from deporting any more Hungarian citizens to Poland.

In the beginning of September, Anikó was moved to a communal cell next to Kató's. She had made repeated demands both to Seifert and to Lemmke to be allowed to see her mother. Lemmke provided this solution: next door still meant total separation and, of course, it ended the daily visual communication across the yard. But at least Anikó's long isolation was finally at an end; she could teach her cellmates face to face.

Her social talents blossomed anew. She began each morning by leading her cellmates through vigorous physical exercises. Then she lectured them about life in Palestine. Her own enthusiasm was so contagious that many who had never cared much about Palestine before now became fervent Zionists. She organized an assembly line for dolls and entertaining parlor games. The women in her cell, who had been tormented by boredom, suddenly found their days too short.

The new optimism was reflected in relaxed regulations throughout the prison. Anikó and Kató met more frequently, since the water tap stood immediately outside their cells. Three times daily a prisoner was allowed from each cell to go and fill a bucket. Everybody looked forward to her turn, because even this symbolic increase in freedom was highly prized. Yet many gave up their turns just so that Anikó and Kató could "accidentally" meet in the corridor for a few precious seconds, to squeeze hands or quickly embrace.

But these relaxed conditions did not last. During the night of September tenth, the lights were suddenly switched on throughout the jail. Soldiers came into the cells with lists of names, nearly all Polish. At last, most of Anikó's cellmates were lined up outside in the corridors, which were reverberating with the heartrending wailing of women. Anikó hurled herself on a bed and cried from sheer anger and frustration, surprising all those who had looked to her for calm and strength.

A short while later, Anikó, too, was taken away. Kató heard the news the next morning.

"Don't worry, she must be going to a better place than this," an outside worker tried to comfort her. Amidst all the miseries of the past few months, Kató had felt real joy in one thing only—being close to her daughter—and now she had no idea where they had taken her.

Two days later, on September thirteenth, it was Kató's turn. As promised, the Germans meticulously returned all her possessions and money. Then she and the other prisoners were driven to the internment camp at Kistarcsa. This was a vast place crammed with people looking for long-lost relatives and friends as each new transport arrived. The prisoners lived in crowded huts, but within the perimeter of the fences there was freedom of movement. They could walk in the open and breathe the air as much as they wanted. After months of imprisonment, intimidation, and abuse, Kató found Kistarcsa almost a resort, and she was happy to see a number of old friends alive. But as she frantically scanned the remote corners of the camp, asking anybody who might know, she could find out nothing about Anikó.

Since there were no restrictions on sending letters or receiving parcels, Kató immediately wrote to Margit, asking her to try to discover what had happened to Anikó. She also wrote to her sister, who was trying to get Kató a Swiss protective pass and secure her freedom.

Not long afterward, Kató was summoned to the camp office. There stood Margit, in the company of another famous actress, Hilda Gobbi. Kató was overjoyed, but as soon as she tried to embrace Margit, the latter rudely repulsed her.

"Madam," said Margit coldly, "I urgently need your signature for renewing the rental agreement. And here is next month's rent." Kató quickly saw through the charade, which was for the benefit of the camp supervisor sitting there. Ordinary citizens still needed a plausible reason for visiting the camp, and Margit had used the only excuse she could. In the commotion surrounding the visit of two famous actresses, Kató asked Margit to use her contacts in finding Anikó.

Finally, on Yom Kippur, by order of the Ministry of the Interior, the whole internment camp was abolished and Kató was free to leave. She had nowhere to go. Since her arrest, all Jews had been ordered to move into the "star-houses," marked with the large yellow star. Most of these crowded tenements were confined to a small neighborhood known as Lipótváros. Kató's sister Irma and her husband, Felix, lived in such a "star-house" on a street that was named—in mockery of the times—after the same constitution that had once guaranteed equal rights to all citizens of the country. The sisters' reunion was joyous, despite their surroundings. Of their family, they alone survived the deportations.

The most important news for Kató was that Anikó had sent word to her via Dr. Náday, a young lawyer who was conducting the defense of Yoel, Peretz, and others involved in the same case. Yoel and Peretz were in a jail on Margit-körút, also in Buda, but Anikó herself had been moved to yet another prison in Pest, on Conti-utca. Anikó was quite satisfied with conditions in this prison. She was sharing a cell with a group of young

Communists, who had at first some difficulties relating to the kibbutznik fighting with the British imperialists. Anikó's winning ways and enthusiastic talks about the labor movement in Palestine soon convinced them that they had much in common.

Dr. Náday had met with her there and offered to represent her along with the others. Anikó had sent word to her home address on Bimbó-út, the only one she knew, seeking advice on whether she should have this or another attorney. Margit received the message and got in touch with Irma.

As soon as possible Kató went to see Margit in the old Szenes house. It was strange to be in the familiar surroundings where she was now forbidden to live. Margit told her that two young men had happened to call just the night before, bringing an envelope from someone called Geri. The envelope was filled with money, and enclosed Geri's greetings to Anikó.

Dr. Náday promised to try to arrange a meeting with Anikó, but only if Kató would risk not wearing the mandatory yellow star. It was nearly impossible to obtain permission for Jews to visit relatives in jail. But it was part of the schizophrenic order of the times that authorities sometimes turned a blind eye if there was no official reminder that a person was Jewish. Within a few days, Kató accompanied the lawyer to Conti-utca. Permission had been given for delivering a food package and a ten-minute meeting.

Anikó was brought in by two guards. She looked radiant and in good health, and was overjoyed to see her mother free. The presence of the guards inhibited their conversation. Kató gave Anikó the message from Geri. When she heard the code name for Reuven Dafni, her face lit up. She did not know where he was or how he sent the message to her, but she knew she had not been forgotten after all. Then she opened the parcel her mother brought, and was moved to tears by a small sewing kit she had been given as a little girl. "Oh, this thing still exists!"

Kató asked if she needed anything else. It was turning cold and the cell was unheated, so Anikó requested some blankets. Even more she wanted books, but she warned her mother that they could not be returned; they would have to be left for the prison library. What she desired most was a Bible—in Hebrew. One of the guards was listening and asked, "How could a Jewish girl have a non-Jewish mother?"

"Of course I am Jewish, too," Kató replied.

"Where's your yellow star, then?" asked the guard.

Kató thought fast. There were at this time several initiatives by the Hungarian government to exempt well-known people from some of the humiliating regulations directed against Jews.

"I'm not required to wear the star because of my husband who was a famous writer!" The guard replied with a touch of pure Budapest: "Ah,

Mr. Szenes, of course. I knew him well when I was a waiter in his favorite coffee house." Anikó glowed with pride. Her father's books might have been burned, but the man had not been forgotten.

Anikó then brought up the question of the lawyer: "I think it won't be long before my case comes up. I do need a defense attorney. You should decide who would be best." All too soon, the ten minutes were up.

Finding the right person to represent Anikó was no simple matter. Kató's brother-in-law was a lawyer, but like all Jewish lawyers, Dr. Felix Barta had long ago been forbidden to practice. Kató turned for advice to Dr. Palágyi, an old family friend and a lawyer. He had not heard of Náday, and thought they should find somebody more experienced. He approached several other lawyers but they all found some excuse to refuse the case. Some well-meaning people suggested that the only way to help Anikó was bypassing the judicial masquerade and getting to somebody with influence inside the military. Valuable time was lost while Kató tried in vain to reach various higher-ups. In the Hungary of 1944 a poor Jewish widow had no strings to pull.

Finally, a Zionist acquaintance told her to seek out the Aid and Rescue Committee. There, a man named Grossman told her that she did not need a lawyer; Dr. Kasztner, the head of the committee, was the right man to help Anikó. He could visit anybody in jail, and even take her food. Grossman refused to give Kató the home address for Kasztner, but she managed to get it from someone else and hurried to see him.

He happened to be in Switzerland negotiating with the SS, so Kató told her daughter's story to the woman she found at Dr. Kasztner's apartment. The woman, she later found out, was the wife of the unfortunate Joel Brand, who was still being held by the British in Cairo.

"We know your daughter's case," said Mrs. Brand. "Dr. Kasztner will visit her tomorrow, upon his return. Go to his office and his secretary will make the appointment."

Kató hurried back to the office of the Aid and Rescue Committee with a package that Kasztner might take in for Anikó. The secretary refused the package and told her to come back the next day. She tried day after day, but Dr. Kasztner was always too busy to see her. On one of those occasions she met Dr. Ottó Komoly, a founder of the committee who knew the Szenes family well. He was horrified to hear that Anikó was in the Gestapo jail. Kató repeated what she had been told about not needing a defense attorney.

"Get a lawyer," Dr. Komoly said, "right away."*

---

*This is the version that Mrs. Szenes maintained in her testimony at the sensational Kasztner libel trial which rocked Israel in 1953–1954. Kasztner had testified in Nuremberg on behalf of SS Colonel Kurt Becher; after his aliyah to the new state of Israel (changing his own name from Rezső to Israel) he was widely regarded as the savior of Hungarian Jewry. When accused of collaboration with the Nazis by a Hungarian Jewish journalist, Malkiel Grünwald, Kasztner was urged by his friends in the ruling Mapai party to sue for libel. Grünwald's defense attorney, Samuel Tamir, asked Mrs. Szenes to testify, which she did, much against her inclination, and despite pressures from government officials. (Yoel Palgi, for instance, who held an important job at the time, did not testify against Kasztner, whom he had known from their native city of Cluj.) In the end Kasztner won, but at tremendous cost: Judge Benjamin Halevi concluded that Kasztner seemed concerned only with saving a few important Jews and that in negotiating with the Nazis he had "sold his soul to the devil." Dr. Israel Kasztner was assassinated in Tel Aviv before his final exoneration in 1958.

TWENTY-EIGHT

THE LIGHT GOES OUT

Finally Kató had to choose the only prospect found by Dr. Palágyi, and on October twelfth Dr. Szelecsényi, who had established a reputation for having won several difficult cases recently, undertook Anikó's defense. The next day huge air raids all over the city forced most people into shelters. So the defense attorney's first meeting with Anikó was on Saturday, the fourteenth. Because of renewed air raids, he was forced to stay at the jail and could spend more time with her than he had planned. Like most people he was enormously impressed by Anikó's courage. Later that afternoon he met with Kató at his office and told her, "I doubt if one among a thousand men would have done what she had."

"What is going to happen to her?" Kató asked anxiously.

"If there is really a trial, they will sentence her, of course. I can't say to how many years—it could be five, two, or seven. What does it matter? When this is all over, all prisoners of war will be freed. And I'm not betraying any secrets, dear madame, when I say that we aren't talking about years here."

"Is her life threatened?"

"No, I don't think so. There is nothing in the law to put her into that kind of danger. I'm not saying this to give you false hope; that's really my opinion."

The attorney promised to give Kató early notice of the trial date. He thought she might have a chance to see Anikó during the proceedings.

"What about visiting her before then?"

"I'm afraid Captain Simon, the military prosecutor in the case, has forbidden any visits except from her attorney."

Kató left Dr. Szelecsényi's office greatly relieved. As she laboriously made her way through the half-ruined city, now under almost daily bombardment from the air, she knew that the war could not last beyond a few months. It was clear to all except the most fanatical believers that Germany could not win. She did not know about the frantic efforts at the highest levels of a divided government to make a separate peace with the Allies—preferably the British—before the Russians reached Budapest first. The next day, October fifteenth, 1944, Governor Horthy renounced Hungary's alliance with the Third Reich and asked for an armistice with the Western Allies. But this attempt failed miserably, and within hours there was a coup from the ultra-right. The fascist Arrow Cross party seized power and its leader, Ferenc Szálasi, formed the new government, enjoying the full confidence of the Germans, who were pleased to be rid of Horthy. The coup began the final act of a national tragedy, ending any hope of achieving early peace and of saving Budapest from being turned into rubble. It was an even greater catastrophe for the Jews. Eichmann returned to Budapest two days after the coup to finish his work. The humanitarian pressures from the neutral embassies, the Red Cross, and the Church were nullified overnight.

Immediately a new array of anti-Jewish laws and regulations was proclaimed. The twenty-four-hour curfew for Jews was lifted for two hours occasionally to allow them to do essential shopping and business. No Jews, unless they were under diplomatic protection, were exempted from wearing a yellow star; anybody caught without one risked immediate arrest and death. Everybody was a potential informer, because the new regime threatened with death anybody who tried to help or hide Jews. The caretakers of apartment houses were particularly zealous in reporting any Jew who tried to sneak past them into the street. Gangs of thugs and death squads roamed the streets, kidnaping people indiscriminately and herding them to the embankment of the Danube, where they were lined up and shot into the freezing river, chained together. The great river became an instant graveyard for thousands of nameless victims.

Since her last meeting with Anikó, Kató had been trying to find a Hebrew Bible. In this, one of the largest Jewish communities in Europe, not one Bible was to be found. Stores selling Jewish books and religious objects had been shut down following the German occupation. People who still owned a Hebrew Bible were reluctant to part with it, especially when they heard that they could not get it back. Finally Kató had to give up her search. It was to be one of her everlasting regrets that she could not fulfill Anikó's request.

It was now too dangerous for her, a Jewish client, to visit Dr. Szelecsényi, an Aryan attorney. To maintain communication, she had to rely on her sister and her husband, Felix, who had managed to acquire diplomatic immunity with one of Wallenberg's protective passports, through some distant connections they could prove with Sweden. Through them, Kató learned that Anikó's trial date had been set for the twenty-eighth of

October. She wanted to know how the new political situation would affect the attorney's earlier opinion about her chances. Jews had long been forbidden access to telephones, but a sympathetic family allowed her to make a call to Dr. Szelecsényi. Despite everything he remained optimistic.

"She may get ten or twenty years instead of five, but everything else I said remains true." He urged Kató to attend the trial, where in all probability she could meet with Anikó.

On the morning of the twenty-eighth Kató hid her yellow star and walked across the Margit Bridge to the military jail on Margit-körút. This grim four-story building was originally designed for three hundred prisoners: now it held eight times that many. The trial was already in session, so she waited in the corridor outside the courtroom where a notice read "Anna Szenes and Associates." At about eleven, the doors opened and people began to pour out, Anikó among them. She was surprised to see her mother and immediately ran up to her and embraced her. One of the guards separated them, saying that no conversation was allowed until the judges returned from a recess to give their verdict. As so often during the past months, Kató and Anikó were standing close, facing each other on opposite sides of the narrow corridor, yet forced to remain silent.

After a tense waiting period, the prisoners were summoned back into the courtroom, and Kató stayed outside. Only a few minutes later, Anikó and her comrades were brought out again. Anikó said quickly, "There isn't going to be a verdict today. Apparently the judges will announce their decision in another eight days, next Saturday."

She seemed calm. Kató, on the other hand, had been preparing herself for this moment, and now she felt a terrible letdown. She rushed up to the defense attorney, who was also just coming out of the courtroom.

"Dr. Szelecsényi, what's the meaning of this?"

"It doesn't mean anything. The judges could not agree among themselves. It happens."

"Mother, please thank him for all he has done; Dr. Szelecsényi conducted a very fine defense," Anikó admonished Kató gently. The attorney was pleased by her praise. During the trial he had endured much abuse from the judges for taking such trouble over a Jewish girl. He now returned the compliment, telling Mrs. Szenes about Anikó's superb speech in her own defense. When the military tribunal charged her with treason she pleaded not guilty, explaining to the three judges that she had had to give up her native land and choose another home in Eretz Israel because the leaders of Hungary had betrayed her country to the Germans. And now they were betraying the ideals of Hungary, by turning their backs on the persecuted. She told them how her father, a Hungarian writer, had always taught her to believe in what was good and do what was right. Now she had come back to save those whom they oppressed, and she warned them of the retribution that would surely come to them for their criminal acts.

The judges were not particularly pleased to hear Anikó's analysis, but the American air raids and the Russian artillery audible from the outskirts of Pest reminded them that at least she might be right about the retribution.

Szelecsényi had to defend another client, and he urged mother and daughter to take advantage of the brief opportunity to talk. Anikó was worried.

"How could you be walking about in times like this? Why can't some of your Christian friends hide you?"

"My only worry is to make sure that your case ends happily."

"I'll manage somehow. But I won't have a moment's peace, Mother, while you take such unnecessary risks."

The guard who had been the waiter at Béla's favorite café interrupted them; he had to take Anikó back to the Conti-utca jail. He was sure that permission would now be given for Mrs. Szenes to visit her there. Kató promised to try the following Monday.

During the next two days the aerial bombardments grew so much worse that Kató could not go out. She finally managed to visit the Conti-utca prison on November first, but the gatekeeper told her it was All Saints' Day and no visiting was allowed. When she returned the next day, the office was open but she was told that it was up to the military prosecutor, Captain Elemér Simon, to grant permission for visits. His offices were in another part of the city at the Hadik barracks. Kató knew the place only too well: it was where Rózsa had confronted her with Anikó on that fateful morning in June, what seemed now a lifetime ago. It was too late to venture that far, so Kató went there the following morning, only to be told that the captain had left for some business in the country and would not be back in the capital until the seventh of November, the following Tuesday. Was there anybody else, a deputy, who might help her? No, only Captain Simon had the authority to grant a visiting permit.

In the meantime Kató was wondering about the verdict; the eight days would be up on the fifth. She wrote an inquiring note to the defense attorney. Dr. Szelecsényi replied that there would be yet another delay, because the court had a new president who would have to study the transcript. He promised to inform Kató as soon as he heard anything.

On the morning of November seventh, eleven days after the trial, Kató went to see Captain Simon once more. The scene that greeted her at the Hadik barracks was vastly different from the week before. With an air of chaos bordering on panic, uniformed men were running about, carrying bags and trunks and unpacked objects that they were throwing into the nearest available trucks. Engines were running and as soon as a truck was filled to capacity, it was driven through the gates and into the road, where at top speed it took off toward the west. The constant roar of the artillery barrage drifted in from a distance of about twelve miles, where the Russians had their forward positions.

The guard at the gate doubted if Mrs. Szenes could accomplish anything; most of the people at the barracks had already fled or were about to. Somehow she found Simon's office. Two secretaries and an adjutant, in hats and overcoats, were preparing to leave. One of the women told her that Captain Simon had been transferred to Margit-körút, where the trial had been held. If she hurried, she might still find him there. She gave his office number and directions to find it inside the jail.

Oblivious to all danger, Kató rushed back from Pest to Buda, taking more than an hour to cover the distance on foot. She arrived at the Margit-körút jail at about half past ten. The prison that had been so busy on the day of the trial was nearly deserted now, as if everybody had already fled. She raced up to the first floor and after a frantic search she found the captain's office. It was empty. A briefcase lay on the desk with a pair of gloves resting on top. Hoping desperately, Kató waited in the corridor outside. Finally she met a clerk who confirmed that Captain Simon was somewhere in the building and would be returning. Kató waited, feeling numbness take possession of her body. Her mind was trying to remember the day's curfew regulations. That morning Jews were allowed on the streets between ten o'clock and noon. Even if she got the visiting permit, it was unlikely that she could get back to the Conti-utca jail and see Anikó that day.

After about forty-five minutes, the captain came and went into his office. Kató followed him in. She introduced herself and asked for the visiting permit.

"This case is no longer mine," he said. She sensed a certain embarrassment in his voice.

"Since when?" she demanded.

"Since yesterday."

"Who's handling the case now?"

"I don't know."

"Who do I have to ask for a visiting permit?"

"I don't know."

"Should I go to Conti-utca and ask the prison director there?"

"Why don't you try that?"

These curt responses brought Kató's frustrations to a boiling point. "The least you could do, Captain, is give me guidance about the next step. I can't understand why it's so hard to obtain a visitor's pass; I know of many others who have been allowed frequent visits. I've only seen my daughter for ten minutes during all this time."

"Really?" Simon was surprised. "I don't remember allowing that."

"Why isn't there a verdict? The eight days are long up." There was a pause. Simon turned away from Kató's insistent eyes.

"Or is there a verdict?" she persisted anxiously.

"Even if there is, I couldn't tell you."

"Why not? Can you legally keep that from the mother of the accused?"

Once again Simon remained silent, so Kato repeated, "*Is* there a verdict?"

The captain stepped behind his desk and sank into his chair. He motioned Kató to take the chair in front of him.

"Sit down," he said reluctantly. "Are you Jewish? Or was it only your husband?"

"He was, and I am. The whole family is Jewish."

"I don't see you wearing a yellow star."

Kató lifted her handbag, which she had used to camouflage her star, and waited for him to continue. Finally, he spoke: "Are you familiar with your daughter's case?"

"Yes. The defense attorney has kept me informed."

Simon launched into an account of Anikó's military career: how she had given up her Hungarian citizenship when she went to Palestine; how she became a British officer, working as a radio operator; how she had been dropped by parachute into Yugoslavia where she had spent time with the partisans. She came back to Hungary with the alleged purpose of rescuing Jews and British subjects; therefore she had committed grave and serious crimes against her native land . . .

Kató interrupted, quoting Anikó's words in the Gestapo jail, that nothing she had done was to harm the interests of Hungary. But Simon went on.

"These are not ordinary times. Your daughter was court-martialed. She had been found in possession of a military radio. The judges found her guilty of treason and asked for the maximum penalty. And the sentence . . . has already been carried out."

In the interminable silence that followed Kató felt her heart stop. As if she had been suddenly turned into stone, she stared without blinking at the impassive military judge. Slowly her mind began to rebel. What if this was yet another sadistic torment? Did not the attorney's note say that he'd be informed when the verdict date was set? And he would let her know? She grasped this straw: "No, that's not possible. I just got a note from the attorney. Surely he'd have to know about the verdict . . ."

"Of course he knows. He must be trying to spare you."

"Spare me? How long could he spare me from knowing? No, the attorney wrote me the truth. There is no verdict yet . . ."

"Who is the attorney?" asked Simon.

"Dr. Andor Szelecsényi. Here's his letter." She handed him the envelope.

Captain Simon quickly perused the letter and jotted down the name and telephone number: "All right then. We'll give him a call."

With this cavalier dismissal, Kató lost all hope. Overwhelmed with grief, she burst out, "Is this the way things are done here? Can this really happen? That I couldn't see her? That I couldn't talk to her, before . . ."

"She didn't want to see you. She wanted to spare you any further excitement." The captain's voice was carefully bland as he told this blatant lie. Then he elaborated, as if wanting to soften the blow: "She did write some farewell letters . . . I'm sure you'll get the one she wrote to you."

There was a long tense silence, which forced Simon to say, "By the way, I must remark upon your daughter's courage, which she exhibited to the very last." Then as if he had found this incomprehensible and yet admirable, he added, "Fancy, she was actually proud of being Jewish! She really had an extraordinary personality. It's a pity that she used her talents for the wrong cause." Seeing that Kató did not respond, the captain went on: "You must accept what has happened, Mrs. Szenes. This war has claimed many victims. You must think of your daughter as just one more."

Kató asked for the letters he had mentioned. He replied that she could pick them up any morning in the Conti-utca jail. The captain busied himself with his gloves to signal the end of the interview, but Kató remained seated. She had no purpose in life now and nowhere in particular to go. Simon looked at his watch impatiently.

"It's that curfew again," he said. "You could get yourself into a lot more trouble. Here, you'll need this to get back home." He scribbled a note on his official stationery stating that he had summoned Mrs. Szenes on official business.

As Kató stumbled down the stairs, she was seized by the certainty that Captain Elemér Simon had just come from Anikó's execution.

She traveled back to Pest on the tram, which stopped at the corner just opposite the yellow-star house where her sister lived. Irma was cautiously peering out from behind the lace curtains on the second-floor window. Regulations prohibited Jews from looking out the windows of their own apartments, but Irma was terribly anxious. Not only was Kató breaking the curfew, but she was also constantly pestering the authorities, who could so easily rearrest her. Irma was greatly relieved to see Kató alight from the streetcar and waved discreetly to her. But she wondered why Kató lingered there, holding on to a post.

Kató did not think she had strength enough to cross the road. But noticing her sister waving, she summoned up her last ounce of will power, trudged across, and dragged herself up the stairs.

"Did you get the permit? Did you see Anikó?" Irma asked eagerly.

Kató looked at her blankly.

"Anikó is no more . . ." she murmured, barely audible. "She has been executed."

Kató sank to the floor, overcome. Felix was not home, so Irma struggled to put her sister to bed, where she spent the next several days hardly conscious of what was going on around her.

As soon as Felix returned, he and Irma decided to call on Dr. Szelecsényi to find out what he knew. The attorney happened to live near the jail on Margit-körút. As Kató had suspected, he had been told nothing about the verdict or his client's execution. By chance he had seen a hearse leaving the prison, which the gatekeeper told him was carrying the British parachutist woman. He launched an immediate protest against what he called an illegal act of judicial murder. Captain Simon was unmoved by the charge, claiming that the military tribunal had finally decided upon a verdict of death. He offered no official document to back up his claim, and Szelecsényi concluded that Simon had acted on his own. It may have been personal revenge for the speech that Anikó made at her trial, or simply the desire to tie up loose ends before he fled his post. Every day scores of executions took place in the Margit-körút jail, and Anikó was just one more Jew.

Simon continued his lies. In response to the lawyer's questions, Captain Simon briefly described Anikó's last acts. Yes, she did want to see her mother, but there was no time to contact her. Simon could not explain why Szelecsényi himself had not been informed. The captain mentioned Anikó's letters, and even read a few sentences from one of them, but he refused to deliver them to Szelecsényi.

The Jewish Burial Society claimed Anikó's body, which was taken to the Jewish cemetery in Rákoskeresztúr. Nobody was informed about the burial. Irma and Felix tried to find out, but they were told that Jews were not permitted to attend funerals of their own kin. It was a miracle that a Christian gardener who survived the war remembered where she was buried.

A few days later Kató roused herself. She knew she had to hurry to gather Anikó's remaining belongings before all traces of her disappeared into the mounting chaos. Braving an air raid and roving gangs of killers, she and Irma reached the Conti-utca jail and asked for Anikó's letters. The surprised authorities said that Captain Simon would have them, if anyone. After several visits Kató gained partial success—she was given a small bundle of Anikó's clothes. Hidden among them she found two carefully folded pieces of paper. One was the poem that Anikó wrote after their confrontation at the Hadik barracks ("One . . . two . . . three . . ."), dated June twentieth. The other was an undated farewell note, written perhaps during the tortures when she did not know if she would survive much longer. It had to suffice instead of the final one that Captain Simon had apparently taken with him or destroyed:

> Dearest Mother, I don't know what to say—only these two things. A million thanks. Forgive me, if you can. You know so very well why words are not needed. With unending love,
> your Daughter.

TWENTY-NINE

DEATH MARCH

During the week following Anikó's death, Irma tried to obtain for Kató a diplomatic pass, or *Schutzpass*. Because of the reign of terror that followed the Arrow Cross coup, Raoul Wallenberg and a few other diplomats were now issuing these protective passes indiscriminately on tenuous or false evidence. In addition, a number of underground Jewish rescue operations forged them on a massive scale. As a result they became devalued, especially in the eyes of the Hungarian Nazis, who had cared very little for diplomatic niceties in the first place.

Irma had heard that the Zionist organization was empowered to issue a limited number of Swiss documents. She was advised to apply to a man named Salamon at the so-called Glass House on Vadász Street. The Glass House, now an annex to the Swiss Legation, was surrounded by mounted police, allegedly protecting the hundreds of people trying to get in. Irma managed to slip by the guards and hand in her petition. She waited a long time, but nothing happened and finally she went home empty-handed.

Kató meanwhile returned to bed. If she had the strength to wish for anything it was to end her miserable existence, and to be freed from the deadening pain that had never left her since her interview with Captain Simon. On the evening of November thirteenth, Rózsi came to see her, bringing a letter from Judith, her new Christian employer and one of Kató's oldest friends. Judith had been deeply shocked to hear of Anikó's death, and she was now terribly worried about Kató. The city was rife with rumors that the long-feared deportation of Jews from Budapest had finally begun; in her letter she begged Kató to come and hide in her house, while she tried to obtain a Christian birth certificate for her.

Nobody in the yellow-star apartment building knew anything about the deportations. Telephones and radios had long ago been confiscated to prevent any communication that might have led to collective resistance or escape. But Kató had no desire to go anywhere, so she sent the tearful Rózsi back with her thanks. She could not accept a generous offer that would have brought her friends into deadly danger.

The next afternoon, the whole building came alive with noise. People were rushing up and down the echoing stairways and banging on doors. The caretaker told tenants that all of them must line up in the courtyard below with their identity cards, or protective documents if they had any. Irma thought that Kató should stay in bed, but a little later Felix brought the news that guards were about to search every apartment. So Kató dressed and hurried down into the central yard. Lads barely out of school, dressed in Arrow Cross uniforms, were deciding who would be deported and who could stay. They took all men and women between the ages of fourteen and fifty, except those with protective passes. Irma and her husband were allowed to stay in the house, but Kató, who was only forty-eight, would have to leave. Irma barely had time to rush up to the apartment for her sister's bag, which was packed in readiness for the constant air raids. When the time came to part, Irma sobbed uncontrollably. But Kató had no tears left to shed.

She was told to join the line of about thirty people who were to be deported from that one house. Then, accompanied by two armed guards, they marched down the street toward the Gothic mass of the Parliament Buildings. At every corner another column emerged from the gloom of this November twilight: silent, defeated men and women marching toward an unknown fate.

By the time they converged on the eastern end of the Margit Bridge, long lines ahead and behind them were lost in the dusk. Kató and her group crossed the first half of the bridge, where the group was forced to detour north through the island; the rest of the bridge had been blown up by an enormous explosion just a few days before. Now with darkness came the rain, and the pathways of the island turned to mud. Finally the tired marchers crossed the Árpád Bridge into Óbuda, where they were herded into the yard of a brick factory for the night. There was a passageway running around the giant kiln, which gave out a little warmth. The luckier ones could huddle there and dry their clothes. After a sleepless night, they were sorted into columns of a hundred people each, to begin the long march toward Austria.

From people in her row Kató learned that the forced marches had begun the week before, when it became clear that the Russians could break through to the capital within a matter of days. The railroads north toward the Polish death camps were already blocked. Open lines to the West were used by the SS to take all valuables out of the country, including whole disassembled factories, to continue the war effort from within the Reich itself. They commandeered for their own escape whatever railroad cars and wagons were left.

Two of Kató's companions were members of the Csángó family, wealthy merchants who had once owned a well-known chain of leather-goods stores. They were in-laws, and though Mr. Csángó was over fifty, he had volunteered to accompany his sister-in-law in place of her injured husband, so that she would not be alone on this frightful journey. Kató heard him trying, in vain, to bribe a guard to deliver a letter back to his relatives, who were still attempting to procure forged baptismal certificates, which were essential for escape.

By the afternoon the doomed columns had slowed down. Added to the fatigue and fear about their future, the rain had soaked through their bundles and clothes. They covered about ten miles during that first day. Arriving at the town of Piliscsaba they were herded into a camp with a number of huts. These were so crowded that the new arrivals simply dropped to the ground and fell into a deep sleep, despite the wet and the cold.

Unexpectedly during the night Kató found relatives in the camp: Béla's sister and her husband. Ilus and Emil had not heard about Anikó; their own news was almost as depressing. Béla's seventy-year-old mother had been left behind with their daughter, who had given birth the week before. Their twenty-five-year-old son was lying in the hospital with pneumonia. Within the next few weeks all three generations would be dead.

They agreed to try to stay together the following day, but when dawn came and everyone fell into line, Kató could not find them. As the columns moved slowly through the villages, large groups of local peasants came to watch them. Few seemed to feel any sympathy. On the contrary, Kató thought she could detect satisfaction on many of their faces. After all, they had been promised, when the deportations began, that their Jewish neighbors would never return, and it would be safe to take over their houses, fields, and stores. Even those who had not been particularly anti-Semitic before now had reason to be.

Large signs were posted everywhere warning people not to provide help to the marchers, except for water. As usual, the promised penalty was death. Even the guards were afraid of the local Fascists (who turned out to supervise the march through their own villages), becoming more abusive to stragglers when they were in sight.

The third night was spent in a large sports arena. Next morning they received a few crumbs of bread, which had to last them the rest of the day. As they marched, people began to drop dead by the roadside, where they were left beside their small bundles.

The day's survivors were herded that evening into an enclosure surrounded by barbed wire. The night was extremely cold, and the air was filled with the groans and cries of the sick. The guards threatened through loudspeakers that they would fire into the crowd with machine guns if anyone attempted to escape. During the night a couple next to Kató died after horrible convulsions. They had swallowed poison. The guards had refused to bring them water. By dawn, many more corpses littered the field.

Kató finally found Ilus, her sister-in-law. She tried to persuade her and Emil to march with her, but they had already made arrangements with their present companions to carry one another's baggage. Kató felt that she could not leave the Csángó family either, even though they had now decided to escape. They would have to act before they reached the Austrian border; once within the Reich, there would be nowhere to hide. Meanwhile word came that at the next stop they would be met by representatives of various rescue organizations. Anyone with the proper documents could return to Budapest.

A number of people drew fresh hope that their families might have obtained protective passports for them. Automobiles flying foreign or Red Cross emblems drew up beside the column, and diplomats called out the names of people who were supposed to be under protection. Kató had no reason to think that her name would be on any list. Her only hope was that she too might drop by the wayside or fail to wake up to this daily nightmare.

Soon the guards had a crisis on their hands. Many people could not continue on their feet and yet refused to die. At length, the guards hired horse-drawn carts to carry the wounded and their baggage—at the victims' expense.

On the fifth night the marchers arrived in the vicinity of Szöny and were crammed into stables, which stank with large piles of human refuse from those who had preceded them. There was no more mention of rescue organizations.

The next day was to be decisive. Csángó had drawn up a plan whereby he would escape when they reached the town of Gönyö. His sister-in-law and Kató would follow. If all went well, they would be reunited in Budapest.

The exhausted group arrived in the town of Komárom by noon. The city was festive, people fresh from church services were strolling about in their Sunday best, barely giving a second glance to the straggling deportees, who had become a common sight. Suddenly air-raid sirens began to blare and in a matter of seconds all the townfolk disappeared into shelters. The marchers were told to keep marching amidst the falling bombs. But the initial confusion lasted long enough for Csángó to disappear. Kató and Bözsi were at the rear of the column. With the guards' permission, several people now went into a pharmacy to buy medication. It was near a corner and as the march slacked off, Bözsi took the decisive step. She turned her back on them and fled down a side street. Two seconds later Kató followed her. Simultaneously they tore off their yellow stars and began to search for shelter. A few houses away, they noticed a tall woman standing in her front garden, apparently oblivious to the air raid. Bözsi walked up to her and asked for a glass of water. The woman looked around apprehensively, but there was nobody to observe them. She locked the garden gate and invited them into the kitchen of her tiny cottage.

Kindly, she offered them tea or soup. Both women wanted to wash first, so she brought them a pail of water and a washbasin, then went on to prepare the soup. Fortunately she was alone: her husband was in the army and her daughter was staying with the grandparents. It was safe for the two women to hide in the barn at the back. The problem would be in the afternoon when the coachmen hired to transport the disabled marchers might return; they liked to drop in for a chat.

When the coachmen came by a short while later, the two women hid. They tried to form a plan that would get them back to Budapest. Bözsi thought it best to get a message to her husband and wait for him to send them faked birth certificates. But their hostess told them that trains no longer ran to Budapest. She also considered their idea of hiring a cart and hiding under bales of hay too risky: she did not think that any of the coachmen could be trusted. As a last resort she would hide them for the night in her loft, for which Bözsi offered a considerable sum of money. But the woman was clearly reluctant to go that far in defying the law: hiding Jews was punishable by death. In the end, she suggested they thumb a ride with a military transport, which sometimes made room for civilians. Their lack of identity cards should pose no problem; since the deportations had begun the military rarely bothered to check papers.

Kató and Bözsi had no choice but to take the risk. They left most of their blankets and clothes behind, as well as Bözsi's wedding ring and some money. After dusk, the woman directed them to the major crossroads on the edge of town, where a growing crowd of people waited for rides. After several hours a truck stopped. Kató and Bözsi squeezed in, their disguise assisted by total darkness. They squatted in a corner near total exhaustion, hoping to remain unnoticed by the other passengers.

Most of the people in the the truck were returning from a buying expedition, as food items were becoming scarce in the capital. Now laden with vegetables, live chickens, and ducks, they were in a jolly mood, singing and exchanging jokes. Somebody was playing the harmonica. Kató heard a deep male voice ask: "You've seen the way they're transporting those Jews? They even provide them with carriages. And they guard them so sloppily that many of them escape!" But the other passengers failed to be aroused to anger by the man's outburst; they continued to sing and joke as if they had not a care in the world. The two Jewish stowaways breathed more easily again.

Near midnight the truck rolled into Budapest, and the two women got off near the house where Bözsi used to live. Her apartment was now occupied by a young Christian couple, but Bözsi said that the caretaker was trustworthy and would probably let them hide for one night. Most tenement houses in Budapest were locked up by ten; without a key the only way to get in was to ring the bell. They waited tensely until the small peephole was pushed open and they felt someone peering out at them.

"Oh, thank God you're alive," a man cried, quickly opening the heavy gate. He seemed genuinely relieved to see Bözsi and led them up to her former apartment, where half a dozen people had taken sanctuary and were sheltered by the caretaker and his wife. The young woman who now lived in the apartment shared in taking the risk. She prepared a warm meal and a hot bath for the new arrivals; the others meanwhile filled them in on events of the past week. The news was almost uniformly bleak. By the following night all remaining Jews were supposed to be inside the official ghetto. Those with protective documents were required to move into special safe houses flying the flag of the country that provided the protection. A great number of these were also in the designated ghetto. More than one hundred thousand people had been herded into this roughly twelve-block area. Many knew that this was prelude to further horrors that had already been inflicted on other Jewish communities under German occupation. So people who had barely escaped the expulsions and forced marches now began another desperate search for hiding places before the deadline.

That night, Kató and Bözsi slept for the first time in more than a week. At seven-thirty in the morning the caretaker came in. He had heard that each house was to be thoroughly searched soon and asked them regretfully to leave, since he did not want to compromise his own position. This was received in stunned silence. There was simply nowhere for them to go except the ghetto, which they were all determined to avoid. Another half hour passed, and the caretaker came back to repeat his warning. Kató felt that she could not place any more burdens on Bözsi, who had already saved her life. Several in the room advised her to go either to the Red Cross or to the Advisory Bureau on Jewish Affairs; if they heard her story, maybe they could give her a Swiss passport and secure her a place in a safe house.

Kató thanked them, although she had no reason to believe that those organizations would provide her with any help. As she passed the kitchen door, the young woman who had welcomed them the night before noticed that she was leaving.

"Where are you going?"

"I don't really know," Kató answered truthfully.

"Do you have any documents? Any paper to show that you are a Christian?"

"No."

"Why don't you take this," she said, offering her a birth certificate. "It is my mother's. It's very dangerous to be on the streets without identity papers."

"I don't know if I'll be able to return it any time soon."

"Take it. We're not in any hurry to get it back."

The Red Cross office nearby referred her to the Jewish Advisory Bureau on the Baross-utca, where Kató found a crowd that filled the lobby of the office block and spilled out onto the street. There were very few hours that Jews were allowed outside the barricades of the newly established ghetto. Anybody who still nurtured the hope of exemption was storming the few Jewish agencies that were allowed to stay open precisely to feed such hopes.

Kató struggled to the top of the stairs on the second floor, where a couple of harassed officials were trying to respond to questions that were aimed at them in the form of desperate wails and angry outbursts. When she finally caught a man's attention, Kató told him that she had nowhere to go. Without a second's pause he shot back: "We're not here to provide a roof over your head, lady. We're supposed to save lives!" and he had already turned to the next person. As Kató pushed her way back through the stream of humanity, she wondered bitterly how the man could not see the connection between the two.

Back on the street, she drifted along aimlessly. She caught herself heading toward Bözsi's apartment, surprised at how the homing instinct, when one is homeless, can assert itself after a single night. She had to force herself into another direction. She wandered along Rákóczi-út, one of the city's busiest shopping streets. It was hard to accept that a few months before the cafés and restaurants had been filled with laughing and seemingly carefree people. Now mounds of rubble rose everywhere in the wake of constant bombing.

After an hour, Kató suddenly remembered her friend Judith, who had offered her home before Kató was taken on the death march. Now that Kató had a Christian birth certificate, the risk to Judith was considerably less. And in truth, she had nowhere else to go. If Irma and Felix were still alive, they must have moved into a safe house or the ghetto, and without a Swedish pass Kató would never be admitted into their house.

Kató took a streetcar to Buda. Judith and her husband owned several small, old buildings near the foot of Castle Hill. Judith's English school had expanded quickly until the German occupation, and these houses around their residence were used both for classrooms and for boarding students. Kató anxiously rang the bell. Her apprehensions were somewhat dissolved when her Rózsi opened the door. She and Judith's mother were beside themselves with joy to see Kató standing there. By coincidence, Judith had just gone out to try to find out what had become of Kató. A short time later she returned, almost in hysterics.

"They took her away . . . The caretaker at her sister's told me . . ." she sobbed to her mother.

"Who? For God's sake, what's happened now?"

"Kató was taken on a death march . . . A week ago . . ."

"Calm down, Judith," her mother said. "Kató is here."

As the whole family sat down to lunch, Kató was bombarded with questions: were the reports of the horrors of the deportations and marches true? She replied circumspectly that no words could describe the actual truth. There was a thirteen-year-old child at the table, and she did not want to go into details.

"I think it would be very good for my son to hear this," Judith replied, "and I hope he will never forget it."

After lunch Judith drew Kató aside and said she had a plan. Not far from her house was a convent. The nuns ran a hospital for women, which adjoined the convent, and the chief surgeon, Dr. Miklós Dubay, was a reliable friend of Judith's. While Kató spent the afternoon sleeping, Judith went to see him.

"It's all arranged," she announced triumphantly, bringing Kató supper on a tray. "Tomorrow morning you have an appointment at the hospital. They're going to admit you to make some tests. By the time the results are known, maybe the war will be over." The optimism was not entirely groundless. The Russian artillery sounded closer each day from the southeast; daily the air raids intensified.

Next day, on the morning of November twenty-second, the two women walked down Fö-utca, which runs parallel to the Danube. They headed north arm in arm, Christian and Jew, in a neighborhood where both had lived more than half their lives. Any number of people could have recognized them, knowing that Kató was supposed to be inside the ghetto and that Judith had no business befriending a Jew. Yet they walked with their heads erect in the biting autumn wind, knowing they had no choice.

In about ten minutes they arrived at Batthány-tér, a busy square surrounded on three sides by elegant eighteenth-century buildings. The fourth side was open, like the proscenium of a stage, with a backdrop of the

Danube and the voluminous Houses of Parliament framed on the far side of the river. The convent on the north side of the square was housed in a two-story neoclassical building with large windows. The entrance to the hospital was on Fö-utca, and Kató could see, no more than a hundred yards farther on the other side, the somber brick prison in which she and Anikó had spent three months. From her present perspective they had been relatively sunny months. Anikó was alive then and they both still had hope.

THIRTY

THE PRICE OF A LIFE

Dr. Dubay greeted the two women with matter-of-fact cordiality. To maintain the impression that this was a routine check-up, he explained the tests and examinations. Since no beds were available in the general ward, he had arranged for Kató to be placed in the section for internal diseases. Then he directed them to the nun in charge of admissions.

Kató had spent the previous evening memorizing the details of her false birth certificate and inventing a fictitious life for herself, places she had lived and what happened to her family and herself in almost half a century. Judith had advised her to say that she had fled from Szolnok, an agricultural town on the Great Plain. It had already fallen to the Russians and there would be no way of checking her story, should anybody become suspicious.

Kató was nervous, like any congenital truth-teller. She had never even been to Szolnok! What worried her most, however, was her complete ignorance of the Christian religion and its customs. Judith taught her how to make the sign of the cross, and told her not to worry—after all, there were plenty of lapsed or occasional Catholics. A nun took down Kató's personal data without suspicion. Judith saw to it that she was comfortably put to bed with a pile of books on her night table, and told her to get in touch if she needed anything.

Kató turned her face to the wall, to avoid conversation, but the other four women in the room at once began to question her. The oldest asked right away whether Kató knew her relatives in Szolnok. Kató was forced to change her story: she did not actually live in Szolnok but was visiting when the Russians reached there. This elicited instant sympathy from the others, a woman and her two daughters. Their estate apparently had been overrun by the Red Army, while her husband, an army officer, served on the front.

After months of prison and terrible privations, the hospital routine provided tremendous luxuries: central heating, a clean bed, a warm bath, three meals a day, and the constant care of the sisters. Unfortunately, it was not to last. Two days later a nurse announced the hospital's decision that patients well enough to walk would have to go home to make room for others. The real reason for this change in policy was a series of newspaper articles accusing hospitals of sheltering Jews and deserters. The Arrow Cross had threatened to search every institution, so the hospital was taking preventive action to protect legitimate patients.

The nurse told Kató that she would have to talk to Dr. Dubay. Kató at once called Judith, who promised to contact the doctor. She did more: she approached the head of the hospital, whom she knew less well. That evening the nurse came into the room and said, "Etelka Kovács wanted on the telephone."

Nobody stirred. Kató was awake reading.

"Isn't Etelka Kovács here?" the nurse asked in surprise. Finally it dawned on Kató that this was the name on her false papers. She put on a dressing gown and hurried to the phone. It was Judith, reassuring her that she could stay on.

Not long afterward, the mother of the two girls was discharged. Listening to her daughters, who spoke very freely, Kató gathered that their story too was largely fabricated. They were posing as fugitives from the country, yet they seemed to know every street in Budapest. After a while it came out that they had gone to the same school as Anikó. Their mother managed to get a cleaning job at the hospital, and spent every afternoon visiting her former ward. She brought her daughters whatever extra food she could find, and what was more valuable for Kató, news of the latest atrocities on the outside.

The approach of Christmas generated a great deal of excitement among the nuns, who were decorating a big tree just as if peace and good will reigned on earth. On the twenty-fourth of December, the traditional observance of the Christmas holiday in Hungary, they invited those patients who could walk down into the central vestibule. A great number gathered there, most of them in perfect health. They could see through the French doors into the big hall, which was filled with decorations. Around the fully dressed tree a small choir of children sporting white vestments and little wings was getting ready to sing. Suddenly the whole building shook and plaster was falling everywhere. One of the wings of the hospital sustained a direct hit from an artillery shell. The siege of Budapest had begun.

During the ensuing panic the nuns ordered all patients to take their bedclothes and essentials into the basement. The two-hundred-year-old convent had enormous vaults, in places six feet thick. They would have made an ideal shelter except for the lack of space. The more agile patients took the available beds, leaving those who were truly sick to chairs and other makeshift arrangements.

The nuns were trying to carry on the festivities and serve the holiday meal when the lights went out. The electrical system had been hit. The following day the water main was put out of action, leaving hundreds of people in the dark and without water.

Air raids rarely lasted more than a few hours, and then life would quickly return to normal. That was what everybody expected now. But the Russians had arrived at the outskirts of Pest and their artillery pounded the capital without relief. Most of the hospitals in Pest were evacuated, and vast numbers of wounded soldiers and civilian patients were brought across the river. Among them were pregnant women and people whose nerves had been shattered by the war. The hospital lacked medical facilities underground, so with each passing day a number of patients died. When the convent morgue became full, bodies were piled up in the courtyard where the unusually harsh winter froze the corpses and for the time being checked epidemics.

At night, during the occasional lull in the shelling, Kató ventured outside into the eerie quiet to pry some ice from the broken pipes. Already some entrepreneurs were selling bottled water for a price. It was too precious to use for personal hygiene.

Conditions grew worse during the next three weeks. By the middle of January the Russians had occupied the eastern half of Hungary, including Pest. The Danube became once again the moat against armies from the East. As the Germans retreated westward across the river they blew up the city's magnificent bridges, cutting the lifelines between the twin cities. They swore to defend Buda street by street, house by house. From the Pest side, the Russian gunners had a panoramic view of their targets across the Danube, including the totally exposed square where the convent stood.

Hospitals are supposed to be neutral ground in war, under the protection of the Red Cross. Against the vigorous protests of the doctors, some Germans barricaded themselves on the first floor of the convent with their light artillery and machine guns. The convent church, one of the finest examples of baroque architecture in the capital, became a stable for their horses. The entire hospital became a prime target for the Russian gunners.

The massive vaults withstood the bombardment for another month, but supplies were running out. Daily rations were reduced to a bowl of diluted soup with one piece of bread. As more wounded were brought in, the nuns no longer had time for the less serious cases in the women's ward. Kató herself went to another part of the cellars to help out. The sick were piled practically on top of one another. Blankets, when available, served for mattresses. The fetid air was filled with the stench of gangrene. Nobody had washed for weeks; even the healthy were tormented by lice. Kató found Dr. Dubay working on an improvised operating table. He had been practically without sleep for weeks, and yet he was even-tempered, knowing just the right words of encouragement to bring a patient back from the brink of despair.

One day water began to seep up from below, forming puddles at first, but soon flooding large areas of the basement. The survivors hastily gathered their belongings and dragged the wounded up above ground. Some sought shelter in the less damaged parts of the convent. Others spent the next two nights in the open during one of the coldest Februaries on record. They were surrounded by piles of frozen corpses, which could not be buried because of the artillery barrage and the intractable ground.

The third dawn Kató noticed people venturing across the frozen river in front. Now the artillery barrage had stopped and there was no sign of the Germans in the surrounding buildings. Only the distant rattle of sporadic gunfire could be heard from the hills of Buda. As they listened to the tense silence, Kató and her companions began to think the impossible: the war might be over at last.

Even though liberation seemed only hours away, Kató doubted she would live to see it. She was so weak that the others took her inside the convent and found a bed for her. She closed her eyes and sank into a comatose sleep.

She woke as warm hands caressed her hands. Trying to focus her eyes, she saw Rózsi, sent by Judith to fetch her. The Schanda residence had been turned into rubble, but the family had found refuge in an adjoining building. Kató promised to join them as soon as she gathered enough strength. Later that day Russian soldiers arrived and distributed cigarettes and canned food. They inspected the sick, searching for soldiers and possible resisters. Military uniforms had long ago been discarded, and they were assured that the patients were all civilians.

Early next morning, Kató set out toward her own house on the Rózsadomb. Normally it would have taken no more than half an hour to walk up the hill. Now the full horrors of the siege unfolded before her. Hardly a wall remained upright. Vast canyons of rubble covered acres where apartment houses once stood. The brick fortress on Fö-utca, where she and Anikó had spent what now seemed such happy days in prison, had huge gashes. Dead horses lay in the streets, their legs twisted around burntout tanks, all the flesh hacked and scraped from their sides by starving people.

The destruction was so complete that Kató, who had lived in that neighborhood for a quarter century, was lost. The streets had simply disappeared. Looking back down at the once-magnificent view of the city astride the Danube, she saw a smoky holocaust. After an hour and a half, she finally found what remained of Bimbó-út. From the outside the little villa seemed to be standing. Going through the gaping hole where once the garden gate stood she noticed that the roof had collapsed. As elsewhere in the city, not a single window remained intact. Inside she found Russian soldiers looking for loot. All the closets had been turned inside out and Kató saw dozens of Béla's manuscripts, his books, their children's letters and photographs, all lying in filthy heaps exposed to the elements. Fortunately none of these precious possessions interested the liberators, and when they realized that she was the owner of the house, they mumbled something in Russian and left.

Numbed, Kató tried to think how to save the family souvenirs. The house was uninhabitable, and she did not know what had become of the caretakers, whose presence might inhibit further looting. She knocked at the neighboring house and the first person she saw was the caretaker's wife, who fell crying into her arms, amazed that she had survived. They had not seen each other since that first afternoon when the Gestapo arrested her. The woman recounted a familiar tale of horrors, ending with her husband's death from shrapnel and his burial in the garden. She herself had moved next door later, when the roof caved in, and after Margit had gone to stay with friends. Now she invited Kató to her new quarters, a one-bedroom apartment crammed with eleven people. Even more generous was her offer to share her stash of canned food; each can now was worth more than diamonds.

Kató promised to return the next day. On her way back to the convent, she met one of her neighbors. His name was Vajda, an architect. Unexpectedly, he knew details of Anikó's last hours. His son, also called Gyuri, was jailed in the Margit-körút prison for underground activities. His work assignment was in Supplies. On November sixth he was given orders to provide an extra portion of food for a British officer accused of spying. He delivered the meal and instantly recognized Anikó. She told him briefly what had happened since she had left for Palestine. The following morning, Gyuri got another order: no portion for Anna Szenes. Alarmed, he hurried to her cell. It was empty. From the courtyard below he heard the sound of a military detail marching. He quickly looked down and from the window witnessed unobserved Anikó's last minutes: her refusal to be blindfolded and her defiant stand in front of the firing squad, which had unnerved even Captain Simon.

With renewed anguish Kató listened to Vajda's story. The morning's events had already drained her limited physical and emotional resources, and she was barely able to drag herself back to the convent. Most of the survivors were still there, either unable to move or with nowhere to go. After months of role-playing, they now revealed their identities. Most of the patients turned out to be Jews or other victims of persecution. The doctors and the nuns had known all along who they were, and had admitted them at great risk to themselves.

The following morning Kató expressed her deep gratitude to these doc-

tors and the sisters and walked to Judith's house. They were still in the
shelter of the house opposite, but Mr. Schanda, an architect, was already
busy renovating. They wanted Kató to stay, but the thought of her un-
guarded house with the precious papers drove her back to the Rózsadomb.

When she arrived there, the caretaker related that Russians had searched
through the house, confiscating most of her canned food and leaving barely
enough for herself.

After a few days next door, Kató became too anxious about further
looting in her own house and tried to fix up a room where she and the
caretaker could live. The latter was terrified to move; she was afraid of
being raped by the Russian soldiers and felt safer with a dozen people
around. None of the men would help Kató rebuild, because they risked
being press-ganged into labor battalions, newly formed now by the Russians. After all she had endured, however, Kató was not afraid. With the
caretaker's help she boarded up some windows and constructed a temporary shelter inside the house, where she began the painful task of sorting
through letters, photographs, and papers to see how many could be preserved. The work proceeded very slowly. With the cold and the hunger,
she had very limited energy reserves, and nearly all of these were consumed
in the daily tasks of survival.

Since Kató felt that her age and debilitated appearance protected her
from rape by the liberating army, she undertook the difficult journey down
the hill to the nearest working water tap. Long lines of people waited to
fill their jars and buckets with clean water, necessary to sustain life. Each
trip took several hours out of a brief day and left her completely exhausted.
Finding food was much harder. Occasionally she was given a loaf of black
bread by a Russian soldier; otherwise everybody had to fend for himself.
There were no stores, only peasants coming into the city to sell their
produce. But this too was in short supply, given the season and the dis-
ruption of the harvest by the war. Money was worthless; only gold and
jewelry could buy food on the flourishing black market.

Judith's mother had given Kató a small container of wheat. She kept it
for a long time, both as a treasure and because she did not quite know
what to do with it. But one day when she felt she could not endure the
hunger pangs any longer, she found her old coffee grinder and ground the
wheat into flour. Adding water she worked it into rough dough, which left
her hands with bloody bruises. This first loaf of bread she made, though
lacking in some essential ingredients, was the best she had ever tasted in
her life.

In March the icebound Danube began its noisy breakup. Crossing was
no longer possible except by boat, an extremely perilous undertaking amidst
the rapidly moving ice floes. Kató had long worried about the fate of her
sister, Irma, and her husband on the other side of the river, but she had

no idea how to trace them. The telephones did not work and regular mail had not resumed, although some of the adventurous rivermen offered to deliver letters between the two cities. Kató decided to send a message to Dr. Palágyi, the old family lawyer; he had an apartment close to the Jewish quarter where Irma and Felix had lived before they were forced to move. To her surprise she received his reply a few days later saying that her sister and brother-in-law had already been to see him: they had come through the siege relatively unscathed. Dr. Palágyi would let them know at once that Kató too had survived.

One day, as Kató was sitting outside the remains of her house, trying to gain a little strength from the feeble rays of the sun, she noticed an old couple stop and look quizzically at her. After a long moment, she recognized Irma and Felix. They had the same difficulty recognizing Kató. They embraced wordlessly, practically the only survivors of a once large family.

A temporary pontoon bridge brought a trickle of foot traffic between Buda and Pest. Soon after her reunion with Irma and Felix, as Kató sat outside her house, she saw a young man coming down the street who looked vaguely familiar. Greeting her, he reminded her of his name, Gyuri Fuchs. He had been one of Anikó's friends and admirers in the Zionist Youth movement. He had been drafted into a forced labor battalion and never reached Palestine. When the Germans came, he joined the Jewish resistance movement; he told Kató how they rescued people on their way to being shot and dumped into the Danube; they even got inside jails, wearing stolen Nazi uniforms. Kató was spared the ordeal of telling Gyuri about Anikó; he had heard about her return and martyrdom while working at the Glass House. He also knew about Irma's efforts to get Kató a protective pass; he was shocked to learn that she had never gotten it. The young man brought a little food with him from his parents' tiny cache, a small piece of bread and the first egg that Kató had seen in many weeks. She accepted it gratefully.

In the last week of March, another young man appeared at the house on Bimbó-út with a letter that came from the other side of the river by hired boat. Kató read: "My hands tremble and my eyes fill with tears as I write this letter . . ."

It was from Yoel Palgi, the only survivor of the three Palestinian commandos who had reached Budapest. He spoke of Anikó's great heroism, and of his certainty that she would become a legendary figure in Jewish history. He wanted Mrs. Szenes to accompany the bearer of the letter to Pest, where Yoel would house her until he could arrange passage for her to Palestine. He begged her to remember how much her son Gyuri, who now worked with Yoel's chaverim at Kibbutz Maagan, missed and needed her. She should pack up her most precious souvenirs and essential possessions and leave Hungary at the earliest opportunity. He also enclosed some money, which he said was Anikó's and therefore belonged to Mrs. Szenes. He apologized for not fetching her in person, but he still carried the responsibility to fulfill the task for which Anikó and her comrades had come—to rescue the Jewish remnant from Europe.

Kató was eager to meet Yoel, but she was uncertain about leaving the country so soon. Much as she wanted to be reunited with her remaining child, there was so much she had to do first. She wanted to find Anikó's grave and learn what had happened to many other relatives. She did not feel she had the strength to go to the end of the street, let alone travel to Palestine, which seemed like the end of the world.

But Yoel's letter had given her back the desire to live, even if somewhere else. What was there to stay for in Budapest? Could she imagine living amidst the ruins of everything that had once been her life, among the murderers of her daughter, relatives and friends? Still, she wanted to see the murderers brought to justice. A few weeks after the liberation she went to see Éva Singer, her good friend Edith's daughter, who had survived the Holocaust, having hidden her small baby with an Aryan working-class family. Éva now had a job with the people's tribunals that were being set up to try Nazi criminals, and she promised to help Kató track down Captain Simon.*

As soon as Kató gathered enough strength, she went to visit Yoel, who lived in the district near the Városliget, a large park at the far end of Pest. Kató walked down to the Danube embankment, across the pontoon bridge, and then several miles to Yoel's address. The east bank had been liberated in mid-January, and great progress had been made in clearing the rubble and beginning general reconstruction. Some stores were open and there was an incongruous normality to the comings and goings of busy pedestrians in the middle of total devastation.

The long journey exhausted Kató physically. Yoel welcomed her as his own mother; his praises for Anikó and Gyuri were greater than any brother could have offered. And of course he had much to relate about the secret details of their mission, which Anikó had kept from her for military reasons and to protect her against possible torture.

*After the war Captain Simon was caught and sentenced to one year in prison by a tribunal. However, he never served his sentence and escaped from Hungary. He disappeared until November 1985, when major Israeli newspapers carried a report that he was alive and living in Argentina. He was interviewed there by Knesset member Dov Shilansky. The seventy-two-year-old Julius [sic] Simon claimed that Chana Szenes had been the only person whom he sentenced to death and that he had no regrets: " 'If I were to start my life over, I would have chosen again to become a military judge and would have sentenced her to death again . . .' He said that Chana refused to ask for a pardon, and if she had, she might have been spared because the Russians were approaching and the judges were nervous . . . but she made them so angry with her Jewish pride that they decided to sentence her to death" (*Maariv,* November 11, 1985).

Yoel lived with a group of young Zionists in a bombed-out villa. He would try to lodge Mrs. Szenes in a nearby hotel as soon as it had been sufficiently repaired to reopen. For the time being he offered her his own room. He would sleep in a corner of his office, where he was working on arrangements for the first aliyah from Central Europe following the Holocaust. Despite the six million Jewish dead, British immigration policy for the survivors had not changed. Yoel had only a limited number of legal certificates, of which Kató would get one. He was also helping younger and more able-bodied people to get to ports on the Black Sea, where illegal vessels were waiting to take them through the British naval blockade to Palestine.

Hesitant to leave her home completely, Kató made the long trek across the river several times a week. Finally Yoel persuaded her that the group might be leaving for Constantsa on very short notice, so it was best to stay close. Meanwhile, he overwhelmed her with small attentions. He told her that she should be receiving some money soon, confirming something Anikó had once whispered to Kató in jail. She had told Kató that the Jewish paratroopers had been offered danger-money by the British before leaving on the mission. They all refused, because they were volunteers, not mercenaries. They asked instead for their families to receive compensation if they did not return, so insurance policies were arranged with the Jewish agency. Anikó mentioned that Kató would be entitled to two thousand pounds sterling, still a considerable sum in those days. Yoel was sure that as soon as the British diplomatic mission returned to Budapest, Kató would be given immediate assistance.

Meanwhile the first newspaper that appeared published a story about the paratroopers and the heroic martyrdom of Anna Szenes. There was a strong human-interest angle and Béla Szenes had been a good friend and valued colleague of many of the surviving journalists. Embellishments and testimonials began to circulate from those who had known Anikó. Others were eager to clear their record and testify before the people's tribunals.

Finally a British military mission did arrive in Budapest, five years after the severance of diplomatic relations. Kató first learned of it through Yoel, who was summoned by a Major O'Rourke. The major had already heard about the newspaper story and was wondering what he could do to help Mrs. Szenes. He wanted Yoel to convey to her that she should not talk to the press about what had happened to her daughter and why the British had sent her into Hungary. Since Yoel was only too aware that the British had done everything possible to prevent the paratroopers from coming to Hungary, he suggested that O'Rourke tell this directly to Mrs. Szenes. The interview took place a few days later. Major O'Rourke expressed his profound regret and repeated his concern that Kató should not speak publicly about what she knew.

"Everybody here has been waiting for the British mission," Kató replied, "waiting for a thorough investigation into Anikó's murder. As she was a British officer—"

"Not exactly, madame."

"—she should have been protected under the normal conventions for prisoners of war."

"Well, she was not a regular soldier, but an agent—"

"I think there are many people here," Kató said with emphasis, "who want to see how the British behave toward those who made sacrifices for British interests. For instance, if she had been really British—"

"The fact that she was an agent, or rather that she was a Palestinian," the major shifted his stance, "does not mean that we are not concerned. But we do not want the Russians to find out about our methods of operation." Kató was confused, having understood that the British and the Russians were allies who had just fought and won a war together.

"We would much rather take this to an international tribunal," O'Rourke continued. "I understand that you want to go to Palestine, Mrs. Szenes. Let me assure you that we British very much care about what has happened and want to demonstrate it." Kató thought that he was going to bring up the subject of the insurance policy, but he did not.

"I can't tell you anything more concrete right now, but I want you to promise that you will come up and see me before you leave town."

That evening Yoel rushed into her room.

"Well, what did he say?"

"Nothing, really," and she recounted the conversation verbatim. "Great Britain is a very great power," she added, "but it can neither buy me nor stop me from telling the truth about what happened." Yoel was surprised to hear her speak that way, as was Kató herself. Both recognized that she had learned this new toughness from her daughter.

In April Yoel left Hungary and told Kató to wait for the arrangements for her aliyah, which should be confirmed any day. He would meet her in Palestine, and promised to find Gyuri and give him the news of her survival. Kató moved into the small hotel, as Yoel had arranged. There was still no glass in the windows and no heat, but at least the weather was growing warmer. Her new accommodation also had the advantage of being nearer to Irma and Felix's old apartment, to which they had returned. Kató still spent most of her energies on day-to-day survival. She weighed barely ninety pounds and food was still extremely scarce. Kató and Irma would spend hours each day in line at the soup kitchen set up by the Joint Distribution Committee with American funds.

After a few days in her new quarters, Kató returned to find the message that a British sergeant had called several times. Major O'Rourke had sent him.

"Mrs. Szenes, could you tell us please where you bank?" The young man did not seem to realize that in a city where practically every vestige of civilized life had been extinguished, where only the necessities for survival had any value, people no longer had bank accounts. A few valuables might have escaped the confiscations, extortions, and pillage by the SS, the Arrow Cross, and the Red Army—if they had been hidden and their owners were not tortured to confess the location. Whatever Kató still possessed had been hidden on the estate of the Sas family in Dombovár, but of course she had no idea what had become of them.*

The sergeant was convinced that the British government had already transferred the insurance funds to the Jewish Agency, and that it was simply a question of wiring the money, perhaps through the Palestine Bank, the one Kató had used occasionally when Anikó needed help. But neither the British soldier nor Kató could guess that it would take several years before she finally received the two thousand inflated pounds that some insurance appraiser had put on Anikó's life.

---

*She soon found out that most of the Sas family had been rounded up, and almost all of them perished in Auschwitz, including Anikó's closest friend, the beautiful Évi.

THIRTY-ONE

SURVIVING

Kató waited several more months for her Romanian visa, which would enable her to board a ship from Constantsa to Palestine. It was not the only obstacle to her aliyah. During the chaotic aftermath of the war, the logistics of organizing such a voyage for Holocaust survivors from several countries posed tremendous challenges for the Haganah and the Palmach, which had to go underground as soon as the war was finished to begin their war of independence from the British. According to the White Paper, 1945 was to be the last year that Jews would be admitted legally to Palestine, even though the meager quota of seventy-five thousand immigrants had not been filled.

The Jewish survivors of the Holocaust numbered in the hundreds of thousands. Liberated from the death camps, they were placed in other camps for displaced persons. Some would wander for years through the countries of Europe, in search of their former identities, families, and homes. When these Jews returned to their native towns, many were accused afresh of causing the miseries of the war and of defeat. If ever there was a moral and physical imperative for creating the homeland that the Balfour Declaration had promised a generation before, now was the time.

Jewish hopes were raised when the British electorate turned Winston Churchill's wartime government out of office, and the new Labour government, under strong international pressure, seemed willing to take the Palestine question to the new United Nations. But when President Truman asked that one hundred thousand displaced persons be admitted into Palestine, Labour Prime Minister Attlee counteroffered a number below twenty-five thousand.

Kató of course knew nothing of these global machinations. Like everybody else in the shattered country, she lived one day at a time. Her most urgent need, before she left, was to tend to the dead: she had to find out where Anikó was buried, and Béla's grave in the Rákoskeresztúri Cemetery had been neglected for many months. On her earliest trip across the river, Kató had sought out the offices of the Jewish Burial Society. During the past year this brave organization had coped with the mounting losses of Jewish lives as best it could under severe restrictions imposed by the Nazi occupation. The reign of terror and the siege of Budapest had produced thousands more Jewish dead each week. Throughout the spring, as the ice melted in the Danube, more corpses had to be fished out, most of them stripped of all identification by their murderers. Others were found under the rubble, in shelters that were sealed off by collapsing buildings. It was highly unlikely that anyone would have kept records about the resting place of one Jewish girl. Kató had to prepare herself for the pain of never seeing her daughter's grave.

Miraculously, somebody at the Burial Society found the name and record of a burial on November eighth, the day after Anikó's execution. Kató took the slip of paper, which directed her to a section and row in the Kerepesi cemetery. After a long walk past the ruins of the Keleti Pályaud-var—the train station where she had seen Anikó off in another lifetime five years before—Kató finally arrived at the famous cemetery, which had a segregated section for Jews. She spent hours walking up and down the endless rows of disheveled graves, yet she could not find the plot. About to give up, she saw a man, who looked like a caretaker or gardener, approaching.

"Who are you looking for?" he asked. Kató told him and showed him the slip of paper. The man looked at it and said, "I know this. The British parachutist girl . . . But she isn't here, madame. These numbers are for the cemetery in Rákoskeresztúr. You will find her in the Martyrs' section. I buried her there myself."

The man's name was János Nyíri, one of those ordinary heroes of extraordinary times. After the Jewish gravediggers were arrested or prevented from leaving the ghetto, he supervised the burial of Jewish victims by Christian gravediggers. Despite the chaotic situation, he honored his promise to the Burial Society that proper Jewish rituals would be observed. He also kept accurate records of each burial, even to the point of noting the exact position of each corpse in multiple graves.

Nyíri happened to be at the Burial Society offices on November eighth when a cart carrying fresh corpses arrived. The Society's remaining employees were trying to determine who Anikó was and how to dispose of her corpse. As an officer of a foreign army she was obviously someone special, and perhaps she could be buried in the section reserved for martyrs. On the other hand, she was also a Jew and in the authorities' eyes, no Jew could be considered a martyr. An added complication came from the interdiction on any Jew giving instructions, even about details of a burial, to a Christian. Even though Nyíri seemed an exceptionally decent person, this was not a time when Jews found it easy to trust anyone. So one of the clerks at the Burial Society phrased his request very cautiously: "I don't think, Mr. Nyíri, that anybody should get into trouble if this corpse happened to be buried in the Martyrs' section." Next day the gardener returned with the exact location of the grave; it was somebody at the Burial Society who made the mistake of filing it under the wrong cemetery.

It would take several more weeks before public transport was restored to distant Rákoskeresztúr, and Kató was on the first bus that left from downtown with its load of sad-looking people. In the cemetery, Kató quickly found the plot indicated by Nyíri. He had marked the grave carefully with a wooden stake that gave her name and the date of burial. Kató wept in the place where her young husband had now been joined by their young daughter.

Yoel was still in Budapest and accompanied Kató on her next visit. Somehow he managed to find a pot of geraniums, which he placed on his fallen comrade's grave. He also left money to commission András Beck, a prominent Hungarian artist, to sculpt a memorial to Anikó. Kató visited the artist several times and saw a model of the sculpture, which was not finished until several years later.

Toward the end of July there was still no visa from Romania, no money from the British, and not much of a life for Kató. Following that first newspaper account, the legend of Anikó's martyrdom circulated by word of mouth in Budapest, and Kató's journalist friends were gently pressuring her to tell the full story. She resisted, remembering Major O'Rourke's admonition, but finally decided that Anikó's mission would only be fulfilled if people knew about her. One afternoon, as she was in the middle of her first such interview with Zsigmond Szöllősi, an old colleague of Béla's, two Zionists came and told her that a car was standing outside, ready to leave for Romania. The visa had finally materialized, after certain palms had been greased.

Kató had been packed for weeks, but she did want to say goodbye to her sister and brother-in-law. The young men offered to fetch them while she prepared to leave. Within half an hour they returned with Felix and Irma, who had managed to grab food for Kató's journey. Kató gave them the money to pay for her room and then a tearful farewell followed: the two surviving sisters—the other two had perished in Auschwitz—knew they were not likely to see each other again. Then, much to the old journalist's amazement, Kató was gone—as if making her aliyah to Palestine was something she had scheduled for that part of the afternoon.

The car, one of the very few private vehicles functioning in the whole country, had a Red Cross painted on it; for added protection, it flew a Czech flag. The young Zionists were staying behind in Budapest, entrusting Kató to an able young lawyer who spoke Romanian and had made the journey several times. Later it turned out that the young man was only a law student, but they called him doctor to reassure Kató and to impress anybody who stopped them for identification.

The car was driven by a Hungarian chauffeur who was not Jewish. He assured them that they would be across the Hungarian border by ten that evening and in Bucharest the following day. The car was stopped frequently at military checkpoints, but they had a prepared cover story about going to Cluj, where Kató would be looking after orphaned children at a summer camp. The Russian soldiers seemed uninterested until they were quite near the Romanian border. Here they were told to get out of the car, so that their luggage could be examined. Everything was brought into an office and taken apart. A Russian woman interpreted the soldiers' questions. One concerned a picture of Anikó in military uniform: they wanted to know who she was. Kató explained that it was a joke: when Pali Sas, Évi's older brother, was drafted in 1939 into a labor battalion, Anikó tried on his uniform. The interpreter supported the story, confirming that the uniform was definitely Hungarian. After the travelers repacked everything and went outside they saw that their car was gone. The entire search had been staged in order to steal this scarcest of commodities.

The Russians pretended to know nothing about the theft and politely offered to phone the local police to see if they could help the stranded Hungarians. By midnight the police arrived and took them into the nearest small town. The only shelter was a jail cell with three beds. The two men were somewhat frightened but Kató felt almost at home. Despite her hunger she slept well.

The next day they found the police station totally surrounded by clamoring people who were similarly stranded. After several hours Kató's party was told what they had guessed long before: it was unlikely that they would see their automobile again. They were advised to get three train tickets back to Budapest.

The young law student was firmly opposed to Kató's return, when she was so close to Romania. She should wait in this little town and he would try to find a car, maybe by offering his watch to a Russian soldier for a lead. He instructed Kató and the driver to find a hotel and gave them money before he left.

By this time they were famished, and the driver went off to the local market. He came back with salami and fresh bread, fruit, and other delicacies that were almost forgotten in the capital. Days passed and there was nothing for Kató to do but wait. One night in the hotel, she was awakened by noise from the next room. Thinking that she had recognized a woman's voice, she asked the front desk the next morning who had checked in during the night. The woman turned out to be a distant cousin of Kató's who had converted from Judaism when she married a baron.

Not only had they survived the war, but their car had too; they had been driving on a food-buying expedition with their son when the Russians performed the same disappearing car trick on them. They too were stranded in the hotel, which was beginning to look like the setting for a French farce.

After long negotiations, a Russian officer guaranteed that the baron's car could be found in exchange for another vehicle. Kató never found out how the transaction ended, after the baron drove her to the border, where she hired a horse and cart to Nagyvárad, the nearest town inside Romania. Kató finally arrived there exactly one week late. She was met by a Zionist doctor who arranged her accommodation. They left at five in the morning to catch the aliyah ship from Constantsa. They drove for two days through Transylvania until they reached their immediate goal: the Palestine Emigration Office in Bucharest. Here Dov Berger, another of the parachutists, whose mission had been to Romania, greeted her warmly. He showed her around the Paris of the Balkans, which exhibited hardly any sign of the war, except for rationing in stores and restaurants. He found her a hotel, where she was to stay for a few nights only, while final preparations for the aliyah were made.

Kató had to wait in Bucharest for three months. She moved in with a Jewish family and developed a circle of friends, some of whom were also from Budapest awaiting the same ship. While there she arranged for the translation and publication in Romanian of *Csibi,* Béla's classic for children.

But Kató's main concern during this time was for Gyuri. All she could find out from the Palestinians was that he had enlisted in the Jewish Brigade and was serving somewhere in Western Europe. Even though her fears about his safety eased as peace gradually took root, she still longed to see him and hold him, the sole reason now for her existence. She needed to share with him the great pain that only they two could fully understand.

THIRTY-TWO

THE REASON WHY

One day in the middle of November 1944, Gyuri was working as usual in the fields. He had been a novice member of Kibbutz Maagan since his arrival in February, and was caught up in the novelty of physical labor. Life in Spain now seemed decadent; in this place work had a larger meaning. The bare, sun-browned mountains rising from the sheer blue of the Galilee surrounded him with stark beauty and desert energy. With an innate gift for languages, he was making quick progress with Hebrew. About half the members of the kibbutz spoke Hungarian, so it required discipline to practice his new language. One powerful incentive was his desire to talk as often as possible to a pretty teenage girl from the neighboring moshav. Ginnosra had soft eyes, jet-back hair and a mischievous laugh. She was a sabra, born in the Galilee, and she embodied a miracle to him who came from the Diaspora: that life was possible for a Jew knowing only Hebrew. And Ginnosra was fascinated by this shy stranger whose childlike smile masked a distant sadness. They began to meet often across the fence from the moshav. They went swimming and hiking together, and Gyuri was delighted when she called him by his new name: Giora.

Absorbing as his new life was, Giora still had much of the former Gyuri in him. By a strange twist he was the only one of his family in this new land. Chana was back in Europe, and he did not know where. For a few weeks after her departure Yonah and Peretz brought short letters from Cairo. Then, just as news of the German occupation of Hungary reached Palestine and he urgently wanted to get in touch with her, she was gone from Egypt and nobody would say exactly where.

From what he managed to piece together at Maagan, Gyuri gradually began to realize how his sister's pretended lightheartedness during their brief reunion had misled him. That last night in Tel Aviv he had merely scanned the long letter she gave him; so overwhelming was Chana's physical presence, her bubbling vitality, that he had failed to read between the lines. Since then he had examined every word, and now knew that it had been a farewell letter. He felt helpless anxiety each time he read the closing words: "I hope you will not get this letter, or if you do, it will be after we meet. Should it turn out otherwise, my little Gyuri, I embrace you with my endless love—your Sister."

The last letter Gyuri received from Chana was written on June sixth, the day of the landing of the Allies in Normandy, and the day before she crossed into Hungary. Without giving the smallest clue about her location, she sent heartfelt greetings for his birthday: "I did so much hope that this time we'd be celebrating it together, but I was wrong—well, next time— perhaps." She asked him to keep writing to her about everything in his life: "Letters will reach me sooner or later and I'm so happy when I can get them."

Since then he had not heard from either his mother or Chana. Worried and restless, he applied as a volunteer for the Jewish Brigade, to be sent back to Europe. The kibbutz withheld approval: he had barely arrived after an adventurous escape, and it was a general policy not to permit more than one from the same family to go into danger. So Giora kept working through the scorching summer into autumn, waiting for news and yet hoping that none would come, since almost all news about Hungary was catastrophic.

This mid-November day, he noticed a man coming toward him in the field. He was wearing khaki, a common sight among the chaverim, but Giora had not seen him before.

"Giora Szenes?" he asked, and introduced himself. He was Shaul Avigur, a high-ranking official of the Haganah. Giora nodded.

"We do not know this for certain," he said quietly, "but our sources tell us that Chana is in very great trouble . . . Indeed, she may no longer be alive. I am sorry. She was a most valued comrade. We will inform you as soon as we know anything more."

For a long time Giora stood there, leaning slightly on his hoe; it seemed utterly impossible that the sun was shining and the grass was growing and yet his sister was no more. After a long time, he went back to the kibbutz and announced that he would join the Brigade at once, leaving the kibbutz altogether if necessary.

Giora became a soldier in early December 1944, but by the time he finished training and was sent to Europe, the war against Hitler was over. There was a small chance of being shipped to the Far East where the Japanese still held out. It was strange for Giora to be traveling again in the Europe he once knew so well, now a place chaotic beyond recognition. And stranger still was the thought that there were few of his people left alive on this continent. He was in Austria, a few hours from the Hungarian border. Anxious about his mother and eager to find out what had really happened to Chana, he asked to go to Budapest. He was told that British soldiers could not go there because of the Russians. To make sure he would not try, he was posted instead to Holland.

One day in Bucharest, Dov Berger came to Kató and said he had an address for her son; she could send a letter to him.

"What am I allowed to write about?" she asked.

"About anything you want," said Berger.

"Really?" Kató had been so used to writing all her letters in code with the censor in mind that the possibilities of expressing herself openly presented a huge challenge. Where would she begin?

Before any reply could have been returned, the aliyah ship was ready in Constantsa. Most of the thousand passengers on the *Transylvania* were legal immigrants with proper certificates, but in the last minutes the Zionist organizers staged loud fights at the dockside to distract the authorities long enough so they could smuggle a few illegal stowaways on board. The boat was crammed full and at first it looked as if Kató would have to spend the five days sleeping on deck. The only unoccupied cabin was the royal suite, reserved for Fülöp Freudiger and his family. Freudiger was one of the leaders of the Jewish community in Hungary who conducted negotiations with the Germans. In August 1944 his escape to Romania triggered wide-scale panic that deportations from Budapest were about to begin. By now he was supposed to have reached Istanbul, so Kató and the mother of one of the Slovakian parachutists were given the luxurious suite.

It was late October and getting warmer as they approached the shores of Palestine. The voyage was uneventful, but on the fifth morning the entire ship was swept by excitement. As Kató climbed on deck she could see the panorama of Mount Carmel, dotted with white villas and ancient trees.

It was Friday, and preference was given to the Orthodox who wanted to celebrate Shabbat services on shore. Kató was content to stay on ship until Sunday; there was a heat wave and she did not expect anybody to be waiting for her. The newspapers, however, treated the arrival of each aliyah ship as a great event and had published the names of the passengers. As a result, Kató was greeted by a small crowd of people as she set foot on dry land in Haifa. Yoel stood there, with Professor Fekete (the family friend with whom Chana had stayed while visiting Jerusalem), who came specially from Jerusalem, and a small committee of ladies from the Women's International Zionist Organization (WIZO), some of whom she knew from Budapest. One of Anikó's requests upon leaving Hungary was that Kató should join WIZO as a volunteer. The Nahalal School was funded by WIZO; Anikó thought that this was an appropriate way of showing gratitude and Kató was glad to please her. Later she joined an informal group of WIZO mothers whose children lived in Palestine; each week they read to each other any letters they got. Anikó's early letters were so informative that they were duplicated for other WIZO groups throughout Hungary.

Thanks to Yoel, Reuven, and other surviving paratroopers of the mission, Chana's story had already spread throughout Eretz Israel. Several journalists—some Hungarian, others from Hebrew papers—came to the docks eager to interview Kató; from their questions she realized that Anikó was no longer just her daughter, but had already become a part of Jewish history.

People were asking about her plans but Kató was too new and felt too tired to have any. Yoel had already arranged for her to come to Maagan and await Gyuri's return. At least there she would be understood in Hungarian until she could learn enough Hebrew. But first she was to spend a few weeks in a health resort to regain her strength. She was admitted at once to a new sanatorium on top of Mount Carmel. A young man called David came to visit her there. He introduced himself, in German, as a member of Kibbutz Sedot Yam and addressed her as "Ima" Szenes, or Mother. He invited Kató to Caesarea the following week for the commemoration of the first anniversary of Chana's death. Would she come and tell them about their chavera—how she fought and how she died?

David also brought with him a slim volume that Hakibbutz Hameuchad, the federation to which Kibbutz Sedot Yam belonged, was publishing for the anniversary. It contained selections from Chana's diaries and poems. Kató was pleased that most of her writings—including the diaries, the script of The Violin, and many poems—were preserved. Before Chana left on her mission, she had packed them up and put the trunk into storage. When Yoel came back from Europe, he brought Kató's request to find these manuscripts. At Sedot Yam, he had found the trunk with its treasures. Yoel was in an ideal position to appreciate the writings, since he knew both Hungarian and Hebrew. Many of the chaverim were surprised to find out that Chana had been a writer.

Yoel had helped select the material for this first printing, which sold out instantly. Many editions followed, each one augmented by fresh discoveries of poems and letters and testimonials by her comrades. Her book fed the growing legend and later became a fundamental text for teaching Israeli schoolchildren and young soldiers about the meaning of heroism.

After two days on Mount Carmel, Kató moved to another resort near Rehovot, where she spent the following three weeks trying to gain weight. The meatless food was plentiful and by the end Kató had gained back half the pounds she needed. On November seventh David came to escort her to Sedot Yam.

The kibbutz dining room was filled to capacity, and a sea of young people surrounded Ima Szenes, the mother of their Chana. Kató thanked them for the opportunity to meet them, and apologized for not being able to speak to them in their language. One of the chaverim, watching her gestures and listening to her voice, exclaimed joyously, "It's as if Chana were back!" That evening a smaller group gathered and, speaking in German, Kató told the tragic but inspiring story of their fallen comrade.

The kibbutz wanted her to stay, but Kató was already committed to Maagan, where she was impatient to welcome Gyuri back from Europe. She promised to visit often, however. Back at the sanatorium, Miriam, Chana's classmate from Nahalal, came to see Kató from her nearby kibbutz. She had just had her first baby, but she rushed to meet Chana's mother. Later, Pnina, the other Nahalal roommate, came to visit from her kibbutz. So from the very beginning, Kató felt that she had acquired not so much a new country as a large family. Of course nobody could replace Anikó, but from all her friends, she felt a special kind of love that said that Anikó was not dead.

Kató went to live at Kibbutz Maagan at the Sea of Galilee and began to work. With two other women she was assigned to look after infants while their parents worked in the fields. The work did not require knowledge of Hebrew and Kató was only required to work half the day. Later she also taught the piano to some of the older children. It was through the eyes of small children that Kató gradually learned about her new home in this ancient land, where everything was different from her former way of life. Yet everything was also familiar because of Anikó's letters over the years describing her own difficulties in adapting to life in Eretz. One afternoon Kató fell asleep outside in the shade and woke to the wet and rough tongue of a cow licking her face. It was the kind of incident that would have made Anikó laugh; Kató constantly felt the pain of not being able to share such experiences with her.

By the time she had been in Palestine for two months, almost everybody had demobilized. Every time Kató saw a uniform in the distance, she would drop everything and run to see if it was Gyuri. The kibbutz leadership also began to wonder what had happened to him. They had put in a request for Giora's return as soon as Kató arrived: it was usual in such cases to grant leave at once. Now they decided to send someone with Mrs. Szenes to the Jewish Agency in Jerusalem. David Ben-Gurion was at the head of the agency, the unofficial Jewish government of Palestine; his executive assistant was Teddy Kollek. When Kató and the chaver from Maagan arrived in Kollek's office, it was empty. The entire leadership was in a big meeting, hearing a report from Moshe Sharett, the foreign minister, about his trip to America. The chaver went into the meeting and whispered to Kollek that Kató was waiting outside. Overhearing this, Ben-Gurion excused himself to the whole assembly: "The mother of Chana Szenes is outside. I must greet this lady." He introduced himself, but Kató was so new to the country that she did not know who he was. He promised to send a telegram to Giora, asking him to return from Holland at once.

Meanwhile Giora had grown tired of waiting and even before Ben-Gurion's telegram had arrived, he took matters into his own hands. He petitioned for a leave and arrived at the end of 1945. Finally mother and son were reunited. There was much pain in their joy. She had found a muscular grown-up man, only the smile reminding her of the boy whom she had last seen more than five years before. Giora was shocked to see how much his mother had aged, but when she recounted the full story of the past two years, he was astonished and grateful that she was alive at all.

Giora was still on active duty, but he could visit Maagan on weekends. During one such visit, one of Giora's comrades asked Kató whether the family was related to Chana Szenes, the famous partisan and parachutist. Giora never wanted to derive any advantage from his sister's growing fame: the pain of her loss remained a private grief.

And Chana's fame was growing daily. In December 1945, a clandestine immigration ship called the *Chana Szenes* was beached at Nahariya with its precious cargo of Holocaust survivors. Schools, settlements, a forest, cultural centers, and dozens of streets were named after her. In Budapest there was the Anna Szenes Home for Girls for the few returning orphans from Auschwitz.

By the time Israel was proclaimed a state and had won her independence, relations with Stalinist Hungary had deteriorated. Israel wanted to bring back the remains of Chana and the six other Jewish parachutists who fell in Europe. The Communist authorities acceded to the request, partly because the Martyrs' section in the cemetery was attracting large numbers of people, the only place in the city where assembly was not forbidden. But they were reluctant to acknowledge that Chana was a heroine who died not just for Jews but also for the cause of Hungarian freedom. Giora had applied for a visa to Hungary, as did a delegation of chaverim from Sedot Yam, but they were not allowed to enter the country. They had to wait for her body in neighboring Vienna, as yet another ideology had closed the borders between East and West.

Chana's body was exhumed very early one March morning in 1950, with only a government doctor present. An anonymous call the night before alerted Pali Sas, Évi's brother from Dombovár, who hurried to the grave with his wife, Lydia. The remains were sealed in a coffin and placed on the train to Vienna, where Chana's cortege was finally greeted by her brother and fellow workers. Her coffin was honored in the Jewish cemetery of Vienna and then traveled by train to the port of Genoa, where fresh wreaths were laid by survivors of the Jewish community there.

When the ship arrived in the port of Haifa, it seemed to Kató as if the whole of Israel had turned out to welcome back her daughter. Chana's coffin lay in state in front of City Hall, flanked by a guard of honor of paratroopers from the new Israeli Defense Force. An additional civilian honor guard was changed every two hours; it included her comrade Yoel Palgi and the prime minister of Israel.

The next day, the procession went by limousine toward Tel Aviv. Children lined the highway, throwing flowers. At Caesarea the cortege turned toward the Mediterranean. Chana rested one night at Sedot Yam. The kibbutz had wanted to provide the final resting place for her and had pleaded with Kató; but the Israeli government also sent a delegation to her, which explained its point of view:

"We want Chana Szenes to be buried in Jerusalem. We are trying to gather there into one place everything that is most precious for Jews in this country and in the world." Kató was inclined to agree. Chana now belonged to the nation, not just to one community.

The triumphant funeral procession continued, stopping in Tel Aviv for more commemorative speeches. Finally they traveled up through the hills to Jerusalem, and to the Knesset, where the entire legislative body accompanied the hearse to the former Jewish Agency building that was now the seat of government. And so the solemn marchers made their ascent of Mount Zion. There, near the tomb of Theodor Herzl, with full military honors, Chana Szenes was given a soldier's burial in the Cemetery for Heroes.

IN SEARCH OF CHANA

I was born in 1944, the year Chana died, in Budapest, the place of her birth and death. A Lutheran baptismal certificate and a Christian family who risked their lives by claiming a Jewish baby as their own saved me. My mother, who had taught Gyuri and Anikó Szenes to dance, had to give me up, since she was doubly persecuted, as Jewish and as a member of the Communist resistance movement. My father found refuge in one of the Swedish safe houses, which was raided by Arrow Cross thugs to celebrate the Christmas of 1944. The SS nailed him and hundreds of others into cattle cars that stood waiting for twenty-four hours at the Southern Station. Raoul Wallenberg pulled him off the last train the Nazis tried to send to a death camp.

Much of this I found out very recently. But throughout my childhood I had met people with numbers tattooed on their arms, and I heard it whispered that they had come back from death. So I had always thought of death as a place somewhere in Poland: it was called Auschwitz.

In my Hungarian childhood I never understood why there were so few relatives in my family, compared to my friends' families. Following the Holocaust a pall of silence shrouded the topic. I was not circumcised until the age of eleven—and then only for medical reasons. At about the time that most Jewish boys become Bar Mitzvah, the Hungarian uprising displaced me to England, to which my mother's parents had fled in September 1939, the same time Chana left Budapest. It was there that my grandmother, Edith Singer, told me the story of the Szenes family, her friends and neighbors on Bimbó-út before the war. She gently broke the news to me that I was also Jewish, which meant something different from being Hungarian. Like Chana, I was brought up in the powerful tradition of Hungarian patriotism and nationalism. I did not understand the difference until my grandmother gave me a Hungarian edition of Chana's letters, poems, and diaries.

A couple of years later I met Giora Szenes and his wife Ginnosra when they were visiting London, and I remember being struck by how little past suffering showed on the surface. By this time I knew a number of people who had lived through the siege of Budapest, or who had come back after years in Auschwitz or the Gulag, some of whom were tortured by the Communist police. Many of them were not merely victims: they had performed acts of great daring and endurance. Unlike the people I imagined in my favorite books or admired at the movies, these real heroes seemed quite matter-of-fact. When they came to visit in London, they wanted to know how to get to Marks and Spencer to buy good underwear.

Several years later, I was almost grown up, facing final exams at Oxford, when my grandmother came back from visiting Kató Szenes just before the outbreak of the Six-Day War. As anxiety about the fate of Israel was mounting, I felt for the first time identified with this brave little country. Like many of my generation in the European Diaspora, I felt an unfamiliar pride at being Jewish. Hundreds of students, Jews and Gentiles alike, were taking special planes to Israel, where people were dying once more for the Jews' right to live.

I was now exactly the same age as Chana at the time of her death and I thought a great deal about going to Israel. But I did not go. Of course there were many good excuses. I was in the middle of exams, and I hated war; I would not know one end of a rifle from another, and there were not enough planes; young people were being turned back from the airports of Europe. But because I did not go, I realized what was special about Chana Szenes.

Chana was a person who did go. No matter what difficulties were put in her way, no matter what others were doing or not doing, no matter what difference her going would ultimately make. When she felt she had to act, she acted.

On the surface, Chana's military mission seems like a futile gesture, doomed from the start. Yet, even in failure, she understood the symbolic value of her gesture. Bernard Shaw wrote in the preface to *Saint Joan* that the Maid of Orleans was martyred not for her military triumphs over the British but for her dangerous ideas. Chana died a martyr's death for the idea that to be good one must act, and that one person can make a difference. In a world that has not been kind to armed Jews or to self-willed women, one that is only beginning to cope with its sins of omission during the Holocaust, the symbol of a young woman dangling alone from a parachute in the dark night of Europe, while the British who sent her would not bomb the railway lines to Auschwitz, is disturbing.

Success did not lie in Chana's individual action, but in her faith that building something is more worthy of human beings than destroying it. She was shaped by the communal experience of the kibbutz; she knew that victory could only come if people put their strengths together. I found the meaning of her victory during two trips to Israel, where I went in search of Chana.

The first journey to Israel is important to every Jew, whether one is religious, or a Zionist, or neither. I was catching an El Al flight at Kloten airport in Zurich on the last day of Chanukah. One of the young interrogators from Israeli security cross-examined me about the purpose of my visit. I said I was working on a film about Chana Szenes. She asked for proof. As I tried to convince this tough, unsmiling sabra that I was not a potential hijacker I realized that she was about Chana's age when she set out on her mission. Later on the flight I got a chance for a more relaxed chat with her. She was a chemistry student at Tel Aviv University. Commuting to and from European airports was like any other part-time job; this one happened to be defending the security of Israel against terrorists.

Within an hour of touching down at Ben-Gurion Airport, I was at the Wailing Wall. The last of the Chanukah lights flickered as the real moon shone down on the half moon of the Moslem mosques. Jewish soldiers, Uzis at the ready, patrolled the eerie plaza, which was reconquered during the bloodiest fighting of the Six-Day War. Another night I witnessed a torchlit swearing-in ceremony at the Wall, where young recruits stood unarmed in front of a long row of tables heaped with Bibles and machine guns. As each stepped forward, a rabbi and an officer placed a Torah in one hand and a weapon in the other. I thought of Chana, a pacifist in the Diaspora who picked up the gun to protect Eretz Israel.

I visited Giora and Kató Szenes on the top of Mount Carmel, where they have lived for almost four decades. After leaving Kibbutz Maagan, Giora and Ginnosra married and moved to Haifa, where their two sons were born. Kató also left the Galilee, where she had suffered from the heat and constant sickness. She considered an invitation to join Chana's chaverim at Sedot Yam, but decided she would rather live near her son and his family. She got a job working in a large nursery, until, after ten years, she lost much of her hearing and retired.

For many years Kató has been living quietly in the tiny apartment at the Parents' Home where I interviewed her several times. Her room is like a shrine. On the walls are posters of Béla's plays. On the shelves are his books and editions of Chana's diaries in a dozen languages. Pictures of them hang everywhere, but there are also pictures of the living: Giora and Ginnosra, the grandchildren, and now their children. She reminds me of my own grandmother, nimbly serving food all the time, and with the same anxious alertness if a guest fails to eat what she considers a sufficient amount. Now ninety years old, Mrs. Szenes is a lively raconteur with an amazing memory. When talking about Anikó or Béla, she knows no fatigue. She acts out all the parts, villains and heroes, in the vast tragedy of her life, quoting verbatim, mimicking every spellbinding gesture.

I spent most time during my trips with Giora, who still has the wonderful smile first described by that Budapest journalist when Gyuri was seven. Now in his sixties, his careworn face tells of a difficult life. He and Ginnosra aged prematurely following the Yom Kippur War, when their son David was missing in action for six weeks. Fortunately he returned from a prisoner-of-war camp and is now finishing his studies as a clinical psychologist in Calgary, Canada. He and his wife, Ilana, have recently had their first baby. Eitan, Gyuri's elder son, was born during the War of Independence. He is an engineer, and has three children.

After leaving her native moshav with Giora, Ginnosra taught kindergarten. She is an irrepressible, youthful grandmother who has known a large portion of Haifa's population from the playpen. Giora has spent thirty-five years working for the Israel Electric Corporation, the country's national power company. For many years he was in positions that did not use his talents and the seven languages he speaks. Gradually he was put in charge of negotiating all of the oil contracts for Israel's power plants. He has recently retired and immediately returned to an earlier passion, philosophy, which he studies at the University of Haifa.

Giora's whole life has been overshadowed by his sister, whom he loved very much, by the guilt that every survivor feels about those who died. The memories, the stories pour out of him. During my visits, he brings out new batches of letters, photographs, whole archives of fading material. This gentle man's patience is tried sorely by a steady procession of people who come to him to learn about Chana: answering letters and phone calls from writers, filmmakers, and students doing their homework essay about Israel's national heroine. He does not mind the work, but the constant reopening of the wound visibly hurts, forcing him to make public his private grief.

The Agricultural School for Girls is still training young people at Nahalal. It has grown greatly during the past forty years. Three or four buildings from Chana's time stand, including the two-story dormitory where she shared a corner room with Miriam and Pnina. The circular moshav around the school, where we visited one of Ginnosra's friends, is much as Chana described it. It is more prosperous now, of course, and some of the streets are paved. But it is still a village, with farm animals and farm smells, in the heart of Israel's agricultural miracle.

My wife and I pulled into the parking lot of the Roman theater at Caesarea, which was excavated from the sand dunes in the 1960s. A sign with an arrow pointed: Sedot Yam. Practically everything is different there from the way Chana knew it, except the sea and the sand of her famous poem. The Crusaders' castle a couple of miles to the north is a busy tourist center; the Arab village that used to be nearby has disappeared. The biggest change is the kibbutz itself. Mature trees cast shade over well-kept lawns and gardens, with paths leading to large modern buildings housing the communal dining room, administrative offices, and meeting halls. Dotted over this verdant campus are the modest private dwellings of the kibbutzniks, each immaculately kept with its own garden. There are playgrounds and kindergartens and schoolrooms. Near the entrance to the kibbutz large workshops produce tiles, which are sold throughout the world. This, rather than fishing, now provides the economic base for the community.

After asking for directions we found the library, which is called Bet Chana—Chana's house. There is a simple profile of her, carved of wood. We were welcomed by Miriam Huelsen Neeman, librarian and archivist, who lectures often to the Israeli Defense Forces and throughout Israel about Chana. She has short silvery hair now; she and Chana came to Sedot Yam at the same time. Miriam reminisced about living conditions in the tents and washing clothes on the beach; they lived like that for many years, long after Chana left and did not return. Miriam showed us photographs from those days and read from minutes of early kibbutz meetings at which Chana spoke, including an impassioned speech she made opposing the chaverim who wanted to spend money on going to the movies.

Miriam's son, Niv, an artist who grew up and still lives at Sedot Yam, took us to the rocks where Chana used to sit and watch the sea. He spoke about her and her poetry, this legendary person of his mother's generation who died long before he was born. Niv also showed us his tiny studio where he carves beautiful sculptures. He finds the marble, including the finest Carrara from Roman ruins, scattered everywhere under the sand. A whole arboretum with classical pillars has been found in the dunes.

Miriam took us to lunch in the vast modern dining room overlooking the Mediterranean. Cheerful old men cleared the tables and I thought about Chana's struggles with her chores. Around the table sat several chaverim who knew her. Malkiel Ben Zwi was on the administrative council that agonized about letting her go on the mission. "She talked all the time about her mother and her brother," he said quietly. "I think it was because of the guilt that she went back." But these old chaverim did not offer much new information about her. Much has happened to them in the forty years since she spent those two brief years with them and was gone. And nobody knew then that she would become a national heroine.

Leaving Sedot Yam we gave a ride to an old man going to visit his grandchildren at another kibbutz. Avram remembered sharing a tent with Chana.

"Did you have fun?" I asked him.

He looked at me. I tried to prompt: "Well, you were young, and I thought maybe you had some fun and games in those tents."

"We worked so hard, we were always tired," he said. But no matter how tired she was, Chana usually was the last to sleep. He remembered her always reading or sometimes writing at the feeble light of a kerosene lamp.

We sat with Reuven Dafni at a Hungarian restaurant in Jerusalem. After the war and the founding of the state, he went into diplomatic service. He was the first Israeli consul-general in Los Angeles, and later ambassador to India and other countries. Now he is a director of Yad Vashem, the Holocaust Memorial on Mount Zion, near the Heroes' Cemetery where his comrades rest. Yad Vashem has the largest archives in the world relating to the Holocaust; here Chana's original diaries and many of her letters are kept. So is the poem "Blessed is the Match," on that thin piece of paper that Reuven rolled into a ball and threw into the bushes forty years ago. He can laugh at that now; underneath there is still the regret, bordering on anger, that he permitted Chana to go. "But nobody on earth could have stopped her," he reminded himself with a rueful smile.

We visited Kibbutz Maagan with Giora and Ginnosra. Her family still owns land in the moshav next door, and we went bathing in the Sea of Galilee on their beach. Overlooking the blue lake and the brown Golan Heights on the far side, we sat in the comfortable bungalow of Yonah Rosen, who originally recruited Chana into the Palmach. The other two Transylvanians on the mission are dead; there is a large memorial building to honor Peretz Goldstein. Yoel Palgi returned to Maagan and then held many important positions with El Al; later he was ambassador to Tanzania. Yonah and his wife, Hava, currently the top administator of the kibbutz, both speak Hungarian, as did many of the older kibbutzniks at lunch. Yonah teased Giora about returning to Maagan just to enjoy the Hungarian cooking.

Driving near the troubled Lebanese border we called on another Szenes family, not related to our hosts—except by suffering. Judith and Saul Szenes spent their teens at Auschwitz and Buchenwald and finally made their aliyah in 1949. They fell in love on their long journey and named their first child born in the free land of Israel—Chana.

I traveled everywhere in Israel in search of the real Chana. The closest I came to imagining her alive was on a quiet Shabbat morning when I went to see Miriam Pergament, Chana's friend at Nahalal, the Miriam of the diaries. Now a grandmother, she had spent a lifetime at Kibbutz Hatzor in special education, teaching many generations of children. Until I met Miriam it was hard to picture Chana growing old, having children, or in retirement: would that intense fire have ultimately diminished, burned itself out?

Miriam's face was completely serene. Even sad memories about Chana's last visit, off to Cairo in her Air Force uniform, made her smile. "She was in such high spirits, talking only about what good times we would have when she returned." Miriam spoke of their first year at Nahalal. "Chana . . . She had such will. And when she was only eighteen, already she was a leader."

In the end I found Chana not in the buildings or the old photographs, not in the museums and cemeteries, not in the stories told about her in the kibbutzim and schools. I met her in the hearts of people who continue to build her dream in Zion. She is in the eyes of young soldiers and kibbutzniks hitchhiking back from leave, eyes that light up at the mere mention of her name. She is alive in the flourishing fields and orchards of the Emek, in the marble sculptures of a young artist at Sedot Yam, and in the laughter of children she did not have the time to bear.

—Peter Hay
Los Angeles
July 1, 1986

FURTHER READING
AND BIBLIOGRAPHICAL NOTES

A. About Chana Szenes and Her Family

Hannah Senesh: Her Life and Diary. Translated by Marta Cohn. London: Vallentine, Mitchell & Co, 1971; Schocken Books in New York. Paperback edition still available in the United States.

There have been thirteen editions of the edited diary in Hebrew since 1945 (which includes selected letters, poems, and writings about Chana by her mother, Yoel Palgi, and Reuven Dafni). A small selection of tributes and diary entries first appeared in Palestine in a periodical of Hakibbutz Hameuchad called *Mibifnim;* this same material was translated, augmented, and published in Hungary; Chana's cousin, Pál Sas (Évi's brother) gave me a precious copy. A much fuller Hungarian edition of the diaries and poems, including the text of the play *The Violin,* was published by Hakibbutz Hameuchad in Israel (1954); it has been long out of print. The full text of the diaries has never been published; the original are deposited at Yad Vashem.

MASTERS, ANTONY. *The Summer That Bled: A Biography of Hannah Senesh.* London: Michael Joseph, 1972. The only existing biography—a very good and straightforward account by an impartial writer.

PALGI, YOEL. *". . . és jött a fergeteg" ("And there came a great wind").* Tel Aviv: Alexander Publishing, 1946. This personal and sometimes embroidered account of the mission by one of the parachutists, published soon after the event in Hebrew and Hungarian, is an invaluable source.

SYRKIN, MARIE. *Blessed Is the Match.* Philadelphia: Jewish Publication Society of America, 1947. In paperback since 1976 with a new epilogue. This is the earliest account in English about Chana Szenes and her place in the Jewish resistance.

SZENES, KATHERINE. *On the Threshold of Liberation.* Yad Vashem Studies VIII. Jerusalem: Yad Vashem, 1970.

B. About the Holocaust (Especially in Hungary)

BRAHAM, RANDOLPH L. *The Politics of Genocide: The Holocaust in Hungary.* New York: Columbia University Press, 1981. The definitive work on the subject so far.

———, (ed.) *Hungarian Jewish Studies* New York: World Federation of Hungarian Jews, 1966.

GÁTI, ÖDÖN, ed. *Memento: Magyarország 1944* ("Remember: Hungary 1944"). Budapest: Kossuth Könyvkiadó, 1975.

GILBERT, MARTIN. *Auschwitz and the Allies.* New York: Holt, Rinehart & Winston, 1981.

———. *The Holocaust.* New York: Holt, Rinehart & Winston, 1985. The most recent and comprehensive picture of the Holocaust.

HANDLER, ANDREW. *Holocaust in Hungary.* University, Ala.: University of Alabama Press, 1982.

HAUSNER, GIDEON. *Justice in Jerusalem.* New York: Shocken Books, 1968. An account of Eichmann's activities by the chief prosecutor at his trial.

KATZBURG, NATHANIEL. *Hungary and the Jews.* Ramat-Gan: Bar-Ilan University Press, 1981.

LAMBERT, GILLES. *Operation Hazalah.* Translated by Robert Bullen and Rosette Letellier. Indianapolis/New York: Bobbs-Merrill, 1974. A highly inaccurate and sentimentalized view of Jewish resistance in Hungary.

LÉVAI, JENÖ. *Zsidósors Magyarországon* ("Jewish Fate in Hungary"). Budapest: Magyar Téka, 1948). Lévai, historian of the Hungarian Holocaust, wrote half a dozen books on the subject in the years following the war, and one in 1961 about the Eichmann trial. He was head of the Wallenberg Committee in Budapest and wrote a book about the kidnaped Swedish diplomat.

MORSE, ARTHUR D. *While 6 Million Died.* New York: Random House, 1967.

Rescue Attempts during the Holocaust: Proceedings of the Second Yad Vashem International Historical Conference—April 1974. Jerusalem: Yad Vashem, 1977.

ROTHKIRCHEN, LIVIA, ed. *Yad Vashem Studies on the European Jewish Catastrophe and Resistance,* Vol. VII. Jerusalem: Yad Vashem, 1968.

SANDBERG, MOSHE. *My Longest Year: In the Hungarian Labour Service and in the Nazi Camps.* Edited with a Historical Survey by Livia Rothkirchen. Jerusalem: Yad Vashem, 1968.

C. The Kasztner and Brand Affairs

This is still a highly controversial area. For the extreme anti-Kasztner view, read Ben Hecht's notorious *Perfidy* (New York: Julian Messner, 1961). For the opposite view, there is *A Million Jews to Save.* (London: Hutchinson, 1973), by André Biss, who worked with Rezsö Kasztner.

The sad story of Joel Brand is told by him to Alex Weissberg in *Desperate Mission* (New York: Criterion Books, 1958), and in *Advocate for the Dead: the Story of Joel Brand,* translated by Constantine Fitzgibbon and Andrew Forster-Melliar (London: Four Square Books, 1959). Both books leave many questions unanswered. A more recent though somewhat fictionalized book about Brand is *Timetable,* by Amos Elon (Garden City, N.Y.: Doubleday, 1980).

D. The Kibbutz

From a vast bibliography I followed mainly sources from or close to the period.

DAYAN, SHMUEL. *Man and the Soil.* Tel Aviv: Massadah Publishing, 1965.

FEITELBERG, LIONEL. *Afikim: The Story of a Kibbutz.* Tel Aviv: Zionist Organization, Youth Department, 1947.

INFIELD, HENRIK. *Co-operative Living in Palestine.* Scranton, Pa: Henry Koosis & Co., 1948.

MAIMON, ADA. *Women Build a Land.* Translated by Shulamith Schwarz-Nardi. New York: Herzl Press, 1962.

SAMUEL, EDWIN. *Handbook of the Jewish Communal Villages in Palestine,* 2nd English edition. Jerusalem: Zionist Organization, Youth Department, 1945.

SAMUEL, MAURICE. *Harvest in the Desert.* Philadelphia: Jewish Publication Society of America, 1944.

E. General Historical Sources

ALLON, YIGAL. *The Making of Israel's Army.* London: Vallentine, Mitchell & Co., 1970.

AVNI, HAIM. *Spain, the Jews and Franco.* Translated by Emanuel Shimoni. Philadelphia: Jewish Publication Society of America, 1982.

BENAS, BERTRAM B. *Zionism: The Jewish National Movement,* Vol. LXV of the Proceedings of the Literary and Philosophical Society of Liverpool, 1919.

BUBER, MARTIN. *On Zion: The History of an Idea.* New York: Schocken Books, 1973.

DAYAN, MOSHE. *Story of My Life.* New York: William Morrow and Co., 1976.

ELON, AMOS. *The Israelis—Founders and Sons.* New York: Holt, Rinehart & Winston, 1971.

GILBERT, MARTIN. *The European Powers 1900–1945.* New York: New American Library, 1970.

HABE, HANS. *Proud Zion.* Translated by Anthony Vivis. Indianapolis: Bobbs-Merrill, 1973.

HERTZBERG, ARTHUR. *The Zionist Idea.* Philadelphia: Jewish Publication Society of America, 1959.

HEYMAN, EVA. *The Diary of Eva Heyman.* Translated by Moshe M. Kohn. Jerusalem: Yad Vashem, 1974.

JOHNSEN, JULIA E., ed. *Palestine: Jewish Homeland?* New York: H. W. Wilson Company, 1946.

KLEIN, EDWARD. *The Parachutists.* New York: Doubleday, 1981. Fiction.

Le Dossier Juif—Documents, France 1940–1945. Paris: Editions S. E. SNRA, 1979.

LEARSI, RUFUS. *Fulfillment: The Epic Story of Zionism.* Cleveland and New York: World Publishing Co., 1951.

LOWDERMILK, WALTER CLAY. *Palestine: Land of Promise.* New York and London: Harper & Brothers, 1944.

LOWENTHAL, MARVIN, ed. and trans. *The Diaries of Theodor Herzl.* New York: Dial Press, 1956.

MARRUS, ROBERT MICHAEL, and Robert Paxton. *Vichy France and the Jews.* New York: Basic Books, 1981.

MEIR, GOLDA. *My Life.* New York: G. P. Putnam's Sons, 1975.

MOSHENSON, MOSHE. *Letters from the Desert.* Translated by Hilda Auerbach. New York: Sharon Books, 1945.

OESTERREICHER, MSGR. JOHN M., and Anne Sinai, eds. *Jerusalem.* New York: The John Day Company, 1974.

SACHAR, HOWARD MORLEY. *The Course of Modern Jewish History,* rev. ed. New York: Dell, 1977.

ST. JOHN, ROBERT. *The Man Who Played God.* New York: Doubleday, 1962. Fiction.

SHULMAN, ABRAHAM. *Coming Home to Zion: A Pictorial History of Pre-Israel Palestine.* New York: Doubleday, 1979.

SILVERBERG, ROBERT. *If I Forget Thee, O Jerusalem.* New York: William Morrow & Co., 1970.

WAREN, HELEN. *The Buried Are Screaming.* New York: The Beechhurst Press, 1948.

INDEX

ABOUT THE AUTHOR

Peter Hay [pronounced "high"] was born in Hungary in the year that Chana Szenes died there. During the Holocaust, he was saved by a Lutheran birth certificate and "righteous Gentiles" who claimed him as their own child. The Swedish diplomat Raoul Wallenberg personally pulled Hay's father off of a cattle-train bound for Auschwitz.

Hay's grandparents lived on the same street in Budapest as the Szenes family, and their friendship has now endured for three generations. Displaced to England by the Hungarian Revolution, Peter Hay was educated at Oxford; as a student he translated Chana Szenes' poems for the English language editions of her diaries.

After a dozen years in Canadian theatre and publishing, he moved to Los Angeles in 1980. He has taught drama at the University of Southern California and at UCLA. He is the author of ALL THE PRESIDENTS' LADIES (Viking/Penguin) and four other anecdotal books about the theatre, business and the law.